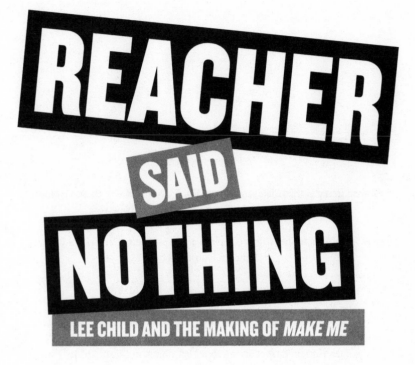

REACHER SAID NOTHING

LEE CHILD AND THE MAKING OF *MAKE ME*

Andy Martin

BANTAM BOOKS

NEW YORK

Published in the United States by Bantam Books, an imprint of Random House, a division of Penguin Random House LLC, New York.

BANTAM BOOKS and the HOUSE colophon are registered trademarks of Penguin Random House LLC.

LIBRARY OF CONGRESS CATALOGING-IN-PUBLICATION DATA
Names: Martin, Andy
Title: Reacher said nothing : Lee Child and the
making of Make Me / Andy Martin.
Description: First edition. | New York : Bantam Books, 2015.
Identifiers: LCCN 2015038231 | ISBN 9781101965450 (acid-free paper) |
ISBN 9781101965467 (eBook)
Subjects: LCSH: Child, Lee. | Authors and readers. | Fiction—Authorship. |
Reacher, Jack (Fictitious character)
Classification: LCC PS3553.H4838 Z75 2015 | DDC 813/.54—dc23 LC record
available at http://lccn.loc.gov/2015038231

Printed in the United States of America on acid-free paper

randomhousebooks.com

2   4   6   8   9   7   5   3   1

First Edition

Book design by Christopher M. Zucker

To all those loyal readers of Lee Child
who may have bought this book by mistake

I love his knowledge, his diffusion, his affluence of conversation.

Samuel Johnson
James Boswell, *The Life of Samuel Johnson*

I think I read in at least two ways. First, by following, breathlessly, the events and the characters without stopping to notice the details, the quickening pace of reading sometimes hurtling the story beyond the last page—as when I read Rider Haggard, the Odyssey, *Conan Doyle and the German author of Wild West stories, Karl May. Secondly, by careful exploration, scrutinizing the text to understand its ravelled meaning, finding pleasure merely in the sound of the words or in the clues which the words did not wish to reveal, or in what I suspected was hidden deep in the story itself, something too terrible or too marvellous to be looked at.*

Alberto Manguel, *A History of Reading*

E-FACE

Aug 22 [2014]
andymartinink to LeeChild
subject: wild idea?

Hi Lee

How would you feel about a "making of" story about your next book?

Thinking about some of the questions that get bowled at you at public events, I reckon most of them concern the process of creation. (Apart from actual marriage proposals.) I was thinking that a genesis-and-what-happened-next type approach could be of wide interest as regards one of your books. i.e. a sort of work-in-progress approach.

Obviously you would have to be up for it, which is why I ask now, so you can blow the idea out of the water entirely if you want.

There are about 10 different ways of doing it, could be more or less systematic and focused, depending. But I guess the minimum is—depending on how it was done—I would need feedback from you on what you are actually getting up to as the story rolls along.

I'm not sure this has been done before—a kind of literary criticism but in the moment, in real time, rather than picking it up afterwards. How This Book Was Written, but actually trying to capture the very moment of creation. I think it could be exciting, but as I say, you would have to really be in the mood for it. You have to admit, it would be different—so instead of the old cutting-yourself-off-in-a-log-cabin approach (or the urban equivalent), you would have someone (i.e. me) looking over your shoulder as you are typing the words.

Not exactly Boswell to your Johnson but something along those lines. Or Ishmael to your Captain Ahab. (Keith Richards to your Mick Jagger?)

Kind of crazy I know and you might say "yes, and TOTAL BLOODY NON-STARTER TOO!" On the other hand, you might feel that it could be a different angle on the whole Jack Reacher adventure. And it would definitely save you having to answer a lot of those questions!

all the best, Andy

Aug 23
LeeChild to andymartinink
Very interesting idea. Much to discuss. Detailed answer Tuesday from New York. Lee

Sent from my iPhone

Aug 24

andymartinink to LeeChild

great!

beginning: where did that idea come from? (one of the great mysteries)

end: getting it out there, reviews etc

writing Reacher could be as strong a narrative as the Reacher adventure (possibly with fewer actual punch-ups, but you never know)

Aug 26

LeeChild to andymartinink

Andy

I'm totally up for this, but we better figure out the how/where/when, because the process is about to start.

Tomorrow I start on the concentrated launch promo for "Personal," and then early next week I'll start writing the 2015 book. So really coverage should start now, to show how writing and promoting are inevitably combined.

So far I have no title, no real plot idea, but I have the opening pages in mind. I hope to get them down soon, and see what emerges after that.

Aug 26

Are you going to be in New York or what? I love the "no title no plot" thing—this is like the genesis moment. Void and without form. A

Aug 26

Yes, in NYC now, doing media etc, then on the road in Savannah, Georgia, Ireland and the UK between September 11th and 20th.

Aug 26

ok if I am going to do this SERIOUSLY (obviously a must), I'd better get right over there and talk it over asap. On the other hand I don't want to get in the way if you are right in the middle of big media hoopla. On yet another hand, big media hoopla is a good part of the story. We start not at the beginning of this one, but at the end of the previous one . . . Basically, I don't want you to start writing before I get there! Sounds as though you're already writing it in your head. I feel I've got to be perched on your shoulder like some kind of pirate's parrot for the first line . . . obviously could catch up with you readily here but I reckon I need to start looking for flights . . . how soon, from your point of view, could I pop up in nyc for purpose of prelim conversation? Am cancelling dinner with the PM of course, Andy

Aug 27

Get here any time, sooner the better . . . but seriously, Monday or Tuesday next week wouldn't be too late.

Aug 27

Sorted. In NYC Sunday. See you Monday? Say where and when and I'll be there.

Aug 28

Excellent. Could start (early) on Monday—CBS TV in the morning, a Simon Mayo phoner to the UK in the afternoon, for a flavor of how it goes . . . plus Monday is 20 years to the day since I bought the paper to write Killing Floor.

Let me know how you feel about that and I'll give you the details.

Aug 28

ha! so you actually had to go out specifically to buy the paper— wow—the next best thing to cuneiform and clay tablets, right way back to the very beginning. Sounds perfect. If you don't mind me being a fly on the wall it would be great to tag along on the publicity train for a while. I was having lunch with Bronwen Maddox the other day—I bought her a copy of The Enemy!*—and she was saying how she had known loads of guys who were dreaming (in vain of course) of doing exactly what you did (the re-naissance thing). So the funny thing is although this is a unique one-off kind of phenom, at the same time there is definitely a universal factor here.*

Aug 28

Cool. Be there at 7:30a.m. Monday and we'll head to the breakfast show. (Note Monday is Labor Day—subways will be running a Sunday schedule, but there should be cabs about and the streets will be quiet.)

Aug 28

see you 7:30 Monday - good early start!

THE END

IT ENDED the way it was always going to have to end. With a burial.

Lee stubbed out a final Camel filter cigarette (except it was anything but final) and breathed out a cloud of *New York Times* no. 1 bestseller smoke. Leaned back in his chair and scrutinized the last sentence of *Personal:*

> O'Day was to be awarded three more medals posthumously, and a bridge was to be named after him, on a North Carolina state route, over a narrow stream that most of the year was dry.

Always good to end with a death, of course. *Posthumously . . .* it was like hammering a last nail into the coffin. Or more, planting a gravestone. There was a finality to it. A valediction. But then it was a pointlessly inadequate memorial. He liked anything to do with bridges and routes (so much sheer hard labor had gone into them), but he particularly liked the dried-up stream. So the bridge was pointless too.

And his own stream, the great flow of inspiration that had kept the novel afloat for the last eight months—hadn't that about dried up now too? "A narrow stream that most of the year was dry." *Could that be . . . me?*

What the hell, it was all like a diary anyway, only masquerading as an adventure.

"THE END." He didn't write it down. Didn't need to. He knew he was supposed to put it in for the benefit of the typesetters, but he didn't see the necessity. That great sense of an ending—the release, the relief, the closure, that satisfying last expulsion of smoke—it all had to be contained in the rhythm and feel of the last sentence. The *End* had to be nailed right there. Those concluding lines, like the final notes of a Beethoven symphony, a coda, had to have some kind of dying cadence to them, a falling away, an elegiac cessation that said, "I've said everything I needed to say." So you really didn't need to write "THE END" too. It offended his sense of economy. Two words too many. If it was the right sentence, the sentence would say it for him.

He couldn't hit SEND just yet though. He would have to wait a couple of days, let it percolate in his head, see what subliminal second thoughts might bubble up. But all the loose ends had been tied up with a bow. *Personal,* his nineteenth Jack Reacher novel—done.

Word count: 107,000. Substantially across the crucial one hundred thousand line. That's what it said on the contract. Anything shorter and it would be too short. Still, 107,000 was relatively short for him. *The Enemy,* for example, was a full 140k. But it was enough. His books had been getting shorter and tighter. He loved the beginning, that gorgeous feeling when nothing has been screwed up yet. Loved the ending too, that great rush towards the finale, when it was all downhill. But the middle—the middle was always a struggle—by around page 2 it was like rolling the rock up the hill again day after day. He'd developed a cunning strategy for *Personal* though, had pretty much outwitted the middle—he just left it out, fast-forwarded straight from the beginning right through to the end, without a pause, nonstop. Problem solved.

Anyway, it had been a blast, the whole way—Paris, London, Romford—so fuck it, it would have to do. He wasn't going to change it now.

He glanced at the time on the computer screen: 10:26, Tuesday night. April 15, 2014. (Reacher, he considered, would know what time it was automatically, without having to check with a mere machine—but of course, he—Lee—was not Reacher, he had to keep reminding himself. There was so much Reacher could do—about the one thing he couldn't do was write a novel about his own experience. Which was why Reacher still needed him.) He'd written the first line on September 1, 2013. It had to be September 1. Every year. *Without fail.* Now it was over.

Lee turned his head away from the screen and looked out of the big window to his left. Tonight the Empire State Building was lit up orange and green—pistachio, like some dumb giant ice-cream cone. It didn't used to look that way. Once it had had only clean vapor lights, white light or maybe yellow, so it was like looking up at heaven. Now, with the coming of LED, it could look like anything anybody wanted—it could be red, white, and blue on July 4, for example. But mostly it looked like a bad 1970s disco light show. It used to be an immense, stately edifice, he thought. Now it's ice cream. Like dressing Jack Reacher up like a disco dancer. It was this view that had convinced him to come and live here, on 22nd Street, on the twenty-fifth floor of a building across from the Flatiron Building. Now—cheapened, stupid, gaudy—the view made it less of a wrench to leave. Farewell, Empire State; I loved you once. Or maybe twice.

He still remembered that feeling he'd had when he first came here. The romance. With the Empire State framed in the window, it would be like living in the offices of the *Daily Planet* in Metropolis: oh look, isn't that mild-mannered, neatly suited Clark Kent up there in the clouds, looking out masterfully on the world (with lovely Lois Lane by his side)? And wouldn't his superhuman powers extend to writing too? It was logical. Wouldn't a writer from Krypton be all-powerful, all-conquering—a Superman among writers?

My Home in America. That other great work of literature that always sprang back to mind—was never really out of his mind. His genesis and exodus. The book of commandments that had guided him here in the first place. He had come across it, aged five, in the old Elmwood Public Library, in Birmingham. It was just lying there on the floor. He'd picked it up. A stiff, cardboard sort of book, mostly illustrations with just a few words. With pictures of children in their faraway homes—he remembered a new England colonial "saltbox," an isolated farmhouse on the prairies, and a Californian beach house with surfboards and palm trees. But the picture he always went back to (he borrowed the book and took it home and eventually returned it, much thumbed, but he had carried it around with him in his head ever since, pristine and perfect, a portable Garden of Eden) was the one of the apple-cheeked boy who lived in New York. He lived on the nth floor of some lofty Manhattan apartment block, reaching right up into the sky, with a bird flying by. And he was looking out of his window at the Empire State Building. Lee Child was that boy, half a century later. He had always wanted to be him, had just temporarily been trapped in the wrong country or the wrong body.

It was like a brain transplant—or metempsychosis—or déjà vu, he must have been that New York boy in a previous life, and somehow he had contrived to get back to what he always had been. A kid in a skyscraper.

And yet now he was leaving.

The apartment he called his "office" had been emptied out. Hoovered clean. The white walls were a blank. It was not just the end of one novel, it was the end of a whole string of novels, the end of an era that would forever be identified with this place. Another time, he might have stood up and picked up the red Fender he kept in the corner for celebratory moments like this one. Plugged it in and switched on the amp. Turned the volume up high. Put the strap over his head and hoisted up the mast of the guitar, stared out into the night and tightened the fingers of his left hand over the frets and wound up his right arm and unleashed the plectrum over the strings. And some mighty earth-shattering chord would rip out into the darkness, accompanied by obscene pelvic thrusting.

Except all the guitars had been shipped back to England. And . . . oh yeah, he couldn't play a note. He was no musician. The guitars were just there for inspiration. Maybe he'd come back as a rock star. (Or maybe a soccer player? Georgie Best or Lionel Messi would do.)

Even his desk had been taken: he was perched on an old dining table, white, circular, sitting on a black dining chair. Not even a decent ashtray (the saucer was full of butts—where was he supposed to empty it? The wastebasket had gone too). He felt like a refugee crouched in the corner of an abandoned building.

Squatting. Like the last man left alive, staring out at the abyss, the ruined deserted city that was once New York. Just him and a few postapocalyptic rats. And a coffee machine.

He took the phone out of his pocket and switched it back on. It pinged with a text from his daughter, Ruth.

"Hey, Doof!" it began (short for dufus).

Lee smiled. Okay, not quite all alone. She was the one who had started it, all the talk about moving. Maybe she was right though, maybe he had been vaguely dissatisfied. And now he was really dissatisfied.

He'd had to finish by April. Moving date was the 24th. Most of the furniture had already gone. The books had all gone. They'd left him the computer, the old Mac desktop. Now it was doomed. He wasn't going to take it with him. He shut it down for the night. It didn't know it was junk just yet. Shhh.

Lee lived upstairs—same building, different apartment. That was stripped nearly bare too. Just a bed. And a coffee machine. He didn't go back to the office all the next day, the 16th. Just wandered around. Sat in cafés or diners, drank coffee, smoked more cigarettes. Came back to it on the 17th. Looked at it one more time. Then hit SEND.

Then he started looking for his hammer. The big claw hammer. That would do the job.

Of course his hammer wasn't in his office. Where the hell was his toolbox? So he popped out the hard disc and put it in his pocket. Went to the hardware store in Union Square. Then he hopped on an uptown C train at 23rd Street, got out at 86th, and went up to the new apartment. Put the disc down on the kitchen table, then he opened up his bag from the hardware store.

It didn't have to be a very big hammer, he knew that. It was just a modest claw hammer, this one, but it would do the job. A hard disc consisted mainly of glass, toughened up with some kind of aluminum or ceramic. He gave it a gentle whack and it shattered into a dozen pieces straight off. Was that all it took? He was kind of disappointed. So much for the *hard* disc. Fragile disc more like. *Mission: Impossible*–style: this disc will self-destruct in . . . about two seconds.

If anyone asked, it was a security thing. Really. He had the new Apple desktop set up in the new apartment, in the office at the back. So the old one was surplus. He wasn't too worried about identity theft. If someone wanted his identity they were welcome to it. There was no such thing as privacy anymore. On the other hand, he didn't fancy people poking about in his old emails. Seeing little phrases popping up on social media. Embarrassing. Potentially.

And really it would be a betrayal of his entire life's work if he wasn't just a little bit paranoid.

But then again: hard disc, hard man . . . Reacher was all over the old computer. He didn't exist as far as the new one was concerned. He loved Reacher, naturally. Reacher was Lee Child on steroids, after all, a surgically enhanced, superhumanly calm hooligan. A Zen caveman. But at the same time, it would be good to have a vacation from Reacher. Reacher had been pounding his brain for the last eight months. Now Reacher lay in pieces over the table. Shattered into little shards. Dust. Random pixels. Stray molecules.

But if there was one thing he had learned about the recurring hero series business, it was this:

YOU CAN'T KILL THE BUGGER OFF!

It would be like killing off the golden goose. You can expose him to mortal danger of every kind. You HAVE to expose him to mortal danger. Bury him. Blow him up. Cuff him to a train. Put him up against an entire army. Put an angry sniper on his trail. But he has to get out of those ridiculously tight situations. Somehow survive, no matter what. Otherwise how could he recur? He couldn't see a metaphysical, ghostly Reacher working. Reacher v. Vampires. Reacher v. Zombies. That was never going to fly.

He wasn't Dracula, but maybe he was a little bit Frankenstein. A monster on the loose. Which he, the mad Dr. Lee Child, had created and unleashed upon the world.

"Predictable." That is what Reacher had said about himself in *Personal*. Predictable that he would live anyway. It was a constraint. Look at the trouble Conan Doyle had gotten into when he bumped off Sherlock Holmes, shoving him over the Reichenbach Falls. The fans had forced him to bring the great detective back again. He'd had to turn the tables on Professor Moriarty after all.

The number of times he'd thought about killing him off. He'd have to go out with a bang, that was his first theory. Shot to pieces while in some way saving the day. He still remembered a cartoon story in *Valiant* so many years ago (or was it *Victor*? or *Hotspur*?). It's the Second World War and a very big guy is given the job of guiding a couple of young kids to safety across enemy territory. They are holed up in a bomb shelter and then some passing Nazi lobs in a grenade. It's about to go off, they are all doomed. And then the big guy hurls himself on top of the grenade in a final, heroic gesture, buries it beneath his massive, muscular chest. He, naturally, is blown to smithereens, but the two kids are saved. He is their savior. A sublime father figure. But dead. It was simple and beautiful, something like that would work.

And then he had thought—wouldn't it be better just to have him arrive at the bus station, at the end of the book, all the bad guys are dead, he's about to hop on the bus, and then he says to himself, "I like it here, I think I'll stay." And he gets off the bus. (Maybe he becomes an upstanding citizen—or a writer? Gets married, settles down, buys a house.) There would be an emotional resolution. He could have ended *Personal* that way. But he hadn't. Medals, bridge, stream. Reacher lives! He had a contract—a three-book contract!—that said he would have to.

All the same he would enjoy having a Reacher-free vacation. Reacher, unreachable.

All May and June he was setting up the new apartment. Stacking the shelves. Putting up the Renoir and the Warhol. Ruth was right, it was a great place, she'd found it, a classy-looking turn-of-the-century building north of the Dakota, and extolled its virtues; he'd bought it on the basis of the floor plan alone, the geometry, he knew it could accommodate all the shelves. He'd have somewhere for everything. So long as he kept on reading he would always need more shelving.

Jack Reacher—huge footloose wanderer, armed only with a toothbrush. Lee Child—tall guy with shelves! Paintings! First editions! Apartment overlooking Central Park. House in France. Farm in the south of England (two farms, to be exact). On the one hand, nomadic hunter-gatherer, on the other . . . farmer? It was easy for Reacher, he didn't have to do any writing. His job was straightforward enough—go about killing people who got in his way, and also not die. Easy. Whereas writing about that . . . it for sure needed more than a toothbrush. He'd still be the boy in the tall Manhattan building.

Sometimes Reacher felt like a reproach. It was like writing about Jesus. The gospel according to Saint Jack. How could you live up to those standards—or down to them?

July, he wrote a TV pilot with his daughter. She was into forensic linguistics. The pilot was CSI but with words, not DNA. It suited Lee. The job was to track down villains on the basis of what they actually say. Everybody leaves verbal fingerprints. There was the case of the guy who murdered his girlfriend—and then texted afterwards using her phone but pretending to be her. The forensic linguists were able to demonstrate that it was really him not her, on the basis of his distinctive punctuation—or lack of it. Lee loved that idea—that you could be sunk by a comma or a hyphen. It all mattered, linguistically. Nothing was too trivial. The best clues were like that—subtle and insubstantial—not a big fat muddy boot print by the garden window.

Most of August he spent in France and England. Eating and drinking. Reading. Smoking. Putting his feet up in the sun.

But now it was nearly the end of August and he was back in New York.

People would often say to him: "How come Reacher is always getting into trouble? Always finding some new drama to poke his nose into? Doesn't he ever take a break?"

"I write about him when he's doing nothing," he would reply. "When he's on holiday and not smashing up bad guys. But they don't publish those ones. They're too boring."

Now it was time for Reacher to get real again. Reacher was back from vacation. Reaching out to him. Again.

2.

CHAPTER 1

WHICH IS WHEN I BLEW into town. To watch it happen. To bear witness to Lee Child writing the next installment of Jack Reacher's continuing adventures. I first picked up a Reacher, purely by chance, in a little bookstore in Pasadena, down the road from Caltech. I knew exactly how Malcolm Gladwell felt when he plotted his incremental curve of addition: you start out reading Lee Child in paperback; then you realize you can't wait that long and start buying his books in hardcover; your next step is to call around to your publishing friends and ask them to send you the galleys. Ultimately, he reckoned, you would have no option but to "break into Lee Child's house and watch over his shoulder while he types."

I had read all the books. I'd reviewed a few of them. I'd interviewed the guy. Twice (once in the U.K., again in the U.S.). Now I was finally breaking in. I had to know what happened next. Before it happened. I was doing what Gladwell had only dreamed of.

There was a date Lee couldn't miss.

September 1, 2014. Labor Day in the U.S. A public holiday. But not for Reacher. It was twenty years to the day since, on the verge of being fired from his job with Granada Television, Lee, nearly forty years old, had gone out and bought the paper to start writing *Killing Floor,* the first of the series. And a pencil (he still had the pencil, much reduced in size). Every year, ever since then, he'd started a new one on the very same day. It was a ritual with him. One he couldn't mess with.

Lee didn't have to become a writer. He had a couple of options after he dropped (or had been pushed) out of television. After being fired, he had taken the trouble to go along to his local "Employment Exchange," as it was then known. More like an *Un*employment Exchange. This was the height—or depth—of the post-Thatcher golden age in the north of England. Manufacturing jobs in the north of England were being slashed—and not that he would necessarily have gotten one even if they had been numerous. There was only one job going, that he was really qualified for. *Warehouseman.* He had given it some serious consideration. Then he had gone out to buy the paper. "We were only just making enough to get by. Then I lost my job. It was fairly desperate."

He wrote the first chapter. *Killing Floor,* Chapter 1. Then showed it to his wife. Everything depended on what she said. He could keep on with *Killing Floor.* Chapter 2. Or he could go and apply for that warehouseman job. She read what he had written and then put it down.

"What do you think? Shall I keep going?"

"Keep going," she said.

He went back to work. The choice had been made. Maybe he would never have made a decent warehouseman anyway.

At 7:30 that morning, September 1, we got in the car to drive to the TV studio. *CBS This Morning.* With Lee Child. There were more people in the car, Lee and his publicist and his editor and his assistant and one or two others—his crew—and me, than on the streets outside. "Everyone's off today and we're working," his apartment doorman had said. As we glided through empty streets, New York on Labor Day reminded me of Lee's description of a backwoods smallville in Montana:

> There were no people on the sidewalks. No vehicle noise, no activity, no nothing. The place was a ghost. It looked like an abandoned cowboy town from the Old West.

"Today we begin!" said Lee, like a kid going to a birthday party, not thinking about the TV interview at all. "I want to get ahead this time, take the pressure off."

"Do you have it in the diary?" I said.

"No, that would be too obvious," he said. "But it is in my head. I can remember it like it was yesterday.

"Around 1:15. My lunch break, because I was still working even though I knew it was nearly over. WHSmith in the Arndale Centre, in Manchester—the one that got bombed by the IRA. I was working all weekend. Then I started writing on the Monday. I had no real time off at all."

"So it has to be today."

"I need ritual. My life needs a shape. It doesn't matter that I'm doing interviews, I have to start today."

"That was a great opening [to *Killing Floor*]," I said. "*I was arrested in Eno's diner. At twelve o'clock. I was eating eggs and drinking coffee."*

"The first day is always the best," Lee said. "Because you haven't screwed anything up yet. It's a gorgeous feeling. I try to put it off as long as possible because when it's gone it's gone."

"Do you have any kind of strategy for writing or rules or whatever?"

"I only really have one. You should write the fast stuff slow and the slow stuff fast. I picked that up from TV. Think about how they shoot breaking waves—it's always in slow motion. Same thing. You can spend pages on pulling the trigger."

"*Die Trying.* All the mechanics and chemistry of firing a shot. Like calculus."

"And what happens to the bullet afterwards. That's the thing most writers forget—they think it's just pull the trigger and wham. But in reality there is a lot of physics. Stuff happens afterwards. Think of *The Day of the Jackal.* The sniper assembles his weapon, fires his shot, but then de Gaulle bends forward to kiss the guy he's pinning the medal on. There can be a lot of time between firing and hitting the target."

This was the day on which Lee would pull the trigger on his new book. The funny thing was that he was having to talk about the old book. Although everyone thought it was new. It was just out—*Personal.* Reacher 19. This was what the interview was all about.

He was wearing denims, a charcoal Brooks Brothers jacket, and shoes with the laces taken out. He has this thing about laces. "Yeah, I got rid of all the shoelaces," he said. "They're a pain when you're traveling."

The studio was great. Some kind of old warehouse in Midtown. We were in the Green Room. Lee went off into makeup. The snacks were great, piles of fresh fruit—pineapple, melon, kiwi, banana, all neatly sliced up—gallons of coffee and tons of croissants. And there were any number of fabulous-looking women just sitting around looking fabulous. Don't know what they were doing there exactly. One was called Whitney. She had "temporary tattooed jewelry."

"I want it to be the same but different." Lee was doing his thing with the TV interviewer. A couple in fact—a man and a woman. His "new" book. Told them the story about his old father and how he had once asked him, when he was peering at a whole stack of books, how do you choose a book to read? And his dad had replied, "I want it to be the same but different." And Lee says, "I applied it to writing this one. It had to be the same—it's the same old Reacher again, love him or hate him—but instead of roaming around America for a change, I have him getting on a plane to Paris, France, and London, England."

I thought he didn't really need to say "France" or "England," but then again maybe he did. He liked to spell things out. It's a salient characteristic of his writing. What time is it? What road is this? Whereabouts are we? Don't skim over the details. So that was the same.

"In pursuit of a sniper who is threatening world leaders. He arrested him once, now he has to nail him all over again."

"So it's 'personal'?"

"Yes, but it's also because his old army general tracks him down using an ad in the Personal column of the *Army Times*."

The thing I liked about *Personal* was that the bad guys were known as the "Romford Boys." Reacher ends up not in the middle of London, at Buckingham Palace, but in the suburbs to the east, in Essex. Romford is where I grew up, so I naturally took this swerve in the narrative as a homage to me. That was probably mad, but every act of reading is also an act of madness, because you have to assume that the writer is writing for *me*, specifically.

I have this relationship thing going on with *the author*. So I was no more nuts than anyone else. Well, maybe a little more.

Lee admitted, when we were sitting about in the café later, that he was probably a little nuts himself. Although he began by denying it. (Obviously, he was still putting off making a start on the new book. He was enjoying the gorgeous feeling too much.) "I'm not a weirdo," he said, knocking back a cup of black coffee. "I know I'm making this all up. I invented Jack Reacher. He is nothing but a fictional character through and through. He is *imaginary*."

He has this way of emphasizing particular words that I can only capture with italics.

"On the other hand, with another part of my brain, I'm thinking—I am reporting on the latest antics of Jack Reacher. *'Hold on,'*" and here he cupped his hand around one ear, as if listening intently. "*'What's that? Let me note that down right now!'* The novels are really reportage."

When he writes, he goes into a "zone" in which he really believes that the nonexistent Jack Reacher is temporarily existent. "I know I'm making it up, but it doesn't feel that way. Okay, so maybe I am a *bit* of a weirdo."

I discover, as we're driving back, that Reacher is very popular in prison. Lee gets fan mail from a lot of prisoners. He once paid a visit to a prison in New Zealand. The prison governor was worried about security. He needn't have worried. Hardened jailbirds love Lee. "I grew up in Birmingham," says Lee. "I've seen worse. And I was in television, therefore I've worked with worse."

Later—okay, let me be more specific, it was around twelve—we're back at his apartment, and Maggie Griffin is explaining how

Killing Floor took off in the States. Maggie was one of the first readers of his first novel in galley proofs in New York, back in 1997. And now she is still with him, as "independent PR advisor." She is probably his number one fan too. Back then she worked on Wall Street and was a partner in an independent bookstore, Partners in Crime. They made *Killing Floor* a "Partners Pick." She would phone people up saying, "Buy three copies! It's going to be collectible." She was right of course. "One to read, another to share, and one to keep pristine. It's going to be worth a lot of money." And it had a great and memorable cover (the white background with the red handprint over it).

She was the one who persuaded him to come to New York, on his own dime (as they say here). "Yes," she would say in her phone calls, lying her head off, "Putnam is flying him over."

They sold a few thousand in the first weekend.

"Yeah, I was a 'cult hit,'" said Lee. "A blip on the radar. I guess it's been incremental since then. The odds against me being in this position are huge. But at the time we were just making it up as we went along. I never had a breakthrough moment really. Just a hard relentless slog in the middle years. Which is why I always have Reacher doing a lot of hard work."

"As in, for example," says I, "*The Hard Way*. '*Yes, we are going to have to do this the hard way,*' Reacher says, being deeply put upon and overworked by his tyrannical author."

"I never like to make it too easy for him—why should he have it easy?"

And then two or three books in, his agent says to him, "Have you heard about this Internet thing?" Dinner at the Langham, next to the BBC. And Lee persuaded Maggie to build him what would become the poster boy of author websites. Streets ahead. Leaving everyone else trying to catch up.

"It probably helped," Maggie said, "when Bill Clinton came out as a fan. Clinton—that was like Kennedy reading the James Bond books."

Maggie said that at the beginning the publishers had "misjudged" the appeal to women readers.

"They like the same things guys do," she said. "Violent retribution. They want blood on the page."

We were just sitting around talking, still delaying the beginning. It was a day of postponement. Lee was pondering Amazon's influence. Amazon has this thing of showing you 10 percent of a book to suck you in. "Some writers," Lee was saying, with a degree of scorn, "some writers have started writing the first episode in their books to fit the 10 percent and kick the book off. They're actually calculating exactly how long their chapters should be." Lee didn't want to be one of those writers. He didn't want Amazon telling him how to write a book. He didn't want anyone telling him.

I knew things went wrong in publishing. Sometimes embarrassing. A friend of mine had her book printed with someone else's cover on it. "They go wrong all the time," Lee said. "This is an industrial process with hundreds of millions of manufactured items." He'd done an industry event recently where the publishers had a big pile of books. A reader came up to him with one of them which had a perfectly fine cover—but was completely blank inside. Lee apologized. Signed the book as normal. But this time he wrote in it: "Reacher said nothing." It was one of his recurrent phrases, almost a catchphrase, if saying nothing could be a catchphrase.

"Reacher often says nothing," Lee said. "He shouldn't have to be wisecracking all the time. He's not into witty repartee. He is supposed to *do* things." Basically, Reacher made Lee Child sound like Oscar Wilde. Not that he was an idiot (Reacher, I mean).

More of a particularly taciturn, very muscular philosopher. Lapidary. Succinct. More at the Clint Eastwood end of the spectrum. With just a dash of Nietzsche and Marcuse.

Then we went to the radio studio a few blocks away (Lee would write about how we turned left, going north on Central Park West, as we came out of his building). Which is when we had the JOHN LENNON MOMENT. (Somewhere between 86th and 87th.)

3.

THAT JOHN LENNON MOMENT

LEE LIVES NORTH of the building where John Lennon used to live and Yoko Ono still lives (I think). Just across from the Strawberry Fields monument to Lennon. I had forgotten all about this until the moment when a fanboy comes running up to us in the street. We had just come out of Lee's building. It was a nice sunny day. Not too hot. We were walking along and suddenly out of nowhere—I think he popped up from the other side of Central Park West. White guy. He had on a black baseball cap, pulled down over his forehead. T-shirt and jeans, I think. Glasses. An intense look. "Hey, Mr. Child," he says, "I'm a great fan of yours."

The whole Lennon story flashed back to mind, the shooting in the street outside his building, *by a fan*. Mark David Chapman probably said to Lennon, "I'm a great fan of yours."

So naturally I thought, *Uh-oh, here we go, when is he going to pull the gun out?*

"I'm grateful to you for your novels, of course," the guy in the baseball cap said, getting into time with us as we walked north, highly respectfully, "but I also admire everything you've written about the art of writing."

"Really?" said Lee. Calm and composed.

"Yes, your work has been a great inspiration to me." Turned out he was an up-and-coming thriller writer. "I really liked that point you made about not giving away too much information—dosing it out. Slow disclosure. I try to keep it in mind while I'm writing."

"Who do you publish with?" Lee said.

"St. Martin's Press," says the guy.

"Good publisher," says Lee. "Well, good luck with the next one!"

The guy thanked him again and backed off (no doubt at the same time loosening the pressure of his finger on the trigger of the handy little weapon he had stowed away in his pocket). Lee has this habit of seeing the other person's point of view. I was seeing a threat to life and limb—an assassin, in short. He was seeing a budding fellow writer. (Really, how much difference was there?) And in his parting words I felt a sense that he was wishing himself good luck for his next one too—given that it barely existed.

It wasn't his own life he was worrying about, it was the life of the unborn book.

I mentioned my John Lennon scenario to Lee as we went on. He laughed it off. "Anyway," he said, "that was on the way *back* to the Dakota. It was outside the building, but he was coming *home,* not going out. He signs a record for the fan. Then the fan pulls out a gun and shoots him." It was a fine distinction. But it was clear he had given the episode some thought. Had seen himself as a possible target. Then dismissed it.

"A writer is never going to be in the same league as a rock star—or an actor, for example. Not even remotely. Writing is show business for shy people. Or invisible people. It's the book that's out there, not the person. We just don't have that kind of visibility—or directness. So I guess, by the same token, we're less of a target." He thought this part of town was more *literary* than his old neighborhood. "I'm more recognized in this part of New York. The Upper West Side. I might have a couple of fans coming up to me if I walk through Central Park. Only one or two a week. No big deal."

4.

CHAPTER 1 (CONTINUED)

LEE IS A DISTINCTIVE GUY to look at. About six foot four. Tall and stringy-looking. Strong chin. Piercing blue eyes. Reddish-brown hair. Late fifties but well preserved. Verging on elegant. Longitudinal. Someone had said to him, "You should play Reacher!" (In the movie.) He had replied, "My body mass would just about fit into one of his arms." (Reacher 220–250 pounds; Child 160.) Still, you can pick him out in a crowd. Or walking across Central Park. He has a long, lazy, loping stride. Half Robert Redford, half Jacques Tati. With a bit of Walter White thrown in for good measure.

He was doing a down-the-line interview with a radio show in England. Now even Lee was starting to worry about putting off the writing. Maybe it was one show too many.

"The book came out yesterday in the U.K. It's already sold a phenomenal amount. So this is not strategic. But I love Simon

Mayo—the guy actually reads the books. I'm doing this show because I want to be on it."

We went in. Bumped into an old guy in suspenders and baggy trousers hitched high. A producer or something.

"So what is this book?" he says.

"It's a thriller. I hope."

"So it's a movie, is it?"

"Well [cue sound of Lee gritting his teeth], it might become one ultimately."

He hates the movie assumption. I have taken a vow to keep off the subject of Tom Cruise (who played Reacher in the *Jack Reacher* movie, based on *One Shot*). He has already received around one million emails from fans saying, "YOU SOLD US OUT, YOU BASTARD!" or words to that effect. He sends out a tweet about what he had for breakfast and they all tweet back to him, "But why Tom Cruise?" Some people said, *What about Daniel Craig?* "Well, what about Daniel Craig?" I said. "He's even shorter!" Lee shot back. (He had actually met Daniel Craig and knew him well enough to call him "Danny." Likewise Clint Eastwood: "They're all shrimps!")

The producer in London is a fan, more well versed than the old guy. "If you ever want a character who's a slightly stressed-out radio producer," she says, rather seductively, "feel free to use me."

Simon Mayo, the presenter in London, says, "We're doing Jack Reacher songs this afternoon. This one is, 'I'm a Wanderer.' "

And then: "Lee Child live from New York . . . The one and only Lee Child!"

Everyone wanted to be a character in a Reacher book. Possibly have a romance with Reacher. Or even be on the receiving end of a crunching Reacher head butt. Mayo launched in with a story about how Lee has a character named Audrey Shaw in *The Affair*.

The real Audrey Shaw's son, aged fourteen, had written to him, telling him she was a total Reacher fan and would he mind using her name. So he did. "She was a fan," Lee explained, "and it's a great name. Perfect for the character."

A lot of people were wondering about Reacher getting older. I'd heard the question asked a few times—how old is he now? Is he over-the-hill or what? Lee reckoned he was around forty-eight now, maybe a bit older. "I used to be very specific, but now I just don't mention it." And they wanted to know if Lee was going to kill him off one of these days. They were expecting it all to come to an end. Twilight of an idol. "It's my readers who are keeping him alive," Lee says.

We walked back to his place. Unmolested by fans or assassins. So far as I could work out, you either wanted to *be* Jack Reacher, make love to him, or kill him off for all time. Or possibly some combination of the above.

The Lee Child apartment was like a very comfortable library. Hushed. Orderly. Lee had had white painted bookshelves installed all around and there was still space for more books. He had a lot more in boxes stashed away somewhere.

"I'm paying for it with the advance on the next book," he said. He looked around and grinned. "I haven't earned it yet. I'm living in an apartment that was bought with a book that hasn't been written."

"Nervous?" I said.

"It's more, I feel I have to really *earn* the apartment. It's like it's on a mortgage—I bought it with promises. Now I have to deliver."

Lee wanted to get down to work, but he thought we'd better have some lunch first. It was about two o'clock. He made us some toast. We had cheese (a choice of cheddar or Stilton—he had a big hunk of Stilton) and marmalade to go with it. And a smoothie (he had apricot, I had strawberry). We sat down in the dining room to eat our toast. It was a lovely old French farm table of some kind, chunky and rustic-looking.

I started telling him about rotten jobs I'd done in the past, how I'd lasted less than an hour in one of them, at a metal factory. Lee had tried a few other jobs, in his youth. He didn't like any of them. It wasn't that he didn't like the work, he didn't like the *workmanship*. In the jam factory, for example. "It was all sugar paste, nothing but sugar paste. If you wanted apricot jam you threw in some orange color. Strawberry—throw in some red. It was like you were *painting jam*. What about raspberry with all those little pips? No problem—here, we'll throw in some tiny wood chips." He was really outraged by how bad it was. "Nothing was real. Nobody cared." He felt responsible for people eating a load of rubbish only masquerading as jam. They were being conned. Lee wanted it to be *good* jam, whatever flavor it was.

He once had a job in a dried pea factory. He couldn't believe it: "Birds were perched up there on the rafters, way over our heads, and shitting into the peas. Nobody cared. That is how it was." And another job in a bakery.

It wasn't a traditional bakery. He wasn't kneading any dough. Or putting loaves in ovens. Everything was on an assembly line. His job was to take loaves off the horizontal belt and stack them on some kind of vertical system. But he couldn't get the hang of it. "There were all these loaves coming off the line. I was supposed to *clamp* seven loaves together and transfer them from the belt to the stack. But I just couldn't manage to do it. Seven loaves, at one time. They would allow you to drop one or two in an hour. But I kept on dropping them. I just couldn't get my arms tight enough around the loaves to hold them all together." He showed me how his physique was all wrong for the job. He was too stringy. His arms were too long. "I kept on dropping them. They were all over the place. They sacked me inside an hour. I deserved to be sacked. I was no good at it." He really wanted to be good—to find something he could be good at. He thought he was good at television. Then he got sacked from that job too.

We were about to go into his office. The novel factory. I think I was more nervous than he was. And I had a sense of quasi-religious awe too—I was about to bear witness to the genesis of a great work, the Big Bang moment. "Do you have anything in mind?" I said.

Because this was the key thing about the way Lee Child writes. The thing that drew me to write to him and break into his apartment and watch him working. He really didn't know what was going to happen next. "I don't have a clue about what is going to happen," he would say. He was a writer who thought like a reader. He had nothing planned. When he wrote to me he said, "I have no title and no plot." But he said I could come anyway. He didn't think I would put him off too much. He relied on inspiration to guide him. Like a muse. Or *the Force* or something. Something basic and mythic, without too much forethought. He liked his writing to be organic and spontaneous and authentic. He feared that thinking about it too much in advance would kill it stone dead. But still he had a glimmering of what would be. He knew the *feel* of a book.

"The opening is a third-party scene, I know that, right at the start. A bunch of other guys. So it has to be a third-person sort of book. Reacher doesn't know what is happening. He's not there yet."

"Do you *see* something in your mind or what? Is that what you mean by 'scene'?"

"It's visual, yes," he replied. "In the sense of seeing the words— I can almost see the paragraph in my mind. The physical look on the page. You have to nail the reader right there, on the first page.

The uncommitted reader. And I can feel it. The rhythm. It's got to be stumbly. It's tough guys talking. I have to get a hint of their vernacular. But, at the same time, it has to *trip* ahead. A tripping rhythm. Forward momentum."

I think it was around then that Lee started talking about euthanasia. He was in favor. There is a lot of *thanatos* in his books, not so much of the *eu*. "I can die right now. I'm fine with that." He dismissed the recommendation of a friend to go off to a mountain in Austria and chuck himself off (he thought you might change your mind by virtue of the fresh air and landscape). Turned out he had some plan, when the time came, involving a veterinary supplies store down in Mexico and a rather powerful cocktail of morphine and horse tranquilizer. Had it all worked out.

"Come on, man," I said, although I basically agreed with him. "Think of your readers! Anyway I'm stuffed if you die. I'll have to finish your book for you. Pretend you're still alive and steal all your earnings."

FINALLY, CHAPTER 1

THAT GOT HIM GOING. We finished the toast and went into his office at the back of the apartment. No Central Park (couldn't afford to spend all his time looking through the window like the boy in the Manhattan apartment). We sat down. Lee sat in front of his desk with the desktop computer on. It was there, waiting for him. It was already switched on. The desk is metal. Riveted. Silver. Huge. Solid. On a bunch of shelves to the right, mugs with pens. And a magnifying lens. On the left—a collection of his own books in hardcover.

The first thing he did was light a cigarette. (Second thing was take a mighty drag.)

"Look, Lee, I'm going to just shut up now. This is like going into church for me. I feel I should be quiet. Anyway I don't want to put you off your stroke."

"It's not a problem."

Lee was sitting in front of the screen of his new computer. An almost empty screen. It didn't even have a page on it. Nothing. I was sitting on this kind of couch a couple of yards behind him. Just perched on the edge of it, not really lying down or anything.

"It's reverse Freudian," Lee said. "You're on the couch and you're analyzing me."

I said nothing.

He flexed his fingers. "Naturally I'm going to start, like all good writers, by . . . checking my email!"

He cast an eye over some kind of Gmail list. "I'm just going to email the editor with the title suggestion. I don't know if it's going to work or not." He pressed the return key and I heard the whoosh sound as the email was sent. "They like to get it out of the way if possible. We'll see what she says."

Then he told me the title. MAKE ME.

"*Make Me* . . . I don't know, it's not definite. Popped into my head last night. But I like it. It's got something. Sounds like Reacher all right. Playground machismo. And then there's that meaning to do with being under surveillance, *making* someone, identifying them, tailing them. And maybe a little bit erotic or romantic too."

He still hadn't really written anything. Then he turns to me in his chair.

"This isn't the first draft, you know."

"Oh," I said. "What is it, then?"

"It's the *only* draft!"

Right then he sounded more like Jack Reacher than Lee Child. "I don't want to improve it. When I've written something, that is the way it has to stay. That's how I was that particular year. You can't change it. It's like one of those old photos you come across. From the 70s, say. And you have this terrible 70s haircut and giant lapels on your jacket. It's ridiculous—but it's there. It is what it is. Honesty demands you own up to it and leave it alone."

He still hadn't written anything yet.

"I reckon around ninety working days. Should finish it around mid-March—mid-April if I slack."

He still hadn't begun.

"And remember, I'm not making this up. Reacher is real. He exists. This is what he is up to, right now. That's why I can't change anything—this is just the way it is."

I was a couple of yards behind him and slightly to the right. I could see over his shoulder. I didn't want to get any closer. It was already ridiculous. Lee told me that he had cut his nails earlier that day. He hated it when the fingernails clacked against the keyboard.

He lit another cigarette and took a deep drag and blew out a lot of smoke then put the cigarette in the ashtray.

"I was thinking—you have a high risk of dying from secondary smoke inhalation here."

I said nothing.

I was thinking: the smoke is all part of it. Like a magic show. Smoke and mirrors. And, quite contrary to standard Magic Circle practice, the magician was tweaking aside the curtain and saying, okay come on through and let me show you exactly how I saw the lady in two and over here is my disappearing elephant, and so on. Everyone wants to know how it's done. And now I was about to find out.

So, I'm behind him. And he is there in front of the computer. I'm trying to keep quiet. Like a mouse if not quite a fly on the wall.

"I'm opening a file here. Microsoft Word doc . . . Now I move it to the middle of the screen."

He was talking me through it, like some kind of surgical operation. "I always use Arial. To begin with, anyway. And ten point. So

I get more on the page. But I crank it up to 150 percent to save my eyes."

It's 2:26 in the afternoon. September 1, 2014. Lee is on the verge of something momentous. At the moment it's a blank page. The file doesn't have a name.

"Then I have to turn off all these red lines . . . Do *not* check spelling. Or grammar. *I* am going to let Microsoft tell *me* what grammar is!?"

It's a huge screen (twenty-seven-inch). Virgin. Tabula rasa. "Single line space. I like to see a lot of text on the page. I don't want to spend all my time scrolling up and down."

He has put his tortoiseshell glasses on. Lit another cigarette. Put it down again. Finally he starts typing. He types:

CHAPTER ONE.

6.

EXIT KEEVER

IT STARTED WITH A BURIAL. It would have to start with a burial.

Lee types with two fingers only, the index fingers.

The smoke was corkscrewing up from the cigarette in his hand. He stopped to take a drag on it. Looked back at what he had written. Crushed out the cigarette. He was looking intently at the screen.

The first paragraph was five lines long. I could almost make out the first word. An -ing word—a present participle. *Something-ing*. Ten point and I'm two yards back. I could see the words, but not read them. Could have been Sanskrit. The suspense was killing me. Next time, I vowed silently, I'm going to bring a telescope. I would have gotten closer, maybe could have gotten closer, but I didn't want to crowd him. I was already nervous about making paper noises as I jotted down largely meaningless notes with a lot of question marks. I was already right on top of a guy in a small room in front of a computer trying to create a novel out of nothing, to conjure it up like a 100,000-word rabbit out of a hat.

Or maybe snake charmer would be a better metaphor—teasing that snake right up out of the basket.

Either way, Lee Child was thinking hard about his second paragraph.

Behind the page, on the desktop—I should have mentioned this sooner—a blue background, plain, no images.

The cigarette went back in the ashtray. The two fingers went back to work. End of second par. He lit another cigarette and then saved the file. For the first time, he was going to give it a name. Stick a label on it. He considered using the title, but then opted for something more neutral. "Reacher 19," he typed.

I leaned forward. I could just make it out. "19?" I said. "Reacher 19?"

"Oh yeah," he said. "Losing it." Deleted 19. Changed it to "Reacher 20." *Personal* was nineteenth. *Make Me* is the twentieth. The file was no longer nameless.

"I'm working up to *Make Me*. Not quite there yet." *Make Me* was fresh out of the oven—he didn't want to drop it.

The second par was longer. The onscreen page was slowly bulking up. He went back and slipped another sentence into the first par. Just a short one. So far he hadn't deleted a thing.

I deciphered another word. "Nothing." No. "Nothing*ness*."

The second par was twice the length of the first. Now he was into the third. The third was only two words long. I could only make out the second. "—enough." *Good* enough? *Bad* enough? Looked more like a four-letter word than three though. A tetragrammaton. Was that an "S" at the beginning?

Lee, stuck in mid-sentence. The cursor flashing impatiently, urging him on, begging for more.

Another cigarette.

That desk: sheet metal all riveted together—made back in England—is that some kind of homage to all those old artisan metalworkers of his youth? Back in Birmingham and Sheffield. Under the railway arches. The craftsmen who knew how to make stuff and make it well. No painted jam. No guano peas. Solid. Dependable.

The fifth par. We're on again! I could make out the beginning: "Only one thing went wrong . . ." A one-line par.

Other books on the shelf. *Encyclopedia of American Police Cars. Webster's. Small Arms.* Tourist guides to Maine, Oregon, California.

Lee folded his hands together under his chin. His face was about two feet from the screen. He shoved it a little closer, peering into the screen like a crystal ball gazer. Now leaning back again, hands behind his head. Rubbing thumb and index finger of his right hand together, as if trying to elicit a flame.

Only backs off for a maximum of ten seconds at a time, then into it again.

An asterisk—or maybe a hash sign? *Center. Return.* We're into a new section. A couple more lines. Then he stops.

3:07: file saved. Reacher 20.

Lee hit a button and the printer stirred. A page slid out. Lee stood up, went over to the printer, took out the page. Then he came over and handed it to me. "There."

I think my hand was trembling. Just a little.

I leaned back on the couch and looked it over, slowly. The first page—or first couple of pages—of the new Reacher. Fresh off the printer. Straight out of the mind of Lee Child. (Maybe with a detour through the collective unconscious.)

Less than an hour. Five hundred words. Two fingers. "I find it's about the right typing speed for me," Lee said. "It's as fast as my brain can keep up with."

It took a while for the text to come into focus. I think I was too awestruck or moved or something to make any sense of it at first. A labyrinth. Utterly mysterious. Then words. Then sentences.

That -ing word right at the beginning. I was right about that. Turned out to be "Moving." This is how the first sentence went:

Moving a guy as big as Keever wasn't easy.

7.

ENTER REACHER

KEEVER. GOOD NAME. I was already hooked.

Lee turned his chair around so he was half facing me, half looking back at his text on the screen. He swung his feet up on the desk.

"I wanted to start with a verb of action," he said. "The participle came naturally." He went over it in his head. "See, I didn't want to write, *Keever was a big guy and moving him wasn't easy.* That's too expository. This way we waste no time. It's compact. I thought about *was not easy* for a moment. But the rhythm was better, *wasn't easy.*"

Here it is, the whole of it, as it emerged, that afternoon, September 1, 2014. That page I had in my hand—now you have it in yours.

Moving a guy as big as Keever wasn't easy. It was like trying to wrestle a king-size mattress off a waterbed. So they buried him close to the house. Which made sense anyway. The harvest was still a month away, and a disturbance in a field would show up from the air. And they would use the air for a guy like Keever. They would use spotter planes, and helicopters, and maybe even drones.

They started at midnight, which they figured was safe enough. They were in the middle of ten thousand acres of nothingness, and the only man-made structure their side of the horizon was the railroad track to the east, but midnight was five hours after the evening train and seven hours before the morning train. So, safe enough. No prying eyes. Their backhoe had four spotlights on a bar above the cab, like kids had on their pickup trucks, and together they made an aimed pool of halogen brightness. So visibility was not a problem. They started the hole in the hog pen, which was a permanent disturbance all by itself. Each hog weighed two hundred pounds, and each hog had four feet. The dirt was always freshly chewed up. Nothing to see from the air, not even with thermal imaging. The picture would white out instantly, from the steaming animals themselves, plus their steaming piles of shit and their steaming pools of piss.

Safe enough.

Hogs were rooting animals, so they made sure the hole was deep. Which was no problem either. The backhoe's arm was long, and it bit rhythmically, in fluent seven-foot scoops, the hydraulic rams glinting in the light, the engine straining and pausing, the cab falling and rising as each bucket-load was dumped aside. When the hole was done they backed the machine up and turned it around and used the dozer blade to push Keever into his grave, scraping him, rolling him, covering his body in dirt, until finally it fell over the lip and thumped down into the shadows.

Only one thing went wrong, and it happened halfway through the job.

The evening train came through five hours late. The next morning they heard on the AM station that a broken locomotive had caused a jam a hundred miles south. But they didn't know that at the time. All they heard was the mournful whistle at the distant crossing, and then all they could do was turn and stare, at the long lit cars rumbling past in the middle distance, one after the other, seemingly forever. But eventually the train was gone, and the rails sang for a minute more, and the taillight was swallowed up by darkness, and they turned back to their task.

Twenty miles north the train slowed, and eased to a stop, and the doors wheezed open, and Jack Reacher stepped down into the dirt in the lee of a grain silo bigger than an apartment house.

"I like the way you use *which*," I said. "*Which made sense anyway*. Subordinate clause, but you give it a fresh start."

"Yeah, *Which* at the beginning of a sentence," Lee said, in a meditative kind of way. "It's an accelerative word. Mostly. I have to be careful not to overdo it though. Becomes a habit."

He stopped thinking about *which* for a moment. He was thinking about the whole of that first paragraph.

"I'm tying my hands here. It's a risk. Who is Keever? What is he? Why is he so damn important?"

"Well, who is he?"

"I've no idea at this point."

I liked that about Lee's writing. He didn't know what he was doing. Didn't need to know. Didn't want to know. Had faith. Blind faith.

"I've made him important though. The fear of the air search. Then you have all the mechanics of burying him. That's what follows. From the sheer size of him and the importance. You have to do a good job of it or it's like he'll pop right back up again. You have to really get him right down there."

I was struck—how could I not be?—by that metaphor in the second sentence. The actual word *size* is explicitly in there, spelling out the governing theme. But *waterbed*? Where did that spring from?

"I slept on a waterbed once. In California? It had a mattress on top, which is strange. But I found myself trying to line up that mattress with the base. Which is impossible. So I thought that was something like the technical problem for the parties unknown."

"You know *Keever* sounds a lot like *Reacher*."

"Does it?"

"Look at it. Listen to it. You've got the "er" at the end and the "ee" in the middle. It's a para-rhyme. Keever-Reacher, Keever-Reacher. Sounds like the train. This is an *alter*-Reacher. And he's huge, just like Reacher. You're suggesting that this really could be Reacher. It is what will happen to Reacher if he's not careful. You always have that. The potential fate for Reacher. Which he generally manages to work around. Unlike a lot of his partners. So you're looking into the void right from the start. You're actually building an abyss. Nothing*ness*."

Child said nothing.

"But you don't start with dialogue. You could have done. You know, 'Hey, what a big bastard he was!' 'What are we going to do with the body?' 'I know, let's dig a hole, a big one,' that kind of thing."

"Yeah." He grinned. "I know what you mean. A lot of writers are like that. They start with dialogue because it looks easier to a reader. Lots of wide-open spaces and air. I very rarely start with dialogue. It's partly tactical. I like it dense. But mostly, Reacher is not a conversationalist. I don't want to give the wrong impression."

"I think Camus said something like that. *Cut out all the chit-chat.*"

Lee took a drag on his cigarette. "I'm taking a risk with this. It's a dense wedge of text. But you're saying to the reader all the time, don't worry, I'm going to take you by the hand and lead you through it."

"'Hogs were rooting animals'?"

"I'm really reacting to the reader's question here. 'Hold on, they're hogs; aren't they going to dig him up again and have him for dinner?' So we have to go down deep."

"With a backhoe."

"I love the backhoe. It's the American word for a JCB in England. A digging machine. A giant shovel. Saves you a lot of time and energy. I'm being a little bit *omniscient observer*. But they are thinking and talking in their vernacular. So we've got to try and stick with that."

"You've got 'steaming' and 'steaming.' And another 'steaming.' I like that. No elegant variation. It's all *steaming.*"

"I really like the *steaming. Shit* and *piss* could change—if I can find some agricultural terms. Reacher wouldn't generally have *shit* and *piss.*"

"You know, I have this feeling you don't much like rural places.

They come up a lot in your fiction as the natural habitat of the bad guys. Is this your take on the American pastoral? Are you being just a bit satirical here about a whole mythology of nature?"

"It's common in Western cultures," he snapped back. "The rural is revered. Farmers are revered." He stood up. Wandered over to the window. Twitched the blind. Looked out on an urban landscape of roofs and windows and water towers. Some sky. A lot of concrete. "But Reacher is all about logic and fact. He would say it's an unexamined assumption. Lots of different kinds of farmers. No doubt some of them are fantastic. But among them are some of the stupidest people doing the stupidest things."

Lee—he loves a good rant. Sometimes it's hard to stop him.

"And if they come up with an innovation it's only to make it even more stupid. Look at chopping up cows in order to feed them to other cows—thus causing BSE. Everybody knows they eat grass. We're turning them into cannibals. Mad cannibals." He turned away from the window, sick of the sight of some distant, seemingly innocent farming community, actually full of unscrupulous maniacs. Nothing like *Charlotte's Web* at all (the one with Wilbur the "radiant" pig). Lee's pigs had to be hogs, not pigs.

"They are not necessarily the repository of wisdom," Lee went on. "They are just as much the repository of ignorance and superstition. And look at the Dust Bowl years. That was all the fault of the farmers. The government was trying to tell them all the time, don't keep planting and harvesting, planting and harvesting every year, year on year, you're going to kill it. And then it dies and blows away. And they're, 'Hey, we didn't know!' They don't know anything."

I had a feeling that *Make Me* wasn't going to be a hymn of praise to that little farmhouse on the prairie. Not one with a backhoe, anyhow.

Lee went and sat back down again, finally running out of steam.

He settled himself back in the chair and put his feet back up on the desk, crossed them, and gazed fondly at the screen.

"I'm feeling good about it. I think it works in and of itself. It's not overlong. And it gets you going. I wish I knew more. But it raises some great questions." It was something he had written for the "Draft" column of *The New York Times* in 2012, under the heading "A Simple Way to Create Suspense." "Ask or imply a question at the beginning of the story"—and then . . . "delay the answer." It was easy for Lee to delay, because he really didn't know the answer. "Who is Keever? Why is he dead? What happened? This is what we want to know. The questions are there. Yes, I'm feeling good at the moment."

He nodded to himself, by way of assent to his own statement. And then he added a qualification. "But also I'm feeling a bit challenged by the next scene. What is Reacher even doing there? How come he's getting off the train anyway? Why here?"

Clearly Reacher has been doing nothing of great import before the book starts up. Just roaming about, no dramas. When he steps down off that train he is reentering the world of action, that realm in which things happen and must be reported on. Lee didn't feel the need to keep tabs on the quiescent Reacher, his well-behaved, decent citizen, peace-loving twin. "Look at Robert De Niro being Jake LaMotta in *Raging Bull*. Classic method acting. He had to *be* Jake. Just as there are method actors, so too there are method writers. They will write out whole bios and calendars for their characters and pin them up on the wall."

I glanced at the walls of his office. They were blissfully devoid of little bits of paper stuck to the plaster.

"A lot of readers come up to me and say—or send me emails and say—'How come Reacher gets into all this mayhem all the time? Can there be that much drama in these little towns?' You could do 'Waiting for Reacher,' but I'm not into that."

He had seen *Waiting for Godot* about "forty times," he reckoned. ("Forty!?" "Thirty-nine maybe.") He denounced a recent production involving Patrick Stewart and Ian McKellen. It was too local, too Northern, and they weren't really trying. Self-indulgent. I said something about *Hamlet,* about how not much happened for long periods, it was all anticipation and retrospective on things that really had happened *off.* Lee didn't fully approve of *Hamlet* either. Self-indulgent. Too long. Were they paid by the minute? "Only *Macbeth* would you leave alone. All the others you would want to speed up. I hate these *Richard III*s which are supposed to be authentic and they're just too long and slow."

He wasn't overly enthusiastic about the comedy in Shakespeare either. "It's just not funny enough."

I asked, "Do you ever want a comic touch in your books?"

"Of course Reacher has more in the way of sardonic humor than he is given credit for. But I'm allergic to comic thrillers. We're talking about killing here. That doesn't seem like the right place for a lot of humor. There are moments—when Reacher leaves a body in the trunk of a car for the rest of the gang to find."

"Classic Reacher sense of humor."

"But I'm not going out of my way to try and be funny. Look . . ." He scanned the screen. " 'Only one thing went wrong . . .' That is almost funny. It's *wry*."

He kept on contemplating what he had written. "It indirectly involves Reacher. The train is Reacher. Another big guy—as you say, an alternative to Keever."

"As big as a silo."

All this talk of size brought us around to the subject of how much he hadn't written exactly. On that particular day. We understood—it was implicit—that it was all about the quality not the quantity. On the other hand Lee liked to crank it out, if possible. Steadily. Day by day.

"So is that the first page, then?"

"It's two pages—of a book. Five hundred words. Half a percent of a book. On day one. That's not bad. On a good day, fairly relaxed, I can do fifteen hundred words." Lee liked to use the word "efficient" or "efficiency" in relation to his work. "The efficiency is severely hampered by not knowing what's coming next. So it's inefficient. But it's efficient because I don't do revisions."

"Not at all?"

"Not much. And I certainly don't let other people do revisions for me." Which started him off on another of his rants. "Look at this word," he says. "*Waterbed.* Or *nothingness* or whatever. Barring catastrophe or the end of the world, I know that this will be published, and in this form. *Waterbed* will remain. Right there, where I've put it. So I care about that word. In the movies, it's a completely unreal feeling. How can you care about this word or that one—because you know it's not going to be there further down the line. A lot of other people are going to come along and rewrite it. *Waterbed* will be gone. You can't care about it in those circumstances. This is why I'm writing novels and not films."

Feeling. It was all about the feeling. Everyone thought that it was the thing that was left out in a Lee Child novel. Whereas the truth was that it was all feeling, all the way through, every last word was feeling. And it had to feel right.

"That is why I can't change anything. The book is like a diary of how I felt at the time. I can't change that."

"I lost count of the cigarettes. Do you think I should be adding up the butts? Making a tally. People probably want to know what the optimal number of cigarettes is, how many per thousand words."

"Too many cigarettes. End of a paragraph; end of a sentence: another cigarette. Normally I'd have had more coffee too." He turned and looked right at me. "I am writing on the verge of a stroke. I'm teetering on the edge."

"Hey, you haven't finished the book yet. You've barely started. We need to know who the hell Keever is."

It was the first time the thought had occurred to me. Is that why he had let me in on the whole thing?—to bear witness, just in case this was the last time. Before it was too late. Despite a solid collection of bad habits, he looked healthy enough. For now. I needed a full medical report. A brain scan maybe. Lungs too.

Lee was like an aging boxer. Muhammad Ali or Joe Frazier coming back for one more big fight. Another twelve rounds in the ring. Another payday. But conscious all the while this could be his last shot at the title. Right up against the odds. And I was his only spectator.

Which reminded me, just a little, of Reacher: this is what he does, he *bears witness*. Without Reacher it's just another tree falling in the forest, silently.

The old split between "office" (downstairs) and "home" (upstairs), in the Flatiron District, had gone. Now it was all one. Which was probably why we were quarantined off, in the dedicated office, at the back of the apartment. Lee reckoned the trouble with working from home was that you are never done, you are always on. And so it proved. He got back to me later that night with some small but significant revisions to what he had already done in the afternoon. A few points had been nagging him.

This is the email he sent me:

Went through what I wrote again and made minor changes that I think snap the voice into better focus—following James Wood's Flaubert theory [in How Fiction Works*], the "semi-*

close 3rd-person" voice there should subtly modify to better characterize the actors. Now I think I have it down, so at the page break we're really going to feel the country villains stepping off stage, and Reacher stepping on.

There was one thing about what he had written that, to my way of thinking, was definitely wrong. But I didn't like to mention it to him. I thought it would be stepping over the line. Like making some kind of sarcastic remark to Reacher.

8.

FUCK YOU, LEE CHILD!

FOLLOWING DAY. Back in the office. The first few sentences remained the same. Keever was still Keever. "I think Keever will always be Keever," Lee said. He admitted later that maybe there was an echo of Cheever in that name (i.e., John Cheever the writer).

But then came the comma. So he did revise after all! He felt the need for a comma. It would make it more "rueful and contemplative," he said.

And they would use the air for a guy like Keever

had, overnight, become

And they would use the air, for a guy like Keever.

The comma picked out and emphasized the importance of Keever—but it also served to draw attention to the thought process of the parties unknown—or rather known but unnamed—who were preparing to bury him. "The punctuation not only makes it stronger—it reflects their being mentally slow. You can hear them saying that."

And then there is a whole word changed in the next sentence. "It seemed to me 'spotter' sounded too trivial." Now that sentence reads: "They would use SEARCH planes, and helicopters, and maybe even drones."

In the second paragraph, "the only man-made structure their side of the horizon" was a problem for Lee. Whose horizon? he wanted to know. It was too definite. And possibly "confusing." "Here they are in the middle of nowhere. They don't even know where the horizon is." In the revised draft this reads:

> "the only man-made structure their side of *any* hori-
> zon . . ."

"It emphasizes their position in the middle of nothingness. They no longer have a clear horizon—it's limitless." It was subtle, but Lee was weaving between the phenomenological point of view of the characters and the omniscient observation of an anonymous narrator. *Horizon* was more him, it was (implicitly) more Reacher.

Lee loves repetition. But he is also sensitive to overdoing it. One of his immediate revisions was to take out one repetition too many. I had become quite attached to the *safe enough* phrase. Ironic (with Reacher in town, who is safe?) and incantatory (like they have to keep saying it to themselves). But where previously he had "So, safe enough. No prying eyes," now he has only, "Therefore, no prying eyes." The second paragraph first sentence contains "safe enough" already. The third paragraph, as we know, is nothing but "safe enough." The point was made. No need to overdo. And maybe he had a soft spot for the word "therefore." Their assumption of some kind of step-by-step irrefutable logic in what they are doing is anything but well founded, especially when Reacher is about to step off the train.

And when it came to the description of the hog pen, Lee wondered if he had been over-embellishing. Enjoying it too much. Rubbing it in. "The dirt was always freshly chewed up," comes out, in the slightly more compressed version, "The dirt was always chewed up."

"We don't need *freshly*. Adverb. One word too many. Better styling. Economy."

I wasn't interrogating him: he was volunteering these thoughts. I wasn't doing any analyzing. He was analyzing himself. Being really rather professorial. Maybe he could get a job as writer-in-residence, at Columbia for example. For the moment, I was his only student. This wasn't an inquisition. Lee had made a big pot of coffee and we were knocking it back, mulling things over. Seminar-style.

There was something he hadn't changed but still wasn't sure about. "I'm still not sure about *shit* and *piss*," he says. "I want something different, but it has to be honest. Would they use 'waste'? I don't know. *Ordure,* for example, is clearly a nonstarter."

I had thrown in "ordure" just for the hell of it and got it thrown right back in my face.

He turned to me and said, with feeling, almost like a reprimand: "But it has to be *honest*." Lee likes to stress certain words, mentally italicizing.

> "Only one thing went wrong, and it happened halfway through the job."

Halfway? On second thought, Lee reckoned, this was "too retrospective." He wanted something more immediate. Now there is no *halfway*, etc. It's "right then": "it happened right then."

I was thinking, there is still a problem with the timing though. If the train comes through only five hours late, that places it at midnight, when they are only just starting work. Shouldn't it be more like six? This was my issue, the one I didn't dare mention to Lee, in case it put him off (or he head butted me in response). He would take care of it, I was sure.

He was more focused on the train going by at that point, what it looked like, not the timetable. The hallucinatory effect. He had swung back to point of view. "It has to be like a vision in a dream. I wanted to emphasize that they were dumbstruck and there was nothing they could do about it. It's beyond their control."

Another thing. Lee didn't want Reacher stepping down into the *dirt*. He often got dirty, of course. But this dirt has been too closely associated with the rural natives and the hogs. We don't want Reacher getting right in the hog pen, surely? So when the train eases to a stop and the doors wheeze open, now we have

> Jack Reacher stepped down onto a concrete ramp in the lee of a grain silo bigger than an apartment house.

It's more solid. "I wanted it slightly higher tech, not dirt. We've had enough dirt. Dirt is for the hicks. And we need to know it's all industrial agriculture, not bucolic at all."

Later that day I'm with Lee in the back of a limousine riding to another TV studio downtown. Chauffeur-driven. All very suave. The sales figures were just coming in from the U.K. First week of publication. *Personal* was number one. But the really interesting thing I noticed, poring over the stats, was that it was outselling the next thirteen combined. "Wow. It's a massacre," I gasped. "The opposition has been comprehensively annihilated."

"I almost feel bad about it," said Lee, barely suppressing a wicked grin.

The also-rans included people like Martin Amis and his holocaust novel, *Zone of Interest*.

"It's good to have the literary guys around," Lee said. He stretched his long legs out comfortably.

"Are they dinosaurs?"

"Writing is essentially a branch of the entertainment industry— like soccer is—and I'm Chelsea, at the moment. Almost exactly. Doing well on the field, but only because there's a lot of behind-the-scenes talent and investment supporting me."

We had been talking about the Premiership earlier. His old team Aston Villa had made a flying start to the season. Seven points out of a possible nine. ("But I'm sure they'll break my heart later. They always do.") Whereas my team, West Ham, had only managed to scrape three together. "Surprisingly, the American system is much more egalitarian. The revenue-pooling system, the draft, it levels the playing field, gives every team a chance. In Britain . . . remember when Villa were winning the league and Ipswich were right up there challenging them? Now . . . the first really are first, and the last are last. It's harder than ever to make up the difference."

A big fat New York bus cut brazenly across our car. The driver was spluttering after stomping on the brakes. "The bus is bigger than you," Lee said reassuringly, leaning forward. "And he doesn't care." He could see the point of view of a bus. He knew what it felt like to be a juggernaut.

*　*　*

I bumped into Joel Rose that evening. Joel is a writer, of the noir persuasion (e.g., *Kill Kill Faster Faster* and corpse-strewn graphic novels), with mad professor hair, goatee, and John Lennon specs. He was less successful than Lee. Everyone is less successful than Lee. So naturally I happened to mention those sales stats. Lee Child annihilating the competition and all that. The Napoleon of literature. We were standing around on the corner of Charlton and Varick in the West Village. Joel thought about it for a while. Weighed the pros and cons. Then gave utterance to his considered judgment:

"FUCK YOU, LEE CHILD!"

9.

THE SONG OF REACHER

"PROFESSOR ANDY MARTIN," Lee says to me. "Come on in."

Apparently Maggie had been checking my academic credentials, such as they were. His people didn't want some maniac creeping up on him in the middle of the night. Or stealing his Renoir or whatever. Technically, I wasn't even a professor (I was only a "Doctor"), but Lee didn't seem too worried about the detail. He had an unwarranted faith in the moral integrity of academics.

He made coffee. He reckoned there was some milk somewhere, but he wasn't too sure about its status. I took it black.

Lee hadn't shaved; he had Reacher-worthy stubble. But he was in a jovial mood, really enjoying being at the beginning of something. He liked it so much he didn't really want to leave the beginning alone.

He had been thinking about the word "like." Of course it was in the second sentence of Chapter 1—simile—but he was thinking of the contemporary verbal tic (I'd mentioned it in some article he had read to do with roaming around New York like a Trappist monk for twenty-four hours). "It's actually quite economical. I like *like*. When someone says to you, 'He was like "I'm so into you,"' it's not that he actually said, 'I am so into you.' It's more, 'He behaved in such a way that a reasonable observer might conclude he was so into me . . .' Which carries an element of doubt. Some kind of approximation has been conceded. So really you're abbreviating the sentence, and implicitly acknowledging the power of impression, while also acknowledging the impossibility of knowing for sure . . . but it's all still there. What was it Ezra Pound said—all poetry is condensation?"

His own Chapter 1 remained stubbornly condensed too. We went into his office and he gave me a fresh printout of page 1. There still wasn't a page 2. It was Friday, September 5. He had started the whole ball rolling on Monday and he was still on the first page. He hadn't added substantially to what he had already written. But he had been finessing. Now he was focused entirely on what Reacher was doing or thinking at the moment he got off the train. Everything was contained in that moment.

"What do you think of the word 'onto'?" he asked me.

"I don't have strong views," I said, knocking back the coffee.

"To me it sounds ugly. I just don't like *onto*. But I've written, Reacher stepped down *onto* a concrete ramp. That is ugly. So I've changed it. Look."

I looked down at the page in front of me. "Jack Reacher stepped down to a concrete ramp." The *on* part of *onto* had gone.

"It's better, don't you think? I'm not having *onto*. Never liked it."

"'. . . down *to* a concrete ramp.' Well, you changed *what* he is stepping down *onto*, I guess you might as well change the preposition, while you're at it. *To* will work."

"I was thinking about what you were saying about dialogue. There's no dialogue at the beginning. But it's all dialogue, in a way, if it's first-person. Nothing but. There's a Nevil Shute novel. The alleged narrator meets some old mate of his in the gentleman's club, who proceeds to regale him with some tale—and that is the story."

"A bit like those old Isaac Bashevis Singer novels."

"Exactly. Shlomo comes up to him and tells him a story. It's all dialogue, really."

"But that was *Personal*. First-person narrative. This is third-person. So it's not dialogue. It's reportage."

"It's funny. I feel as though I'm still just quoting. I did do two first-person narratives in a row. But generally I try to vary it. This time, I didn't feel it *had* to be third-person. There was no real sense of obligation. But the thing is, I knew it was something happening beyond Reacher's knowledge or perception. So it couldn't be his voice at the beginning. It had to be someone else's. Third party, so it's third-person. It's all down to the voice—or *voices*."

I was back on the couch. Lee had given me his one-page printout and I was—I was going to write leafing through it—but how could I be *leafing through* a single page? Anyway, I was reading it. And naturally I was wondering what was coming next. Where does Reacher go from the concrete ramp?

But before we got onto—or rather *to* [delete on!]—that, we had to consider the question of "bigger than" versus "as big as."

"Hold on," says I. "You've changed this bit, haven't you?"

"It had to be," he said. "I was trying to work out why I wasn't really happy with 'a silo bigger than an apartment house.' Obviously it's adjacent to Reacher himself, so I wanted to associate him with the silo. But then he is associated with Keever too. So I realized I needed to echo the first sentence."

Moving a guy as big as Keever . . .

a grain silo as big as an apartment house.

It made sense. The first section starts with the mysterious Keever. The second section switches to Reacher. But there are parallel constructions—to do with comparative sizes—hooking the two of them together. At one level, the novel was all about momentum, forward movement, the sprung or "tripping" rhythm that would "lead the reader by the hand" through the narrative; at another, it was all about the links that cut right across the story line—little subterranean echoes, rhymes, parallels, repetitions, variations. There was a horizontal, linear, syntagmatic axis, propelling you forward, but there was just as much a vertical, paradigmatic axis, a network—at the level of phonology and semantics—holding everything together, keeping it tight and connected. It was prose, of course, but it was just as obviously poetry. *Make Me* is the song of Reacher.

Make Me, that hugely resonant and imperative title, had just acquired another meaning in my mind: this was the novel itself speaking to its author, its maker, crying out to him, *Go on, then, Make Me, and make it as good as you've ever made anything.*

THE LAUNCH (BARNES & NOBLE, UNION SQUARE, SEPTEMBER 3)

JOEL (text): I have tickets for Yankees v Red Sox. Virtually the last game of the season.

ME (text): Damn. Have to go to book launch. *Personal*!

JOEL (text): And they're good seats! Near the front.

LEE (voice): Go to the game! I would.

In the car

KATE (editor): So I hear you're in love with Jack Reacher too.

ME: I used to be. I fell out of love when I realized that coming out with lines like, "You can either walk out of here, or you can be carried out in a bucket," could get me into a lot of trouble.

LEE (laughing at his own line): Carried out in a bucket.

ME: Now I try to stay detached and cool.

LEE: Critical distance. You need that.

MAGGIE (minder): I love *Make Me*. It has to be *Make Me*.

KATE: We're already working on the jacket.

SHARON (publicist): And I'm writing the copy.

[Sound of a phone ringing]

LEE: I don't want to sound like a drama queen, but I need to take this call from Hollywood.

Union Square interview

DAVID GRANGER (editor, *Esquire*): So you bought into the American hard-boiled tough guy tradition?

LEE: It's not an American invention. It goes back to the Middle Ages and beyond. The Scandinavians before that. It was a European tradition for sure. Something to do with the Black Forest—full of peril. Then the Black Forest became sanitized, controlled. Wolves all died out. You didn't need tough guys anymore. So the myth migrated to the U.S.—where there is still a frontier feel. You needed the tough guy all over again. I guess America gave it a particular urban resonance.

DG: *[Some kind of movie question]*

LEE: If you're on a plane and you let the guy sitting next to you know you're a writer, his second question is always going to be, "Have any of your books been made into a movie?" As if the book doesn't really exist until it becomes a movie. As if the book was only a chrysalis waiting to burst forth as a movie. I don't see it like that. A book is a book. A movie is a movie. But books managed perfectly well for hundreds of years without movies to justify them.

DG: Do you do a lot of research?

LEE: I don't *do* any research. Your entire life *is* research.

GUY IN AUDIENCE: Do you ever get writer's block?

LEE: I'm not worried about writer's block. It's not real. This is not rocket science. It's not curing cancer. You just have to sit there every day and write.

The book signing

OLD LADY: I just love Jack Reacher.

LEE (whispering): And he loves you too!

GUY IN HIS TWENTIES: My dad—he died of cancer last year. He hadn't read a book for twenty years. But he read all of yours.

LEE: I hate to lose a reader.

WHITE-HAIRED GUY: Now I have to wait a year for the next one!

LEE: I just can't write them any faster. It takes me a year to write and you're done in a day.

TEENAGE GIRL IN PINK SHOES: What a thrill! This is for my mom. She introduced me to Reacher.

LEE: Always listen to your mom.

The following day

JENÉ LEBLANC (email): I was astonished by the interviewer's assertion that there is no sex in *Personal*. I wanted to stand up and say, "No sex, are you kidding? What do you think goes through the mind of all women when they are reading about Jack Reacher?"

THEN REACHER STEPPED OFF THE TRAIN

LEE WANTED TO KNOW what I thought about the launch at Barnes & Noble. Invited me over. I said I was impressed by *the sea of humanity*. It was the phrase that sprang to mind when I looked out from the stage and contemplated all the people lining up to get their copies of *Personal* signed. It was a real cross-section, a spectrum of society. Demographically diverse. Black and white, young and old, beautiful people, not so beautiful. There didn't seem to be any rhyme or reason to it. Any and every segment of the population could be up for reading Reacher. And in fact Reacher is the strongest brand in fiction. It was in *Forbes* magazine. How likely is the reader of one novel by an author to buy another by the same author? Lee Child came out top. Stephen King was second, Grisham third.

"That's the power of a series character," Lee said. "It's not really me that comes out top. It's Jack Reacher."

Another piece of research had been carried out in the U.K. Apparently Lee Child was the author more readers wanted to get to know.

"Yeah," I said, "I'm living the dream right now."

Lee said, "Maybe a degree of mystery is better."

The second subject in the U.K. research was to do with blurbs on the covers of books. The mini-eulogies excerpted by publishers in the hopes of pulling in more readers. According to the survey, readers didn't trust extracts from newspaper or magazine reviews—they assumed they had been bought and paid for and were automatically untrustworthy.

"Funny, isn't it?" Lee said. "Reviews—no one ever pays a cent for them, as you know."

"Please, somebody, anybody," I said, "come and corrupt me."

Whereas (according to the research) people trusted comments from other writers. Journalists were lying (or saying anything they were told to say), but novelists were telling the truth, only saying what they sincerely believed.

"Even though we are paid to make stuff up."

Which is what got us onto (now I can't help myself) the way authors are perceived at large. I said that thriller writers were seen as a species of idiot savant. Lucky fools who had chanced upon some winning formula.

Lee swatted that idea with a dismissive hand. "How can you write—or even just read—and not be attentive to language and how it's put together?" He loved to read books about how it's done. Stephen King, for example, on his own writing. Or James Wood's critical essay on Flaubert. He admired King's recent novel, *Under the Dome,* in which a giant dome comes to be plonked down on top of a whole town, and saw it as a sly critique of the Republicans. But the only writer he thought was similar to him was Michael Connelly with his detective hero Harry Bosch. "He has a flat, deliberately affectless style that suits the subject."

He was sympathetic to Joel's *Fuck you, Lee Child!* "I would probably feel the same way," Lee said. "In fact I have said something like, 'Fuck you, Tom Clancy!,' in the past." Now he faced the perils of popularity. Every time he had a book come out he would get letters saying that he had stolen someone else's story in a blatant act of piratical plagiarism, but they would be prepared to settle out of court for $10k or whatever. "I just ignore them," said Lee. "No one can say they invented the lonely hero, that's for sure. It's a big tradition. But there is a whole scam industry out there. I imagine they send out these letters to all authors. Maybe they even sucker a few of them, maybe because they really have plagiarized someone."

He wasn't about to say, "Fuck you, J. K. Rowling!" Lee Child and J. K. Rowling were the only two authors who bestrode all the bestseller lists simultaneously on both sides of the Atlantic. But he admitted that she outsold him by a huge margin. "She's a billionaire!" he said, with a degree of respect. "If you look at writing as on a par with music—she is Paul McCartney. The pay scales are eerily similar."

But he wasn't tempted by the Rowling tactic of adopting another name and writing a completely different kind of novel. "Why does she even need to do the typing?" he wondered. "She should just lie on her sofa daydreaming."

He stood up and stalked around the room. "That's what I'm paid to do. There's the relatively boring business side of writing— you know, the typing, the publishing minutiae, getting the book out there, marketing, selling it, if you can. But the first half is daydreaming. I live in a permanent daydream. I get paid to daydream narratives."

At breakfast in a SoHo café that morning, a friend had wondered why it was that Lee Child wasn't seen out and about town more often, being photographed going into clubs and suchlike. "I can't stand clubs!" Lee said. "For one thing." But there was something else too. "I don't think the paparazzi are even slightly interested in taking my picture. Why would they be?" Every now and then he would be recognized in the street, maybe once or twice a week. "But get real. I'm never going to sell a single newspaper or magazine."

He had written an article for *The Wall Street Journal* on the subject of William Styron and *Sophie's Choice* which argued that Styron was really the last of the big lions of literature. "The last of the guys big enough to be photographed going into clubs," Lee said. He included Norman Mailer in that list. Arthur Miller. It was a short list and they were all dead now.

I told him about the time I had gone up to Norman Mailer in a bar in London and how we had fallen into conversation, mainly about blondes as it turned out. Lee had once done something similar with Jimmy Greaves, the soccer player. He'd seen him hanging about in a television studio and had gone up to him and said (as I did), "I don't normally do this sort of thing," i.e., accosting a celebrity. And he told him he thought he had been the greatest thing ever when, as a kid, he had seen him play back in the 60s. Greaves had looked up at him with his big spaniel, veteran alcoholic eyes and said, "But what do you think of me now?" Lee had gone to the same school as Enoch Powell (the Tory politician), Jonathan Coe (novelist), Ken Tynan (theater critic), and (an earlier generation) J.R.R. Tolkien. One of the old direct-grant grammar schools, in Birmingham. "It was a high-powered school, but I didn't particularly enjoy it," he said. "I guess that is just me." Jonathan Coe's novel *The Rotters' Club* had been based on a sixth-form (the first year of high school, for Americans) club at the school. It was a book I liked a lot but Lee didn't think too much of it. "Look at Julian Barnes's *The Sense of an Ending*. All that stupid nostalgia for schooldays! What is it about these guys? What is their audience? They are all fifty- or sixty-something white males who think that the most fascinating people they met were in the Lower Sixth. A pretty narrow constituency. And they're all dying anyway."

Lee lamented the passing of the great writers, the "public intellectuals" of the past. "It's just politicians and comedians on *Question Time*. They don't know who to put on anymore."

Oddly enough I had recently given a paper at a conference on the fate of the public intellectual. From Zola onwards. "J'accuse . . . ?" and all that. Lee went and poured himself another cup of black coffee in the kitchen. "The public intellectual is dead in America," he said. "Over the last fifty years we've had them. Now we're at the end. There is no more Gore Vidal or Norman Mailer. Maybe that's a good thing, I don't know. Maybe we overestimated them in the past. Now we underestimate." In America he thought the decline of the intellectual went back to Reagan and the 80s. "We had a smart generation of people coming out of the 50s and 60s. The Reagan era demolished all that."

His wife has an MA in Anglo-Saxon. Lee was sympathetic to academic institutions, but also conscious of how crazy they can be. "There's this guy. Built his whole forty-year career on just this one word. It's in a poem about the Battle of Maldon. One word in it, nobody can really figure out what it means. That's the word. This guy has taken possession of it. It's his territory. He owns it. One word."

He looked at me quizzically. "I guess that's the kind of thing you do, right?"

I looked down at his page. "I was thinking *waterbed* . . . or maybe *nothingness*. More philosophical. Do you think I could make a career out of that?"

But the reality is that Lee himself was liable to get pretty worked up about a single word. Or a phrase. Or the weight of a sentence. And this sense of the consequences of what he wrote next was holding him back. "Everything hangs on this next sentence or two," he said. "First of all it's, what does he see? It's his point of view. But then—what is the town like? Who's in it? What's in it?"

"Like Margrave in *Killing Floor*. Everything so spick-and-span and polished and manicured—and it's all a lie."

"Exactly. Just describing a place and we're already getting some sense of the weight of the plot. It all matters. It matters a lot. And he's going to run into the no. 2 character. Potentially this could be a colleague of Keever's. A *she*? Looking for him. But then Reacher maybe looks like him. As you said, Reacher even sounds like Keever. I can imagine her making out the silhouette of Reacher as being Keever. Yes, I can see some play with that."

Reacher, stepping down [on]to that concrete ramp. One more step and everything else would follow on, automatically.

"I need to chill and ruminate," said Lee. "Is it purely local—or could it be something more global? A terrorist thing? I have to get the *density* of it. To set up the scene." He lit a fresh cigarette and took a thoughtful drag. "This is the downside of not having a plan. Or a plot. This is *distributed* thinking. It's all about mood and tone and foreshadowing. It's not a plot, it's more like a symphony—all the meaning has to resolve itself into that final chord."

The end was entailed by the beginning, but it remained somewhere over the horizon or around a mountain, like a train, even if you could see the plume of smoke and feel the rail vibrating.

Lee hated injustice—and it was everywhere. He had been reading a book set in the 50s—"within my lifetime, or almost"—somewhere down south. *Devil in the Grove*. Florida. A black kid working in a store—"he just used to sweep the floor and did a fine job of it"—sends a Christmas card to a white girl also working there. Says, "I hope you send me one." For that he is lynched. Or rather, he is taken out and marched away to be lynched. But, as if that wasn't enough, his father is marched right up there too and made to watch and is unable to do anything about it and has to say sorry to his son that he is powerless while he is right there in front of him, being hanged, for no reason by a bunch of white supremacists.

"That is so terrible. At least in Ferguson," said Lee, bringing it right up to date, thinking about the recent police shooting of Michael Brown, "there is rioting too. There is protest. Back then no one even noticed. No one thought of getting justice."

Then Reacher stepped off the train.

MOTHER'S REST

"I DON'T WANT TO BREAK UP the party or anything, I was just passing."

"Come on in, you bloody sociopathic loner, I've got some important news for you." Lee ushered me in.

His daughter, Ruth, was there, and his brother, Andrew. A bit of a family reunion. They were going out somewhere fairly suave. Looked pretty dressy. It was a hot September day in New York and I was in cutoffs and flip-flops. Feeling underdressed as I sipped a cup of tea.

He and his brother ("*younger* brother," Andrew stressed—by a decade and a half—married to historical novelist Tasha Alexander) were about to go and do a joint launch of their books in Chicago. Andrew had a stand-alone thriller, *Run*, coming out (amateur caught up in fiendish plot, or plots, a bit *North by Northwest*. Funny moment where the hero, under siege, toys with the idea of running out and killing a few bad guys, then escaping à la Jack Reacher—and then thinks better of it, and comes up with a techie solution involving a microwave and a can of Coke).

The vital news was this: Lee had come up with the name of the place Reacher had stopped at. "Mother's Rest." Which also explained why he had stopped there. Liked the sound of the name. Classic Reacher—purely whimsical. "He's sentimental about it. Thinks it's something to do with wagon trains having a break on the way west. So he gets off the train. It'll probably turn out to be a corruption of some original Indian name meaning shit hole."

He had also knocked off a short story the night before to meet a deadline. "The Picture of the Lonely Diner." It had to be based on a place in New York. Lee chose the Flatiron District. Reacher turns up, it's all cordoned off, DO NOT ENTER, so naturally he enters anyway. New York with no one in it (the word "nothing" comes up a lot), except a doomed spy and a sympathetic woman FBI agent (SHE: "Why were you born in Berlin?" REACHER: "I had no control over my mother's movements. I was just a fetus at the time.").

I'd noticed that Haruki Murakami, the great Japanese novelist, had come out as a Reacher fan in *The Guardian* (Murakami: "I like Lee Child. . . . So far I have read ten of them." Steven Poole: "What do you like about them?" Murakami: "Everything's the same!").

"Yeah, I love Murakami too," said Lee. "You know they think he's not literary enough in Japan. He's sensitive about it. So it was brave to say he likes me. Fuel for the fire."

Ruth wanted to know what they thought about her father in Cambridge. I told her that there was some git in the English department, Justin I think his name was, or Alex maybe, who had made some snooty, pompous remark about the Child *oeuvre* when I had suggested inviting him over to give a talk. I thought it was fairly typical of the academic mindset.

Ruth said, "Harold Pinter was pretty darn snooty too."

"Then there was that guy in *The Guardian*," Andrew chimed in. "About how every numbskull on the train was reading Reacher or *The Girl with the Dragon Tattoo*."

"Whatever," Lee said, taking it all on the chin.

Ruth kindly suggested that maybe I should be translating Lee's books into French. Reacher wasn't selling in France. Maybe the translation was at fault?

"I was doing a signing in Lyon last year," Lee said. "I was with two other guys. They had queues going out of the door. I had three people." He couldn't understand it. "I even made his mother French! Reacher speaks French! What is wrong with them?"

I wondered if it could have something to do with the Napoleon syndrome. I had just been reading a couple of books by Pierre Lemaitre, whose detective hero is less than five feet tall. "So maybe Reacher is just too big for French taste?"

He said he was thinking of pulling his books out of France altogether, even though they had a house there. "It would be nice to have a country where I don't have to do anything," he said.

Lee was being honest, the way he always was. To the point of expressing vulnerability. He regularly claimed to have no feelings. "Feelings?" he snorted. "If I ever have one you'll be the first to know!" But, right now, contrary to his ironic remarks, he was *having a feeling*. He was especially sensitive about his writing. In *Die Trying* he had written that "Nathan Rubin died because he got brave." It was the first line. The editor had crossed out "got" and put in "became." Lee was furious and had put it right back in again, but the editor, a guy called David, wouldn't give up on the point until Lee finally exploded, "David, you are fucking with the wrong marine!"

"Every now and then I write something gemlike—and nobody notices. It's not that I want to draw attention to technique or anything. But you'd think just once in a while a critic would take note. But no. I have a great sentence, a great paragraph—and it's like it's invisible!" He had been asked to write a short piece for someone on a political theme. So he wrote what he called "a bland defense of democracy"—"It probably still needs defending"—but the key thing was that he had written only five sentences, and each sentence had started with the following letters: O, B, A, M, A. The whole thing was a subtle acrostic.

"And nobody noticed!" he lamented. "In fact," he said to me, "you're about the only guy who does. You and Janet Maslin [a *New York Times* critic, one of his greatest fans]. I'll never forget that line of yours: 'Reacher is a liberal intellectual with arms the size of Popeye's.' I liked that."

He took me into the back room for a minute away from the rest of his crew. Showed me how Reacher had moved on, going further into *Mother's Rest*. But he—Lee—had had to go back again. That one line had been nagging at him. The one about the hogs' "steaming piles of shit and their steaming pools of piss."

Now it read: "steaming piles and pools of waste."

"One less *steaming*," I said. "Pity. I liked the *steaming*."

"It's not that there is anything wrong with *piss* and *shit* as such," Lee said. "But, I don't know, I feel the groove is not there."

THE GOOD, THE BAD, AND THE UGLY

(Lunch with Lee and Joel)

"I CAN SEE you've made an effort," Lee said. "You're wearing shoes." His own outfit was only marginally above the sartorial standards set by Reacher.

We met at Mae Mae on Vandam, in the West Village. It had a bookish feel about it, mainly because it had actual books—as well as bottles of wine—on the shelves. So it seemed appropriate. The three of us had a table in a booth, tucked away at the back, known as "the library." Which probably explains why we were talking baseball mostly. Turned out Reacher had been making progress in Mother's Rest, but baseball came first.

Joel (big blue overshirt, John Lennon glasses, cloud of hair): "How the fuck did you get to throw a pitch at the Yankees?"

That was mainly what he wanted to know, having been a Yankees fan since he was a kid and his dad, who was a waiter, got a lot of free tickets to the games. He was asking Lee rather than me of course, since Lee was the one who got to throw a pitch at the Yankees.

It wasn't the greatest of pitches, but it wasn't the worst by a long distance. 50 Cent, for example ("And where the fuck did that dumb sonofabitch name come from anyhow?" says Joel), threw it high and wide. Lee wasn't trying to impress anyone. And, although also a keen Yankees follower, had never played baseball as a kid in Birmingham. It wasn't too fast, and it had a bit of a loop to it, but it was straight and not too high. The catcher caught it, so that was okay.

"Michael Connelly did it before me. So that provided a model. And Harlan Coben. And Karin Slaughter, but she has a genetic advantage. Her great-uncle was Enos Slaughter, one of the best baseball players of all time. Great name too," Lee said.

The pitch was back on September 10. Lee had practiced over the summer in England. Probably not the optimal place for playing baseball, more into cricket. But he had it all worked out. Thought about it, mentally prepared. Come the day, scorned the chauffeur, took the subway to Yankee Stadium. Walked out onto the field, brimming with confidence. Cheers of the crowd. Then a Yankees guy leans over and whispers to him, helpfully, "Hey, Mr. Child, remember you're on a mound. You're going to throw low. So pitch it up. Aim high."

That threw him. It was one more thing to think about. One too many. He was okay till then. "I can't pitch and think at the same time," he said.

Anyway he was so tall it was like living permanently on a mound.

He'd once had a conversation with Joe Girardi, manager of the Yankees. "There are two kinds of people," said Girardi. "Those who think two fifths of a second is a short time, and those who think it's a long time." If you are one of those rare few who think it's really quite long, then you can play baseball, otherwise forget it. "Baseball is basically impossible," says Lee. "The time between throwing the pitch and trying to hit it is so short. The ball is coming at you so fast. And the bat in your hands is so slim—and round!—there is no chance of hitting it. That's what makes it so great."

Lee was ordering. I remembered Reacher ordering coffee and eggs in the diner at the beginning of *Killing Floor*. I thought Reacher's willingness to go into cheap eateries and have a pot of coffee was the link with Haruki Murakami (whose heroes love a good Dunkin' Donuts). "I don't have any sense of how good food is," he said. "I like it, but I can't really tell the difference." He and Joel ordered some kind of meaty sandwiches or burgers; I had a salad.

Joel loved the fact that Lee had written *Killing Floor* in pencil. It was so *not* prima donna. Not even a typewriter. September 1, 1994. Three pads of A4, the kind with lines. One pencil. One pencil sharpener. And an eraser. That was what he had bought at the Arndale Centre. It cost £3.99 (he remembered precisely). He wrote the whole of the first draft in pencil; the second in pen; and the third on someone else's laptop. It took a day and a half for the printer to print it all out. (He still has the pencil stashed away in Sussex. He tends to hold on to stuff like that.)

"I felt I had to make it clear to *me*—this is NOT a hobby. I had to *earn* the computer. Till then it was the pencil." He'd been thinking for a few years he could probably write something, but doing television had stopped him. It was John D. MacDonald's Travis McGee series that had first convinced him or inspired him. "He made me think it was possible. I could see how it could be done. I love to see how things work on a granular level. When I lost my job it was there in my mind. If you look carefully there is not a huge distance between Travis McGee (six foot four) and Jack Reacher (six foot five)." McGee's job was "salvage."

Lee doesn't really think he has invented anything. It's all borrowed. Partly from MacDonald, mainly from antiquity. He is preoccupied with what Reacher is doing right now, getting off the train in Mother's Rest. But he also has a long nothing-new-under-the-sun view of everything that puts it all in perspective.

"We have a prehistory of around seven million years. We have been recognizably modern for only thirty thousand years." We tossed different figures around, depending on what Ice Age exhibition we had been to. "Still, for every year we've been modern we've been premodern for five hundred."

"Do you mean two hundred fifty?" I said, jotting numbers on my pad.

"Whatever." We were still cavemen at heart, paleo-thinkers, filled with atavistic fears and tribal habits.

"But think what this does for storytelling," says Lee. We've been telling stories for maybe 100,000 years. But only very recently have they appeared on the page. "When most writers talk about 'voice' they mean something rather obscure; when I say it I'm really thinking about talking to somebody, for me the voice is really a voice, it's oral. Everything is oral. I'm sitting there trying to draw you in with my voice." Lee was like the opposite of Derrida, who said there is nothing beyond the Text. For Lee there was nothing beyond the Voice. A pencil maybe.

His great-grandfather in Ireland had been illiterate. He was a miller. He and his wife had managed to make enough to send their kid to school. So his grandfather was the first to get an education. "Marks on the paper are secondary," he said. "Everything comes out of syntax. But that was verbal. The difference is then it was narrowcast. If you were a storyteller in the past you could

only impact on a few people at a time, maybe hundreds or a thousand over time. Now it's millions."

Joel muttered something about how he had only about nine
people turn up to one of his book launches. "Sounds like one of
my classes," I said.

So these were the two types of story, according to Lee. He was
strictly structuralist and binary about it. Reminded me a lot of
Claude Lévi-Strauss, the great French anthropologist, who also
reckoned that all stories were an exercise in *bricolage* or recycling,
picking up old bits and pieces and refashioning them into something new.

1. "There's something out there!" You're sitting around in
   the cave and there are noises outside. Scary noises.
   Coming from the world beyond the cave. "Half the stories
   in the world right there," says Lee.
2. A guy leaves the cave. And then comes back. "That's all
   the other stories."

"Plato's myth of the cave," I said. "In *The Republic*. He comes
back and then everyone else wants to kill him to shut him up.
They don't believe all those stories about the sun."

JOEL: I was telling Andy about Elmore Leonard and his rule about
writing.
LEE: Which one?
JOEL: If it sounds like writing, cut it.
LEE: Of course you could read his books and find every single one
of those "rules" of his broken. I think he wrote that piece for
The New York Times. Probably signed up to do it a few months

before and then suddenly it was the deadline and he just shoved that down without enthusiasm and without thinking about it. I mean, "Don't start with the weather." You know, if the weather is important—think of Alistair MacLean—start with it. It all depends. Maybe you wouldn't have "It was a dark and stormy night."

ANDY: I still like "It was a dark and stormy night."

LEE: And "Never use an adverb." "Never" *is* an adverb!

ANDY: Was that an exclamation? He said you're supposed to go easy on the exclamations!

LEE: It's moved on.

ANDY AND JOEL: Whoa.

He was talking about the plot of *Make Me.* Joel and I were instantly enthralled. He would have been good around the campfire, Lee—he would definitely make you forget about the wolves or the saber-tooth.

"It's all dialogue, remember, or monologue anyway, the voice of the narrator, or voices I suppose. But I felt the page needed breaking up. It was time for the next character. An encounter."

ANDY AND JOEL: Who?

"It's a woman. Has to be. She is looking for Keever. Sees Reacher coming towards her away from the train station."

"What time is this?" says I. "Is it still dark?"

"Yes," said Lee. "The train has only just pulled out. So it's not long after midnight. Maybe there is a pool of light. Vapor lights. I felt I had to get right in there, not wait for morning. She is looking for Keever. Sees Reacher looming up. Thinks it's him. She could be . . . another member of the same firm, maybe the same detective agency, something like that, maybe only half knows him or knows of him. Of course we know Keever is already dead, but she doesn't know that. She thinks Reacher is Keever."

"Reacher doesn't care," I said.

"Right," said Lee. "He's indifferent. He's looking for a motel or a diner. Doesn't want to know about Keever. Not interested."

"He'll get sucked in somehow though," says Joel.

"Always does," says Lee. "All he wants is coffee."

"The Murakami thing," I said. "Dunkin' Donuts."

"My problem here is . . ." Lee started.

"The punch-up," said I.

"Random acts of extreme violence." Joel.

"Readers are going to start to complain. You wouldn't believe the number of messages I get. Amazon or wherever. 'There weren't enough fights so I put it down.'"

JOEL: When's it coming?

LEE: See what I mean? They demand a fight in the first ten pages. But we can't just have a couple of hicks come up to him, challenge him, and get their asses kicked.

JOEL: Why not?

LEE: That is exactly what it's like. Ten pages and where's the fight scene? Readers are ruthless.

ANDY: Okay, Lee, listen, I have the solution, this is what you ought to do . . .

LEE: Come on, let's go and have a cigarette.

JOEL: Good idea.

I followed the two of them out of Mae Mae onto Vandam. They were already puffing away. "Better give me one of those," I said. Lee gave me one of his Camels. I thought I'd better check it out. I struggled a bit with the lighter, finally got a flame, lit it, took a drag. Managed not to cough. "I want the joint next time," I said.

I wasn't kidding. I really did. It was a matter of trying to get into the Lee Child mind. Because he is one for the substances. Recreational. Only "weed" though so far as I know. And, here is the thing, he is a firm believer. Evangelical in fact. "I don't think weed should be made legal," he said. "It should be *compulsory!*"

Another definite exclamation. Sorry, Elmore!

He had this theory about how it helped him "make connections." He used to smoke one in the evening, now he'll sometimes have one in the day too. I mentioned that the last time I'd smoked a joint was one dark and stormy night somewhere down south with Kiefer Sutherland. Lee easily topped that pathetic boast. Turned out Kiefer's father, Donald Sutherland, had written to him saying he could have played Reacher back in the day. The world is full of Reacher fans.

Lee thanked cigarettes for suppressing his appetite and said that at least being into soft drugs had stopped him from becoming an alcoholic. "It was an economic thing," he said. "You couldn't smoke and drink too. You had to choose. I don't drink much to this day. And I never got into cocaine or heroin—couldn't afford it. Not without robbing somebody."

It was while standing out in the sun on Vandam smoking a Camel that I learned the following about Lee Child. He was fourteen and a half when he lost his virginity. Twice. Kind of. Lucky bastard. His friend's parents had gone away—this was in 1969, April—one weekend, there was a party of some kind. "A weekend bacchanal. Friday, Saturday, and Sunday." He smoked his first ever joint.

"I benefited from how behind the times my parents were. They worried about me drinking. I could operate with impunity. They thought I'd been on some kind of study weekend. Or hiking in the hills."

And he got lucky with a girl. His first. And then again, half an hour later, with her older sister. His second. They were all high.

In the middle of all that I managed to slip in that I had once taken a quarter of a tab of LSD, on Hampstead Heath, probably around the same time as Lee was having his first joint. But it was no match for the two sisters story.

I guess it was only after Lee had gone and Joel had gone back to his mighty artistic struggle and I was left alone ruminating that I worked it out. Of course! The punch-up has to happen with the bunch of guys who think they've buried Keever. It was obvious. They bury the big guy. The backhoe, the hole, the rooting hogs, cover it all up. Head off into town for a drink and . . . fuck me, it's him again, the big bastard, I told you to bury him properly!!!

The specter of Keever, haunting *Mother's Rest*.

Then I rushed back to the apartment and had half a grapefruit to get rid of the taste of the bloody cigarette.

14.

ON THE MONEY

FOR SOME REASON Lee's eyes looked a steelier kind of blue. And he had a lot of stubble. He was well into the "middle" phase of the book, rolling the stone right back up the hill again. We talked about my solution to *the punch-up problem;* he dismissed it and came up with something much better. (More nuanced: the locals don't think Reacher *is* Keever, he is only *similar,* therefore ... connected?)

Then we started talking numbers. That is what I was here for. The economics. He was giving me the lowdown on how much he got paid. No hazy euphemisms, no mystification, no nonsense. The raw figures, hard cash. He showed me a check he had just received. It was sitting on the desk in his office. He'd only just taken it out of the envelope. "There you go," he said. "This is how much I'm worth." The check was from Paramount Pictures in

Hollywood. So I knew it was going to be big money—telephone numbers. I had a close look. "Wow!" I said, eyes wide open. "I can't believe it."

Paid to Lee Child (at his old office address) in the amount of:

$28.72

I took a photograph of it for posterity.

"That is serious money," Lee said. "Acting residuals, from my cameo in the movie. DVD, and on-demand and so on. I really feel I earned that. Everything else is just . . . Monopoly money."

The rest of the time we were talking about the Monopoly money. He was doing most of the talking. I was mainly just chipping in gasps of amazement. We went through to his living room, the one looking out over Central Park, a few muted traffic sounds floating up from twelve floors down. He lit a cigarette. We started where he started, with *Killing Floor*.

"I was laboring under a misapprehension," Lee began. "I'd written the first half. I thought it would take months for an agent to get back to me. I'd heard that on the mythic grapevine. So I sent it off saying I'd finished the novel and here's the first half, what do you think? I picked him out of the *Writers' and Artists' Yearbook*—he was the only one who said he made money for his clients. The agent got back to me in a few days. He actually wrote me a letter, which shows how long ago this was. He read it straight off. Then he says, 'I like this, send me the rest.' So I had to reply something like, 'Just fine-tuning the last chapter. Will send soon.' Completely caught me out. Anyway, he agreed to represent me. So I go and see him in London.

" 'How much are you looking for?' he says.

" 'I'm out of a job,' I said. 'I need to replace my salary. Aim high. How about the Prime Minister's salary?'

" 'I can't get you that,' he says. 'I can get you more or less. There is no middle ground.'

" 'Okay make it more, then,' I said."

The graph of his income from the Reacher series shot up, steeply, like a space rocket. I kept on adding zeroes. So much so that I actually ran out of notepad around here. I had only a thin little exercise book that I'd bought round at the old NYU store. Small one. Lightweight. Not big enough for those numbers. Lee noticed. "What kind of journalist are you? First you don't have a pen, now you don't have any paper!"

I think he liked the fact that I preferred a pen and paper to, say, a tape recorder. It was old-school. It was how he started with *Killing Floor,* after all. Paper and pencil. He got up and went into his office. I trailed along behind him. "People keep giving me notebooks. Here, have this one." It was a serious black notebook, which appropriately enough had the words "SERIOUS NOTE-BOOK" stamped in a fine red font on the front cover. In parentheses, it said, "To make it look as if I know what I am doing." Strangely reassuring.

I filled a lot of that one too. Finally looked up.

"What do you do with all this money?"

"I don't know what I do with it really. I give some of it away." And it was true—he had given a lot of scholarships to a couple of British universities, and saved a lot of animals, and randomly bought things for people down on their luck. "Don't know where the rest has gone. I feel a bit like George Best." Lee was referring to the legendary Irish soccer player who played for Manchester United. "You know, *I spent most of it on women and booze and fast cars. And the rest I squandered.* It's going to sound trite—but I am not that into money. I spend money on convenience. I'll pay for the lunchtime flight rather than getting up in the middle of the night. But I'm not particularly interested in being rich."

"It's art for art's sake, then, at some level?"

"Has to be. Art for art's sake. It's a joy and a pleasure. But it's also a job. That pays for your family's welfare."

"So you're a poet . . . and a ruthless bastard at the same time?"

"One does not impact on the other. They are parallel. The one is uncorrupted by the other."

There was one word Lee kept coming back to. It was the difference between books and movies. The word was *trust*. "They trust you," Lee was saying. "The publisher trusts you. The reader *trusts* you. In the movies it's more, 'Oh, he's a good storyteller—and we are going to change it all anyway.' I really enjoy writing screenplays—but really, why bother? You know it will either never be made or it will be unrecognizable. It's an unreal feeling."

"But when you're writing books . . . ?"

"When you're writing books you take extra care. Because of the *trust*."

Maybe that is why he could trust himself to do the job. I mentioned a friend of mine, a writer/director, who was forever worrying about some other great work out there—*Hamlet*, for example, or *Boyhood*. Feeling undermined or eclipsed by it all. Lee had some sound advice for him. "Name any author. He or she is the best in the world at writing his or her own book. No doubt about it. Me, for example. Lee Child is the best in the world at writing a Lee Child book. No one else could do it. Michael Connelly is the same. Could I write his books? No way. I'm always knocked out by other people's work. But that is them and this is me!"

It was all in *the voice*. The voice was everything. But Lee still didn't expect to write the perfect book. *Make Me* wasn't going to be perfect either. "If *Make Me* was perfect, I would feel . . . what's the point? It's done. Theoretically, it would be disabling. But in practice you will never write the perfect book."

"So how do you feel at the end?"

"It's great," he said. "You're feeling great. But it's not a hundred percent—somehow it never quite lives up to the hope." Success was always tinted with the color of failure.

15.

THE QUIXOTIC MATADOR

LEE CHILD ONCE MADE A BARGAIN with himself. It was on a Saturday, late in 1984, maybe. In his car on the way to Leicester. Aston Villa was playing an away game against Leicester City. At the time Leicester City was a top team, with an attack led by Gary Lineker, star center-forward for England. Lee vowed that he would forever give up smoking if only Aston Villa could be granted a victory. It was a pact with God, to forswear nicotine henceforth and for all eternity, if only . . . In the event, Aston Villa lost 5–0. They were slaughtered. So either there was no God or he was an evil bastard who took pleasure in tormenting his own children (and one Child in particular). He felt betrayed. Naturally, Lee took revenge by smoking even more on the way back to Manchester. And has loyally, implacably, continued to do so ever since.

Which sort of explains why he was in such a hurry to get off the plane and out of the terminal and light up. I had a puff to keep him company. But Itziar de Francisco was really smoking. She was the young, attractive, dark-haired, dark-eyed, multilingual woman the publishers had sent to act as his minder in Madrid. He gave her one of his Camels. He was there to pick up a literary prize. Following in the footsteps of Philip Kerr, Michael Connelly, and Harlan Coben, he had been awarded the VIII Premio RBA de Novela Negra 2014. It was worth some six-figure sum.

"I shouldn't even be doing this," he said, back in New York. "I should stay home. I have a book to write."

"It's a prize," I said. "A *literary* prize. And there's loadsamoney attached. And it's Madrid. What is your problem? Are you going to do a Sartre and turn it down? I think he always regretted it."

"This is not the Nobel for one thing. No one in their right mind is going to give me the Nobel Prize for literature."

I'd always loved those stories of Sartre and Camus accepting or not accepting the Nobel, and Solzhenitsyn making his great speech about literature and human rights and the fate of the world. So I was envisaging something along those lines. Or like the scene from *Star Wars* in which Luke Skywalker, Han Solo, and Princess Leia receive some kind of medal and are applauded by the masses on account of saving their planet from the dreaded Death Star.

It turned out Lee had sent along his foreign rights agent to accept the prize the month before, who gave some gracious acceptance speech on his behalf. All he was doing himself was a ton of interviews with the press and TV. And speaking—and then it was a little bit more *Star Wars*-y—at the Getafe Novela Negra literary festival on the outskirts of Madrid.

It was his first time in Madrid, he was telling Itziar. But he had a strong connection with Spain nevertheless. Just as Flaubert went off on his tour around Egypt and the Orient before returning to Normandy to get down to work on *Madame Bovary,* so too Lee (together with wife and daughter) went to Spain for a holiday shortly before he wrote *Killing Floor*. "We had a great time on the beach, somewhere down south, in Andalusia, on the Mediterranean," said Lee. "Swimming, sunbathing, eating paella. Then I got back and found this message on the answering machine telling me I had been sacked. So Spain was a real high point for me." It was the end of his previous life, the last act of Jim Grant, before he morphed into Lee Child. "So Spain is always linked to Reacher in my mind."

Hace calor. I was reminded of my old Spanish lessons as we drove into town. It was a cloudless blue sky. *El sol brilla.* Shirtsleeves at the end of October. Itziar was telling us about how some of her old ancestors had been shot somewhere around here by Franco. "What am I doing here?" Lee muttered. "I should be writing, not talking!"

Lee is like the sun—it takes him a while to warm up in the morning. Which is why he only gets started on writing in the afternoon, around two (about the time I am thinking of a siesta). Except all he was doing in Madrid was talking. We kicked off at the Prado. Somehow the newspaper had impossible-to-get permission to shoot in the museum. He was photographed in the midst of some vast gallery, surrounded by great works of art, looking huge. He particularly wanted to see *The Colossus* by Goya. There was a definite Reacheresque quality to this hairy giant looming over some little village. "It's obviously not by Goya," Lee said.

He was drawn to another one of some poor bugger getting his liver pecked out by vultures.

There was a reason, other than having to get up early to catch the plane, why he was grouchy though. He never got writer's block, he said, but he admitted he was "stalled." Or possibly "side-tracked." In all his interviews he said, with total conviction, speaking of the new novel, "I don't really have any idea just now what it's about," "not a clue." He was "excited to find out," just like the reader. At the Getafe festival, he said he was open to ideas, but he wouldn't be paying for them. "Ideas are free," he said. He still hadn't worked out what the hell was going on in Mother's Rest, why Keever had gone there in the first place, and why he had to die, and what exactly Reacher was supposed to do about it. In fact he was right up against a brick wall, going nowhere.

Also there was no way he could write while he was on the move, he said. Reacher was the nomad. Child was sedentary. The hunter-gatherer of old had to be holed up in his office in NYC. I, on the other hand, was writing in cafés, on planes and trains, or in airport lounges.

"Oh well, I'm done after this week," he said, knocking back a glass of rioja.

We were sitting in some bar somewhere, the kind of "Clean, Well-Lighted Place" that Hemingway spoke of, where the characters are preoccupied with the intuition of *nada* (or nothingness).

"Then it's your birthday."

"Okay after that. When I'm back in New York."

"Then there's California in November."

"You know what," he said, lighting up another Camel. "Maybe I'll never finish this one. Or it'll be a real disaster. It's possible."

"I have faith," I said.

"I just don't know," he said.

We had to go outside, even in Spain. He had a few puffs. "Do you ever think it's fundamentally ludicrous to write eighteen or nineteen novels about the same character?"

"What about twenty?"

"Well," he said, expelling a Camel-shaped cloud, "once you've done nineteen you might as well do twenty."

Despite all of which, he was in a generous mood. He offered to pay for me at the Hotel de las Letras. You could tell it was a classy place. Four-star. Expensive. With poems by Pablo Neruda ("Oda a las cosas") on the wall. Roof terrace (where he was doing the interviews). Cue momentary wrestling with my own conscience. I had to turn him down (reluctantly).

"Artistic integrity?"

"I'll find a cheap dive in the back streets," I said, with some notion of doing an Orwell.

In reality, I got talking to *una chica muy linda* working the desk and wearing a Ralph Lauren shirt (*"Me gusta su camisa,"* I said shamelessly), haggled them way down, and then got an upgrade thrown in. They took pity on my pathetic Spanish, which was better than *nada*. I ended up with a room better than Lee's, with its own terrace, garden, and lounger in the sun. And I had no qualms about accepting free meals on the RBA tab. So my integrity was definitely compromised. I wanted to keep my independence, but (I reasoned) there was no point killing myself.

He was between interviews up on the roof, sipping a Coke with ice and lemon, as the sun went down. The photographer couldn't get his lights to work. "It's okay," Lee said. "I look better in the dark anyway."

Which is why he was happy to stick with writing. He could make it *work*. Lee knows how things work. He thinks of writing as a form of *tekhne*. Just fairly primitive. "Look at that pen you're holding," he said. "It's an amazingly sophisticated piece of equipment. A masterpiece of technology. Do you know who invented it?"

"Mr. Bíró?"

"That's right. Back in the 30s. Hungarian guy. László Bíró. He made pens so cheap it was the beginning of consumer culture. Stuff you could throw away. Did you ever buy a space pen?"

"I didn't think I would need one on earth," I said.

"You know it's a myth, don't you, about the Russian astronauts using pencils?"

"Like you, you mean, writing *Killing Floor*."

"They couldn't have used pencils. Think about it. The graphite dust would have killed their machines. You know they liked to use the old vacuum tubes in their fighter planes rather than transistors? Old technology, but they knew they would survive the electromagnetic pulse from a thermonuclear blast. Transistors would be fried. Sometimes old technology is smart."

Of course Reacher speaks French, but, as we wandered about Madrid, or sat about elegant roof terraces, I kept wondering if the Child *obra* could have some secret Spanish literary genealogy. After all, Lee had said Reacher was "linked to Spain." Maybe it was more than paella. Speeded-up, our intermittent, rambling conversation went roughly like this:

ME: Cervantes? Don Quixote. But tilting at real monsters rather than windmills.

LEE: No Sancho. Reacher mustn't have a sidekick. Sidekicks are always stupid in the end. Like Tonto [the Lone Ranger's loyal "native" companion, whose name means "stupid"]. His collaborators have to be his equals. Almost.

ME: Borges? (Of course Jorge Luis Borges is Argentine, but he writes in Spanish, so I allowed it.)

LEE: Not in Spanish.

ME: Hemingway. *For Whom the Bell Tolls*?

LEE: Everyone owes something to Hemingway. But I'm not that into Hemingway.

ME: Machismo?

LEE: I don't think of Reacher as particularly macho. Macho implies sexist. Which he isn't. Or even having to overcompensate a bit. Reacher doesn't have to compensate for anything.

ME: Matadors, then?

LEE: *Death in the Afternoon*. Yes. There is something of that. One man in an arena, up against some great force of nature. With the sun burning down. Gradually circling one another and closing in for the kill. Everything but the tight clothes. He has to be scruffy and not care.

He came up with two other answers (nothing to do with Spain). One was Goliath. "I always liked Goliath," he said, as we were walking along some *calle* somewhere. "I never liked David. I think Goliath was actually ill when that fight took place. Some say that he was blind. So it was not a fair fight. I thought—what would it be like if Goliath was the good guy not the bad guy?"

Another time we were having one of those charitable lunches at the Hotel de las Letras with Itziar. Big white plates, tiny nouvelle cuisine servings. It inspired reflectiveness. Maybe nostalgia, because we ended up talking about his childhood.

"Did they call you 'Lofty' at school?" I said. It was what we called very tall kids.

"They called me 'Grievous,'" he said, happily.

He was a great scrapper as a kid, just like Reacher. Always getting into fights. He came from a rough neighborhood but won a scholarship to the classy grammar school on the other side of town, King Edward's. He had to wear a dark blue blazer with a complicated badge on. So he had enough trouble walking through his own neighborhood (where the blazer was abnormal). But when he got to school he assumed that, having arrived at a bigger school, the fights would be bigger too. So on the very first day he picked a fight with some passing kid. Didn't just punch him to the ground but gave him a good kicking while he was lying there too. Really worked him over. The other kids were appalled. "I *destroyed* him. I thought that was what was needed. But I had the logic all wrong," Lee said. "There was no real fight imperative. No need to pick on anyone. And especially no need to go in hard. They all thought I was a barbarian." Which is how he got the nickname, on his very first day at school, short for "Grievous Bodily Harm" (in the U.K. legal lexicon, an extreme form of physical assault).

"Basically," Lee said, "Reacher is me, aged nine. I used to fight all the time." And it was true, I checked: in *Echo Burning,* Chapter 7, Reacher recalls a parallel experience at a new school—everything but the nickname: "hit hard, hit early, get your retaliation in first."

And Lee was now pondering the first major fight scene in *Make Me* (Reacher versus Mother's Rest).

"Did you have a death wish when you were younger?" I said.

"I still do," he said. "I don't want to die peacefully in bed."

Technically, Reacher is thirty-six in the era of *Killing Floor.* By the time of *Make Me,* given the itinerant chronology of the stories, he is perhaps another twelve years older. But he always retains something of the young boy. No responsibilities and no cares. No career. No house. No mortgage. Not even a suitcase. Only a folding toothbrush. He sometimes wonders about this when he compares himself with his peers (as in *Bad Luck and Trouble,* where he is reunited with his "Special Investigators" team). "Is there something wrong with me? Why don't I plan for the future?" And the answer is, he is only a boy, after all (albeit a rather large one)—so why should he? He can live for today, not for tomorrow.

The childlike quality of Child's creation also explains why he tends towards short, declarative sentences. Reacher is no Proust—no labyrinth of subordinate clauses, nested like Russian dolls. Nothing is hidden, there are no secrets, no hidden depths. The Spanish newspapers used the word *sencillo* of the Reacher style, "simple," "easy," or "plain," but a word that might be better translated as "degree zero," thinking of the Roland Barthes book *Writing Degree Zero*. Barthes contrasts Albert Camus' *The Outsider*—stylistically stripped down and minimalist—with the more ornate nineteenth-century novels of Balzac and Flaubert. It's the difference between Bauhaus and Baroque. Lee Child is like Camus, only with more fighting. Reacher is like Meursault, living in the present, indifferent to marriage, speaking the truth, incapable of hypocrisy, but capable, by the same token, of an enhanced sense of physical well-being. The difference is that if he decides to kill anyone he is not going to allow himself to be caught, arrested, and put on trial.

The beginning of *Killing Floor* is an echo of *The Outsider*: "I was arrested in Eno's diner." But the rest of the novel, swerving away from the old Camus narrative, is all about how to avoid getting executed and thereby return, at the end, to some level of existential freedom: "I didn't want elections and mayors and votes and boards and committees . . . I wanted the open road and a new place every day. I wanted miles to travel and absolutely no idea where I was going." Likewise, the author.

At one point, Lee compared reading a book to driving a car to Barcelona from Madrid: "Do you want a fast, comfortable, exciting ride—or a slow and uncomfortable one?" Like Thomas Hood, he thought that easy reading was hard writing (and that the converse was also true—the more tangled, the more Proustian, the easier it was to write).

An old friend had asked me, "What genre is Lee Child?" I said I didn't know.

"Genre is about *retail*," Lee said. "Bookstores want to know what shelf to put the book on. But there are really only two types of book. There is the one that makes you miss your stop on the subway. And then there is the one that doesn't."

It was our last afternoon in Madrid: he was going on to Barcelona, I was shoving off (I had a class to teach). Lee agreed that he liked Camus. "Especially the smoking. They all had cigarettes stuck to their lips in those days. Gauloises probably." His interpreter, Helena, who used to live in Edinburgh, was pregnant with her first child and had given up smoking. Lee said when his daughter was born even the doctor who was looking after her was a smoker. "I was smoking in the delivery room. Everybody smoked." Lee had even given a cigarette to President Obama one time, when they happened to be standing around together outside a hotel in New York, and he was on the campaign trail. "He had said he wouldn't smoke during the campaign—but he really needed one. No smoker ever quits for sure."

Reacher used to smoke but doesn't now. Not for health reasons, but because he doesn't want to carry stuff.

Lee still didn't know what Reacher was supposed to be doing in "Mother's Rest." "I'm going to have to smoke a helluva lot of weed when I get back to New York. That'll help."

During that time in Madrid, he must have been interviewed by about twenty different people, men and women, guys with pens and notebooks and TV guys with cameras rolling, heavy, muscular, bearded dudes and pencil-slim scholars in glasses. Skeptics and fans. And one Spanish critic who years before had come up with the nickname "Sherlock Homeless" (which even made it into the movie promotion). I said something vaguely sympathetic after yet one more Tom Cruise–related question. We were sitting in the white-upholstered hotel lounge. "Must be hard, all these interviews."

"Yeah," he said. He looked out of the windows, across the street, at a guy propped up against a wall, sitting on cardboard, with a crumpled hat stuck out in front of him. "Only not quite as hard as being that guy over there."

16.

AN OBJECTIVE REPORT CONCERNING THE RELATIVE STANDING OF DR. LEE CHILD AND DR. ANDY MARTIN

LOCATION: Waterstones on Regent Street, London, just up from Piccadilly Circus.

Date: 23 October 2014

Time: The lead investigator entered the bookstore at 3:05 pm.

Objective: Obtain copies of two books: (1) Lee Child, *The Enemy*; (2) Andy Martin, *Stealing the Wave*.

DURATION:

(1) It could be said that copies of Mr. Child's most recent work, *Personal,* were spotted in less than zero seconds, since they were displayed in the window, in a significant pile. Finding his earlier work, *The Enemy,* took a little longer, approximately thirty seconds.

(2) Dr. Martin's work proved rather more elusive. Having climbed up several flights of stairs in pursuit, the

investigator was then sent down into the basement. A prolonged search was conducted, in the end involving two employees. "I am sure I've seen it here somewhere," said one. A phone call was made to an adjacent bookstore. Finally, a copy of said book was retrieved from an unexpected location. "Very sorry, love," said the employee. "Hope it was worth the wait." Time: approximately 25 minutes.

SUPPLEMENTARY DATA: a few weeks later, shortly before Christmas, the lead investigator attempted to find another copy of Dr. Martin's work in Heffers, Trinity Street, Cambridge. The bearded, long-haired employee assisting the investigator made several pertinent remarks.

(a)   You want that one? It's great. Bradshaw versus Foo. Battle of titans.

(b)   He works around here at one of the colleges, I think. Surfer, isn't he? I heard a rumor he'd shoved off to Hawaii.

(c)   Bugger. I could have sworn I saw it here. Don't worry, I can order it for you.

17.

A CHILD IS BORN

HE HAD STARTED WRITING "Bad Luck and Trouble" (as it was then known—*Killing Floor* as it would become) in the first person. That way he didn't have to name his protagonist. His name didn't come up in the first chapter, while he was being arrested ("I was arrested in Eno's diner . . ."). In the second chapter he was "a murdering outsider bastard," or "this guy," nothing more, until, finally, having been read his rights and now being interrogated, he is required to reveal his name. "Franklin"—Jim Grant's first thought—was okay, but he wasn't totally enamored of it.

He thought for a day. Paced up and down. Sat and stared out of the window. Smoked a lot. Nothing.

The next morning, still nothing.

Then, the supermarket. Grocery shopping. Broke, out of work, watching the pennies. High stress. And as always, a little old lady asking the much taller fellow shopper to grab her a bargain can from the high shelf. And his wife, watching, then offering the kind of black humor she knew was sustaining him.

"You could be a reacher in a supermarket," she said. "You know, if this writing gig doesn't work out."

The eureka moment, in the Kendal Asda.

"My name is Jack Reacher," he wrote that afternoon. "No middle name. No address."

That was it. *Reacher*. Simple. Perfect.

There was only one remaining problem. His own name. Jim (or James) Grant was never going to fly. *Grant*. People didn't really get it, the first time they heard it, especially over the phone. Brown? Brant? He was forever having to spell it out. And then, was it "Grænt" (like "ant") or "Gra:nt" (to rhyme with "aren't")? "Jim" or "James"? The hero had a name, but now the author needed one too.

He came up with the answer for that on one of his trips to the U.S. It had started when he was on that train out of New York, going to Westchester to visit his in-laws, before Ruth was born. The guy next to him had started the conversation when he heard Jim's English accent. He was originally from Texas, it turned out, with a strong drawl. "I have a European car though," he said, with a degree of pride. He wanted to stress that he was a man of the world as well as a Texan. It was a Renault 5, which was marketed in the U.S. as "Le Car," to draw attention to its French origin. Its French style was its selling point. *Très chic*. But the Texan didn't call it "*Le* Car": he called it "*Lee* Car." "I just love Lee Car," he said. The "Lee" word stuck in the Grant household and soon they were saying, "Can you pass *lee* salt, please?" or "Shall we listen to *lee* Beatles?" and so on. When they had their daughter, Ruth, pretty soon she was being referred to as "lee baby" and then "lee child." The "lee" was adopted, but the "child" was really theirs.

Jim Grant screwed up the title page and threw it in the bin. He wrote it out again:

BAD LUCK AND TROUBLE
by
LEE CHILD

Again, simple, monosyllabic, strong. And the "C" was a gift. It would be right next to Agatha Christie on the bookshelves. And Raymond Chandler. Ideally placed for Western alphabetical left-to-right browsers. Of course, it could have been "Lee Carr" (or similar), but he liked Child better, because it was also a common noun, and one with positive connotations (for most people).

And lo, a Child was born.

His wife was a historian by instinct, currently studying Egyptology, and before that mostly Anglo-Saxon stuff. A lot of her long historical perspective rubbed off on him. It gets into Reacher, but it also inspired one of his earliest pieces of writing. "The Ruin" is one of the oldest extant pieces of Anglo-Saxon writing, a poem written by an eighth-century Anglo-Saxon gazing on the ruin of a colossal Roman villa or pool somewhere in England (possibly Bath). It was like an early "Ozymandias." What gods or giants could have lived here? the writer wanted to know. It was an elegy, a melancholy evocation of lost splendor and old warriors. But there was a stanza missing, as a result of the manuscript being burned at the edge. Lee took on the challenge of writing the missing stanza. He had no difficulty identifying with an eighth-century Anglo-Saxon conjuring up lost gods and heroes.

Reacher is like that too—a remnant of the lost warriors of yore. More myth than modern man. Walking amid ruins. Or a desert: "a bone-dry gulch scraped out a million years ago by a different climate, when there had been rain and ferns and rushing rivers" (*Echo Burning*, first paragraph).

"They had no clear timeline back then," Lee said. "They had no idea how many centuries had gone by. Everything was 'a hundred generations' before. It was all myth and legend. Do you know why there are so many 'Devil's Bridges'?"

"Are there a lot of them?" I said.

"They're all over England," he said. There was one back in Kirkby Lonsdale, for example, where he had once lived. "It was because they would build a great stone bridge—and then time would go by and within a generation or two they had forgotten who had built it and even how it was built. So it became the *devil's bridge,* conjured up by some satanic architect of old."

They had not one but two farmhouses in England, one next door to the other. A small farmhouse empire. The second one was the equivalent of Lee's shed at the bottom of the garden—it was where he went to work. There were box-loads of his old stuff kicking about. Over the door to one of the rooms upstairs Lee had stuck up a sign he'd swiped from Granada Television way back:

CENTRAL CONTROL ROOM 2

He liked the idea of control. That was his old job: "controller." Like a flight control sort of guy who "had to juggle around lots of different programs and slot them all together. In the right order. Or there was chaos. It was all about the timing."

As I was leaving, I peeked through the window of the garage. There was an old Bentley, a green one, the size of a small ship, with a big letter "B" on the hood, just like the one Reacher drives in *Killing Floor* (having borrowed it from Hubble, the banker). And there was another car, a Range Rover. It had a distinctive license plate:

LI KAR

THE STORY OF
THE BLIND WOMAN

SHE HAD BIG BROWN EYES. Blond hair. She came right up to me. Nuzzled me. I was just sitting there, in Long Beach. And then she licked my hand. Her name was Eden and she was a golden Labrador. A guide dog to a woman named Terry.

"Do you have kibble in your pocket?" said Terry.

"I wanted to go up and stroke her. I think maybe she read my mind."

"She doesn't normally do that."

"Excuse me for asking—but I assume you are visually impaired." Her eyes were bright but dreamily unfocused.

"I'm a blind woman," she said. "But I can make out a few things. Big buildings and such. It makes life interesting." She laughed, shaking her head, her wavy red hair flying around.

Terry had read all the Reachers, it turned out. Except she hadn't actually *read* them. More listened to them on audio. She didn't like braille much. "It's only six dots. But the books are hundreds of pages long—they are huge. And it's hard as Chinese to learn." She could read enough braille to work out public bathrooms and the different floors in elevators.

She came at it late. Her eyesight only started deteriorating when she set out on a career in librarianship. "That's pretty ironic, I guess. Maybe it was all the reading that killed my eyes, I don't know."

She could still read a little, on a very big screen with the magnification ramped up to the max. But still audio was easier. And the Reacher novels worked well on audio. "I can keep track of what Reacher is doing. He's easy to follow."

There was only one problem as far as she was concerned. "They sure as hell picked the wrong guy to play Reacher."

"You don't like him?" I was taken aback. I had thought for once I was going to have a conversation about Jack Reacher that didn't automatically rustle up the name of Tom Cruise. I had done nothing to prompt her. It was just something she had to get off her chest. Maybe it was the proximity of Hollywood, just a few miles away to the north, that inspired her to think along these lines.

"He's so obviously the wrong guy!"

She spoke in an exclamatory way. Emphatic. Confident. Not unlike Lee Child himself, but with a Southern accent, even though she lived just a few miles away in Fountain Valley, inland from Huntington Beach, to the south of Long Beach. She said "dawg" rather than "dog," for example.

I couldn't just let it go. For once I thought Cruise would at least get the benefit of the doubt. Logically, if you can't see him, you can't object to him. But no. "Surely you, a blind woman, should be more forgiving of Tom Cruise? Does it make all that much difference to you who is playing the part of Reacher?"

"Tom Cruise," she said, "is not how I PICTURE Reacher. See"

(she said "see" quite often), "Reacher has got to make you shit your pants when he walks in the room. He is intimidating. Tom Cruise isn't like that at all. I can remember what he looks like. He's too good-looking. Gotta be rougher as well as tougher."

"Isn't it more important to you what he sounds like? He sounds pretty tough, doesn't he?"

"Nope. He sounds like a little guy!" And she added, just to emphasize the point, "Even my dawg knows that!" I'm not sure if Eden the dog was actually at the showing of the film or if she just somehow knew that anyhow. Or if that was just extra abuse on top, like marmalade.

Not all films were geared for audio commentary, as she explained to me. Apparently there is a conflict in the industry or the government over copyright. And of course not all books were available on audio. She said most of the Reacher books were. I mentioned to her how Jorge Luis Borges had a young Japanese woman reading books to him after he became blind. "Wouldn't it be nice if I could get the authors to come and read to me?" she said.

I promised to go and read my book to her in Fountain Valley after it was done. Even though it wouldn't be Lee Child as such, but only me talking about Lee Child. "Next best thing," she said. "And a damn sight better than that Tom Cruise!"

LONG BEACH

LEE CHILD WASN'T THAT EASY to find, even with his considerable height. There were about a hundred or a thousand other writers roaming around in Long Beach (California) too. We were all at Bouchercon—the annual jamboree of thriller and mystery writers from around the world (named after Anthony Boucher, who started the whole thing many moons ago). And their readers. It was a cynegetic paradise, headquarters of the hermeneutic code. Over three days, in November, I must have gone to dozens of panels, discussing "Belfast Noir," "Jewish Noir," "Murder Ancient and Modern," "Tall Men Telling Tall Tales," "Beyond Hammett, Chandler, and Spillane," "From Page to Screen," and "Kick-Ass Women." I think Eden would have enjoyed the one on "Cadaver Dogs." I listened to Jeffery Deaver (lifetime achievement award) and Michael Connelly (author of the Harry Bosch series, set in

L.A.) and Eoin Colfer ("Where do your ideas come from?" asked someone; Colfer: "My audience is mostly nine-year-olds—I normally get asked whether I like snowmen").

I was weighed down with free books, given to me in a bag sponsored by the Mystery Writers of America. Titles included *The Catch, Dreaming Spies, A Dark Redemption,* and *The Deception at Lyme.* I went to an "Author Speed-Dating Breakfast," sponsored by Smith & Wesson, where a different couple of authors would spin up to your table every minute or so, in between mouthfuls of cereal, and deliver a rapid-fire pitch and hit you with leaflets and bookmarks and occasional trailers. Cindy Sample offered a series with titles like "Dying for a Dude" and "Dying for a Dance." There had to be *Dying for* and a *D.* Someone suggested "Dying for a Donut." Another woman was carrying a shoe in one hand, something to do with getting stabbed on a dance floor. Mike Befeler, who wore a straw boater for several days (the ribbon advertised one of his books), had written some stand-alone paranormals and vampire novels, but was a specialist in "geezer lit." His senior citizen 'tec, who lives in a retirement home, struggles with short-term memory loss and keeps forgetting vital clues. "Maybe I should do one about an aging vampire," he said.

I liked the sound of *Horizon Drive,* written by a Japanese American brother-and-sister team, who had adopted the joint moniker of J. M. Zen, and handed out an origami bird emblazoned with a review extract ("compelling noir entertainment with a sharp edge of modern relevance"). Kathy Bennett, a retired LAPD cop, and author of the Maddie Divine series, had tried to write a "romantic suspense," but she kept postponing the romance because "I've gotta get the killing right!" Before I'd even gotten to my second cup of coffee, I had heard about a wave of surfing psychos, *Dead Heat,* set in San Antonio, the *real* Miami (a hardboiled-hitman-with-heart story), and someone who was a mix of Clive Cussler and Scooby-Doo. And an author of a casino plot had given me a handful of $250 chips (chocolate ones).

One line sticks in my mind, I just can't remember the book or the author: "Two gravediggers walk into a police headquarters—then it gets weird."

Margaret was sitting next to me. She had already piled up thirty-something free books. "That's nothing," she said—her record was 147 freebies at Comic-Con in San Diego. She might have passed for a rather serious and mature grad student, with her hair in a bun and her studious glasses, except that she was also wearing what appeared to be a tiara of rainbow-colored plastic flowers. "If I never read another FBI-profiler I'll be happy," she said. She was a member of the Goat Hill Literary Society, worked in the Newport bookstore, and basically read everything. Except romance. "I love Reacher," she said. "There aren't many series that are still as enthralling on the twentieth as on the first." She asked me if I remembered what Michael Caine had said about the making of *Jaws 4* (about a shark looking for revenge). I said I didn't. "He said he couldn't remember much about it, but he liked the house he bought with it."

Another morning I witnessed "65 Men of Mystery," all lined up as if in a Miss World contest (only with a lot less hair). They didn't seem that mysterious. None of them was Lee Child. Lee didn't appear at a single panel or breakfast or awards ceremony. He really was mysterious. Long Beach reminded me of a line of Bertrand Russell's. Russell once asked how anyone could know that Sir Walter Scott was *the* author of *Waverley* (this was the "problem of denotation"). He reckoned that in order to demonstrate that Sir Walter Scott was the author of *Waverley* you would have to survey the universe and show that everyone in it either was Sir Walter Scott or was *not* the author of *Waverley*. Long Beach was my shorthand way of surveying the universe. Everyone else in it was not Lee Child.

Effortless, languid, Lee glided around the Hyatt Regency, surrounded by an entourage of attractive women, occasionally manifesting himself to sign books (long queues). He put me in mind of Ted Hughes, then Poet Laureate, in the days when I published with Faber & Faber: he was the star, treated like royalty, while everyone else was doffing the cap. In Long Beach Lee was the *grand seigneur,* the lord of all he surveyed, the leader of the pack. King of the underdogs. He was becoming the stuff of fiction. One writer had invented a character going under Lee's original name, Jim Grant: "a rogue Yorkshire cop at large in America where culture clash and violence ensue."

Since I was effectively stalking or maybe staking out Lee Child, it was useful that I got surveillance training, given by an ex-DEA guy called Mike with a droopy Mexican mustache. He taught us the "ABC method." Which sounds simple enough. Only it wasn't. Wandering the streets of Long Beach, I encountered a blonde; a woman in a trilby hat; a guy with tattoos up his arms and a sleeveless vest which showed them off; a woman with a limp; a fat guy in shorts; a Starbucks; a park; a bench. Maybe it was jet lag, but I had no idea what was going on, nor did they.

Another time, sharing a ride, I overheard a conversation between a couple of guys in the back of the cab that went something like this:

"He writes so well."

"I loved the Scudder books."

"Do you know Soho Press?"

"But he has such a sad life. Both his daughter and grandson offed themselves."

"He wasn't doing too well so he had to write some sex books."

"Reacher? He's the hero, right?"

"I don't know his stuff very well but I hear he's very good at conventions."

"He's like Harlan Coben, but in Minnesota."

"Kaminsky was with them for a number of years."

"When he was dying he needed a transplant."

"He wrote so much you can't read it all."

"I teach this class in Bethesda. There was this kid, had a novel—he'd had a few stories published—couldn't get it out there. I got him to send it to my editor. And she wouldn't have it either. They've cut their list by a third."

"I read all the Sara Paretskys."

"Harlan Ellison has a background too."

"You know, whatever brings you the money."

"Were you at the St. Louis convention? It's basically awards and a buffet, but there is camaraderie."

"I'm not big on dinners."

"Didn't he do one of the Bond books?"

One woman I spoke to said she only ever read the first thirty pages of a book and the last thirty and skipped the middle entirely. Sometimes Long Beach felt like being somewhere in a dark intermediate incomprehensible labyrinth, a noir literary underworld, desperately looking for the clue that would make sense of it all. For me it was not a whodunit (they all dun it), more a whydoit?

Having bumped into Vicki Doudera at a stoplight on my first day, I bought a copy of *Deal Killer*, involving her real estate agent/amateur sleuth heroine, Darby Farr ("medium-boiled"). She bought me a pizza in return. And she took me along to an interview with a writer she called "the bitch with the laugh." It was a fair description. She (the other writer) had actually met a real-life serial killer and carried a loaded weapon just in case. I also went along to the "Cute and Sweet, but with a Twist" panel, since

Vicki was speaking. I had a soft spot for her because (a) she occasionally went under the name of "Martin" on account of Doudera being too weird; (b) she spoke French and had studied at the Sorbonne; (c) her hair was a similar color to Eden's; (d) when she asked her middle son if he would like a copy of her latest book, he replied, "Mom, I only read *serious* literature" (he was into Dostoyevsky); (e) she was planning to write a book about chickens.

I introduced her to Lee. "Darby Farr, meet Jack Reacher," I said. Lee had just finished signing a hundred books. I was wearing my "Hard-Boiled" badge, picked up at the speed-dating breakfast.

"You've heard what he's doing?" said Lee.

"Looking over your shoulder while you write?" Vicki said. She was polite but skeptical. "Isn't it just a little like watching paint dry?"

"It depends on the painter, surely," I said. "In this case it's 'Hey, Leonardo, love the smile,' that sort of thing."

"This is what he does," said Lee. "Bullshitting—he's quite good at it."

"'Course it won't be as good as one of yours," I said.

Lee guffawed. "Impossible!"

"It has to be better."

"Ridiculous!"

"They are already eating it up in Stockholm."

For once I wasn't bullshitting. I had just given a paper at the Stockholm Business School (entitled "Lee Child and the Making of His Next Bestseller"). "They say every author is going to want one of these from now on. No book without a meta-book to go with it. The boxed set."

Turned out Lee and Vicki had a lot in common. She had actually sold a house in Maine to the guy who was producing the Reacher movies (she, like Darby Farr, was a real estate agent in her spare time).

"I've been goofing off," said Lee. "A lot." We had gone to the fairly swanky Tides restaurant by the pool to have lunch. Fans would keep coming up to him or waving as they went by. In the distance you could see the Queen Mary, in its final resting place. "Working this month would have needed a heroic effort. And I haven't been feeling all that heroic." *Mother's Rest* had come to a complete halt.

But still he had gotten Reacher into the motel—and out of it again. Reacher takes a room. The motel guy makes a call. "She met a guy off the train." So Reacher is labeled one of "them," even though we don't know who "they" are at this point. Even though he is poking around town in all innocence, looking for the origin of the name "Mother's Rest." In the latest development, the motel guy's grandson is shadowing him. Reads too much into his random movements. "They think he knows much more than he actually does," Lee said. "In fact he knows nothing. He doesn't have a clue what is going on. Doesn't even know anything *is* going on." The woman—who may be a detective of some kind—knows there is something going on, and is still expecting to find Keever somewhere, but even she doesn't really know either. So there is a haziness. Keever knew, presumably, but Keever is dead. "We don't want to know too much too soon," said Lee. The blankness of the landscape—the "nothingness"—is a metaphor of the information deficit. Lee liked it that way. He wanted the slow build. "You want it to feel fast but you have to write it slow."

But it also reflected the fact that he didn't know what was going on either. "I'm still waiting for illumination," he said. "It'll come." Beyond trying to work out the plot, which at that moment did not exist, there was one other big problem looming. The title.

"They don't like it," he said.

I thought that was about the craziest thing I had heard all the

time I was in Long Beach, right up there with a headline some-body quoted, "ELECTRIC CHAIR DEEMED DANGEROUS."
"Who is *they* exactly?"

"The organization."

"What's their problem?"

"They think *Make Me* will only appeal to guys."

I remembered something he had said to me way back. "I have no title and no plot." Sounded as if he was right back to square one. He was due to have a title showdown lunch when he got back to New York.

Another time I bumped into him outside the hotel, sitting on a bench, having a fag. As usual. "I'm going for total cardiac catas-trophe," he said. "I don't want any resuscitating." Turned out he had had a major bout of rheumatic fever around the age of seven—spending four weeks in hospital—and his heart valves and ventricles were all messed up. The episode had had a massive impact on his attitude. Up until that point he had considered himself immortal, like any normal kid. But afterwards, nobody expected him to live much beyond fourteen. Then it was twenty-one. His mother ("hypochondriac, touch of Munchausen's by proxy") used to really rub it in. "I had the clear idea that life was temporary. I'm impatient about waiting for stuff. I'm also irre-sponsible, because I think I'm doomed anyway, so what the hell."

He became fatalistic, but at the same time incurably optimistic. "I never really worry about what will happen next year or further down the road." He took another drag on his Camel. "Presumably I'll come unstuck sooner or later."

It was that time we were having breakfast back in Tides (he had bacon and eggs and pancakes; I had oatmeal and banana) that he explained what he was doing at Bouchercon. Other than nothing, that is. And goofing off. "I love this place. It gives me a much-needed boot up the backside. And a new burst of energy. With all the talent here all working away and producing good stuff, I've really got to keep on rolling and do my thing."

As he spread maple syrup over his pancakes, he reminisced about the Bouchercon that took place shortly after 9/11. In Washington, D.C. Bethesda. The hero of the event was S. J. Rozan, a small but tough woman from the Bronx, who went on to write what Lee thought of as the best 9/11 book, *Absent Friends*. Lee, meanwhile, was reeling with a personal crisis. The twin towers were destroyed in September. The Yankees were competing in the World Series in October, only seven weeks later, against an Arizona team, the Diamondbacks. "The Yankees *had* to win," he said. "Every fiber of my being told me that it just *had* to be that way. It would be a consolation. A reaffirmation of life after all the death and disaster." The reality was they lost, three games to four. "The narrative failed for me. It didn't happen." Lee had effectively become a New Yorker, having lived there or thereabouts since the 90s. He was about an hour out of town, having only recently finished *Without Fail* (the one about assassinating the vice president), when the planes hit the World Trade Center. But in some odd way, the Yankees losing had more of an impact on him than 9/11 itself.

He more or less expected 9/11. It was the ultimate noir narrative sprung to life. An al Qaeda plot to destroy New York—what else do you expect? It was predictable, it was inevitable. New York in ruins. Of course. Isn't it always? And then the Yankees have the opportunity to restore the morale of the city. But . . . they blow it. "It was a crisis for me," Lee said. "I realized I'd spent my entire life coming up with happy endings. But it didn't really work like that. Not in New York, anyway."

Without Fail was published in May 2002 (while he was rolling on with the next one, *Persuader*). Reacher saves the VP. The plot gets turned on its head a couple of times, but ultimately there is no failure. It is *without fail*. Lee—and by extension everybody else at Bouchercon, all the men of mystery and the real estate sleuths of the world—were offering to fix things up, to compensate and console. "Everything is doomed to failure," as Jean-Paul Sartre wrote. Everything would fall apart; it was the second law of thermodynamics; it was entropy. The novel was a species of *negentropy*, a practically pointless protest against the fate of the universe. Fiction rectified the world in accordance with metaphysics. For one thing, a story, if it was good enough, would live on, even when we had long since turned back into cosmic dust. It would live so long as it had readers.

The noir writers of the world were its angels, its saviors and redeemers. Or they wanted to be. But they knew what it was like to fail. Technically, all their works were *failed performatives*. The performative is a statement that does what it says and makes something real: for example, "I now pronounce you husband and wife." That was a performative, delivered by a vicar. "I do," another performative, uttered by the bride or groom. So too, delivered by a king or queen (or captain of industry?): "I name this ship *Queen Mary*. May God bless her and all who sail in her." *I name this man Jack Reacher* had to be seen as a good try, but in the last analysis a failed (or "infelicitous") performative. It took the form of a prayer or a promise. Reacher wouldn't be coming to rescue and redeem anybody. But maybe somebody would. Maybe Reacher would inspire someone else to make good on the Reacher promise. Tom Cruise maybe.

20.

UNDERWORLD

ROB, ONE OF LEE CHILD'S LEGION of readers (and one who had emailed him), had once seen a fellow passenger on a London Underground train reading a book. The guy was sitting opposite him. The book—Rob could clearly make out the title on the jacket—was Don DeLillo's *Underworld,* a massive, sprawling complex novel spanning several decades, with a lot of critical heft to it. Definitely a serious book. A *literary* work.

The next day Rob was back on the train, heading off to work again, around the same time, and by chance the same guy was on the train too, still reading his book. But this time Rob had taken the only remaining seat on the car, right next to the guy reading the Don DeLillo book. Except it wasn't *Underworld* at all.

Inside the Don DeLillo cover—as Rob could plainly see when he peeked over—was *61 Hours.* Rob recognized it because he had

been reading it himself only shortly before. So the guy was reading Lee Child and wrapping it up in a Don DeLillo cover.

Lee was *undercover*. Which I thought he ought to feel pretty
pleased with—but he wasn't, not really. He wanted to redeem the
world but he stood in need of redemption himself. Even with the
chauffeured car and the Brooks Brothers jacket, he remained an
outsider, beyond the reach of respectability. Like an outlaw, a
ronin, a surfer. Like Jack Reacher, in fact, wandering the world
without a suitcase.

THE STONY LIMIT

THIS WAS THE TRIP WHEN just about everything went wrong. Catastrophically. Beginning with the airport. In fact even before the airport because Joel thought I was supposed to be arriving the day before. Which obviously I wasn't. He assumed I was lying mugged and bleeding and left for dead somewhere in darkest Queens. Instead of which I ended up dead in Manhattan.

It all started with the bag. I carry this backpack straight onto planes and straight off again. No luggage in the hold. I take practically nothing. (I even forgot underwear and had to go and buy some from a bargain basement store around 33rd Street. Pure Reacher.) So the woman at the Norwegian desk at Gatwick says to me, "Seven kilos." And then added, "To New York." There could have been a question mark in there somewhere.

"Is that heavy or light, to your way of thinking?"

"Oh, that is light," she said. "Very light. For New York."

"That's good, right?"

I mean, they're always having a go at people with these giant overstuffed cases and they have to throw out their favorite socks and teddy bears and whatnot. You'd think they'd be grateful for the light guys. But no.

"Excuse me, sir, can I have a look at that?"

It was polite, but there was no *please*. I hate the "sir" routine anyway. This was a guy, sticking his oar in, suddenly. Backup. Popped up out of nowhere. Had been keeping an eye on me apparently. American. Suit of indeterminate color. But buttoned. And he had an earphone. Everything but the shades.

He was asking to see my old passport. The one with the visa. The thing is, I have this great visa, given to me by some surfer dude who happened to be working at the American embassy in London the day I went in, back in 2006. But it's nothing but trouble because immigration guys can't believe I have such a visa, which in theory entitles me to do anything I like, but in practice looks suspicious. I have to swear that I lead a life of pure pleasure and never do any work, ever.

So he hit me with a barrage of questions. What are you doing in New York? How long are you there for? Where are you staying? That sort of stuff. And we're still at Gatwick.

"What is the problem?" I say, starting to lose it slightly.

"At the moment I have you down for working illegally in the United States."

I was about to say, "You have got to be kidding me, man!" Except I didn't want to sound too much like John McEnroe right then and there. "I notice you're using the participle form," says I. "But this is not the present tense. I *used to* work in the U.S. Past tense. Imperfect. But that was years ago. Anyway, how can I be working *if no one is paying me*?"

I thought that was a clincher. "I need to make some calls, sir. Wait here."

He makes a ton of calls. I'm just standing there. Finally he comes back. Seems I checked out okay. He has a smile on his face, just a little bit. And a sort of twinkle in his eye. "I understand, sir. So you have this thing going on, do you, with a party in New York?"

"Just old friends," I said. But I was thinking—does he know about Lee? Maybe I should have opened up to him and he would have understood. It still wasn't "working" exactly. What I didn't realize is that the honeymoon was over. Divorce was imminent.

"A major fucking existential crisis has blown up," said Lee, opening the door of his apartment. "While you were in the air. Or I would have warned you."

He sat me down, almost solicitously, and brought me coffee too. Black. He was wearing a black leather jacket, unzipped, some grungy old T-shirt, and blue jeans.

"They were on the phone to me yesterday. It's brand management," he said. "I don't like it, but I understand it. You have to understand it too."

"What are *they* panicking about?"

"Your work." They had read a few chapters, apparently. "They think I should stop talking to you. They're using the word *toxic*."

"That's interesting," I said.

"*Interesting!* That is so academic." I almost wrote, "he spluttered." Truthfully, it was more that he had stood up and was stomping around throwing his hands in the air. There was no actual spittle. "This is the end of the world and you say it's interesting?" He lit another cigarette and stared out of the window in the general direction of Strawberry Fields. "They've had some bad experiences recently. Wounding. They are hurt and bleeding." He mentioned a couple of authors who were in his exalted bracket. Right at the top of the tree. And they had been virtually assassinated by social media. One tiny little unscripted remark to an interviewer and *wham*! The trolls were descending on you in their droves. And in a matter of minutes it's *oh my God it turns out that X is some kind of monster after all* and it's all over the *Mail online* too (or the *New York Post* or whatever). Then it's apologies all round. White flag. We surrender.

"They are running scared," he said. "They really fear social media. They are worried that the stuff you are writing is going to be picked up and turned into a thousand different ways of destroying me."

"That would be bad," I said.

"I wanted warts and all," he said. "And they want to shut it down. You can see why, can't you?"

"They want control."

"And at the moment they don't have control."

"Napoleon felt the same way. *Nous verrons!* he said. But you know, nobody has control. Anybody can say anything."

"And you're giving them the ammunition. The business is shrinking to a handful of brands. I'm one of them. So they have to be protective. I mean, I can see their point. They've worked hard for twenty years. A lot of effort and money. They don't want a wild card to come along and screw it up now."

Lee has this problem with his legs. They are too long for most practical purposes. He doesn't really know what to do with them, like most people don't know what to do with their hands. He was wriggling around on the sofa (having sat down again), trying to get them out of the way somewhere, tucking them under or folding them up at the knees. There is a cartoon of the very tall General de Gaulle where the cartoonist has chopped him in two around the waist and stuck the legs next to him in a separate panel. Lee reminded me a lot of General de Gaulle right then.

"It's apocalyptic is what it is," he said. "It's all going down the toilet."

"How's the work going by the way?"

"I've just written this four-word sentence. I'm pretty pleased with it. Nobody will even notice it."

"I need to have a look at that."

"See, now I want to say, it's a bit like Shakespeare in that line of his. Not blank verse of course. But if I say that then you're going to quote me and social media is going to start up, 'LEE CHILD THINKS HE IS SHAKESPEARE. #PretentiousGit.' Not good."

"But obviously you are Shakespeare, in a way," I said. He gave me a bit of a look. Skeptical. "So am I," I added. "There is a continuum. Every writer is Shakespeare at some level. Just as Borges is Dante. It's the 'spirit of literature.'"

"You want to know the thing that kills me about this whole who-wrote-Shakespeare drivel—it's a class thing. He couldn't possibly have written *Hamlet* because he's just a grammar school boy from the Midlands. Like me."

"It has to be some dude from Oxford, right."

"And an earl at that."

"The class struggle in literature."

"He was from exactly the same sort of school I went to. It was set up around the time of Shakespeare. Probably hasn't changed all that much."

"What was that line you were thinking of?"

Lee has this great memory. Obviously he remembers the names of the two sisters he deflowered decades ago, anyone would. But he can even remember what day of the week it was. It's some kind of weird memory syndrome with him. The opposite of amnesia. And he is also good at recalling poetry and theater. Could probably recite all of *Waiting for Godot.* "It's in *Romeo and Juliet.* The balcony scene, I think. Act two, scene one. How the hell did Romeo get over the orchard walls? But Shakespeare doesn't call them walls. He writes, 'the stony limits.' It's staggering that he would write that."

It was the Lee of old. Ranting on about Shakespeare, summoning up obscure lines of poetry. But, at the same time, it was like *The End.* This was the final chapter being written right there. The Shakespeare stuff was some kind of sign-off line. Tragedy. It all ends in tears. He wasn't even supposed to be talking to me. *They* had told him not to. Or else. We had bumped up against the *stony limit.* I knocked back the coffee and stood up and looked out the window. He was still wrestling with the sofa. There was an icy blue sky over Central Park.

"I'd better have a look at it," he said. "If they can see it, I can see it."

"I didn't want it to mess with your mind. Not, I mean, that your mind necessarily would be messed with, but, you know, the observer always changes the thing he is observing. Which would be you. I don't want you to get all self-conscious on me. You're okay the way you are. Nobody should be trying to sanitize you. Who is going to believe that stupid stuff?"

"Here, shove it on this memory stick. I've got to see for myself how 'toxic' this thing really is."

"I guess you can just shut it all out. If you can shut out everybody bitching about you on Amazon, then you can shut this out."

Just to be fair: not *everybody* is bitching about Lee on Amazon. But he got the point—they were a whole lot worse than anything I could come up with.

I went back to the apartment the following day. Not too early. His mood doesn't really pick up till after the sixth cup of coffee. Around 10:30 or 11. "You fancy a walk over Central Park?"

I said. It was freezing but sunny. I still had all my gear on, the flying jacket and the hat and the scarf, the works. December in Manhattan.

"Nah," he said. "Soccer's on."

We went off to some room with a big screen. The sofa was bloody huge too. Too big for my legs really. I had to stick some cushions behind my back to even get my feet on the floor. General de Gaulle had his legs stretched out in front of him on a dedicated leg rest, a bench of sorts. Like the sofa had a separate mini-sofa in front of it just for his lower half. It was a kind of solution.

We were watching Chelsea versus Hull in the English Premiership. Every now and then we'd get the scores flash up of West Ham (my team) or Aston Villa (his). We were talking about some of the great names players had. I thought Mertesacker for Arsenal was pretty good. Intimidating defensive player. German.

"Ever hear of Beenhakker?" said Lee.

"Nope."

"Coach now. Or manager. But his name means something like 'Leg-biter' in Dutch. Or 'Butcher.' I always thought that was a great name for a soccer player." A very brief pause. "Did you know 'poppycock' is Dutch?"

"Really."

"One of the very few Dutch words to make it into English. *Pappekak*. Means something like 'soft shit.' Hence, bullshit." A beat. "So thinking about your book . . ." He'd read a few chapters overnight.

"Toxicity? On a scale of one to ten?"

"I sort of see what they are getting at. You're going to have to cut that bit about [x]. And there's that line about [y]. That is obviously illegal. Or impolitic. Or something. Is that against your ethics?"

"I don't really have ethics. I have aesthetics."

"But can you cut one or two of those things?"

"So long as the whole thing isn't bent completely out of shape."

"The whole thing is just fine," he said.

"It was only a first draft. Your guys rushed me. We can make it a little more . . . economical. Slim, trim, tailor. So long as we don't have to prettify."

Lee really didn't mind the project. "You've got *the voice*. And it definitely had me going. All that postponement. Is he ever going to start?"

Chelsea scored some stylish killer goal. Hull were goners.

"Is he ever going to finish?" I said.

"Yeah, all that. That's exactly how it feels. The anxiety. It's a suspense story. I get that."

Now Arsenal was slaughtering Newcastle. "You know what I'm going to do?" Lee said. "Tell them to fuck off. What's the point otherwise?"

I felt a little as Stendhal must have done, standing next to Napoleon (he was his catering manager or something like that), and listening to him issuing orders to the troops. Not in himself powerful, but adjacent to power. It was a buzz, I admit.

"Well, you know, I'll probably put it a bit more diplomatically than that. *Let's think this through* or something."

I was putting my hat and coat back on by the front door. I was finally going for that walk across Central Park. "Hey, you know that title argument?"

"What?"

"They didn't like *Make Me*. Wanted you to change it."

"Oh yeah, they just didn't get it. It's a great title. I tried explaining to them. Went and had lunch and said, 'Let's think this through.'"

"Like trying to explain a joke. Still nobody laughs."

"Here's one thing they ought to know. A fact in my defense.

Since Edward Heath in 1970 I have correctly predicted the outcome of every single election. On both sides of the Atlantic. You know what that means, don't you?"

"You should be running the next Democratic electoral campaign?"

"I know what people want. What they are thinking and feeling. How they are going to react. Because I am one of them. I *am* people. They ought to trust me more. Instead of all this pointless pathetic pettifogging." Pause. "Is that a verb or a noun?"

"Gerund," I said. "It's probably Dutch. Like poppycock."

"I sort of see their point," he said philosophically. "It's like the cover, it's all marketing. But I can't back out of the title now. Too late. I've committed to it in my head."

"You can't back out anyway. You said, 'This is not the first draft—it's THE ONLY DRAFT.' Nobody messes with . . .'"

Pause.

"You really are fucking toxic, you know that?"

I was in some bar in Brooklyn later that night. Really small and really crowded. With some visceral rhythm throbbing in the background. Drinking Beyond the Pale Ale from the bottle. I was giving Steve Fishman the rough gist, half distorted by ambient noise. "Wow," he says. "Your ass was actually saved by Jack Reacher. That is something."

22.

NO X, NO Y

IN THE MIDST OF all this drama, Lee was quietly plugging away, rolling his stone up the hill. He had finally stopped goofing off and was now well into his stride. Mid-December, three and a half months in. Chapter 16.

"I'm really enjoying it too," he said. "It's pure pleasure." So long, that is, as he stopped at around a thousand words a day. He didn't want to feel pressured into doing the second thousand, just because of the schedule. He had to shut out all the reasons to speed up. *It's coming out in September; you have to finish by March; we need more, more, more.*

I admit: those reasons were partly my fault. I had spoken on the phone to his editor in London. "How is he getting on?" she asked. A definite note of anxiety. "Is he making progress?" She was already panicking. "The last time I saw him," I said, "he was goofing off in California. Said he was still waiting for some kind of light to go on." "I'm calling him right now," she shrieked.

Now time had rolled on. I would have to answer, in all fairness: *Yes, he really is making progress.* But I really wanted to know about the four words. I liked the idea that it was four. Like the Four Horsemen of the Apocalypse. The Sign of Four. $400. *Four*—as the omniscient narrator points out in *Make Me*—is "a number of moderate technical interest, and most famous for being the only number in the entire universe that matched the number of letters in its own word in English." Also, it was like the opposite of Proust, whose sentences don't really get started until around the four-hundred-word mark. Lee Child, the anti-Proust. At the top end of the spectrum, I had recently been reading (partly for the sake of counterpoint and in a spirit of scientific inquiry) Mathias Énard's *Zone*: more than five hundred stream-of-consciousness pages, only one sentence (with a lot of commas). A 150,000-word sentence (approx.). In the case of the four-word sentence, the funny thing was, it was really more like three words, or maybe just one, repeated again and again.

Lee gave me context first. We were sitting in his office. "Reacher and this woman detective go back to Kansas City—to Keever's house. In search of information."

"Hold on. What is her name?"

"Stashower."

"Stashower. Great name."

Lee had taken the name from an author at Bouchercon: touting around his latest work of nonfiction, *The Hour of Peril: The Secret Plot to Murder Lincoln Before the Civil War.* He'd known him well before that though, thought it was a great name, had intended to use it before but got sidetracked.

"Anyway. There is a poignancy to it. This [Keever] is a guy who has broken up with his wife. His kids haven't visited—yet. Now they never will. Reacher and Stashower arrive at his house. They're at the front. It's daylight. The practical issue—how to break into a house in broad daylight? I had to have verisimilitude in mind. So I described the street. Here it is:

> "The street was quiet. Just seven similar houses, three on a side, plus one at the dead end. No moving vehicles, no pedestrians. Not really a Neighborhood Watch kind of place. It had a transient feel, but in slow motion, as if all seven houses were occupied by divorced guys taking a year or two to get back on their feet.

"I thought it was okay, but then I went back. Was I really getting the point across? So I put this in, between 'pedestrians' and 'Not a Neighborhood Watch':

> No eyes, no interest."

"No eyes, no interest," I said, mulling it over. "I like it. It's not a double negative—Reacher wouldn't do that!—it's a double negation." It was true: Reacher, for all his rough-hewn manners, was a stickler for grammatical correctness.

"It's funny," said Lee. "It's like I'm more into Reacher's thoughts when I'm doing third-person. It's his point of view. Right there on the page."

He printed out thirty-five A4 pages for me and I took them all away to meditate on the four-word sentence. I couldn't really get beyond the four.

Lee liked it because of the Flaubertian point of view: the sentence is registering Reacher's perception, as he studies the road, of something not being there—and the thing that is not there is anyone else's POV. No eyes. We are focused on Reacher's POV exclusively at this point. He has eyes and it is through his eyes that we are seeing things. No one else's.

And then there was a slightly military feel to it. A little like "no guts, no glory" or "no pain, no gain." But these were conditional phrases: in effect, *if you do not have pain, then you will not have gain.* Was "no eyes, no interest" like that? Or was it more parataxis, where the two clauses are not logically related? (Lee was more parataxis as a rule, stacking up clauses one after another in an egalitarian way, deemphasizing logical links, light on "because" and "although" and "therefore.")

But the thing that caught my eye was, of course, the comma. In the dead center of the sentence. He had added a comma, way back on the first page, to produce a "rueful, contemplative" effect. And here it was again. Maybe the "no eyes, no interest" sentence could be read as half an iambic pentameter (thinking of Shakespeare), but to me it looked more like a compressed alexandrine, like two half hemistiches rotating around a caesura. The comma is like the fulcrum, with the two clauses seesawing around it. Phonologically it was five or six syllables, depending.

And then it hit me (I was sitting in Think Coffee at the time, on 4th and Mercer, at the counter, on a stool), the crucial thing here was: what was *not* here. The clue was in the sentence itself: it was saying, *Look at what is not here:* 2 x *no*; 2 x noun. But no verbs. No action. It was pure description (of the negative kind). This was what was surprising about a sentence that the author himself was so fond of: the action hero was really an *inaction* hero at heart. He liked doing nothing in particular. And here he favors the absence of "interest."

It was an amazingly bold statement for any kind of author to write, because in effect it was saying: "Right now, this is actually kind of boring. There's nothing much going on." It was really throwing down the gauntlet. *Go on, then, throw the damn book down, see if I care. And while you're at it why don't you start bitching on Amazon about how there isn't enough "action" in this Reacher novel and poor old Lee Child is really losing his touch and to think he used to be a good writer.*

I could hear, in Reacher idiom, the "double-tap" (as in *Echo Burning,* "He fired a double-tap, two shots in quick succession, with his hand rock steady"). The four-word construction was like a *double-tap,* Lee firing off his two-shot, sawn-off syntax, blowing away all verbs.

In the same paragraph, another very similar sentence: "No moving vehicles, no pedestrians." And then, for no reason, I happened to be flicking through *Persuader* (the one where Reacher goes undercover as a "cop-killer").

> No creaking, no cracking . . . No talking, no movement. (*Persuader,* Chapter 5.)

And then, later in the same chapter:

> I saw nobody. No cops, no ambulances, no police tapes, no medical examiners. No unexplained men in Lincoln Town Cars.

Not as elegant as the four-worder. But a lot of *no*'s. A world defined by absence.

Again, no-no, the double-tap: "No desk, no computer."

I went back to *Make Me.*

"No museum, and no monument." (Reacher looking for the origin of Mother's Rest.)

"No cell phone and nothing to do." (Stashower saying it feels like Sunday in her freshman year in college.)

Make Me was the Book of No: "No briefcase. No computer bag, no fat notebooks, no handwritten pages."

I slammed the pages down on the counter. Not in disgust, but in astonishment. The double-tap was one of his most characteristic moves. If Lee Child could be programmed, the Reacher app would be firing off a double-tap every few pages. Pow-pow.

23.

AT LAST,
THE WHOLE POINT OF REACHER

IT WAS WHEN I was not reading anything for once, just walking along Houston in between Broadway and Sixth, with my collar turned up against the wind, going west, on the north side of the street, near those NYU Pei-designed blocks, that it all fell into place for me. I started remembering some stuff Lee had been telling me about the plot. Which he still didn't know that much about. He had only inklings, glimmerings.

I rehearsed the conversation in my head. We were in his back office at the time.

"What I'm trying to do is . . . I'm asking myself: What is the *pitch* of the bad guys here?"

"Okay, what is their pitch?" I was fishing, but there was no fish. Maybe a shrimp.

"I don't want to escalate anything. I'm aware of that. Think of

Personal. It's America and Europe. London, Paris. A lot of international flights. This is the opposite of that."

"Great."

"I wanted to go back to Reacher's terrain. His home ground. Really, where he was born. The normal Reacher milieu. It's nowheresville. The bad guys are fairly normal-looking. We get a good picture of the town in this section. The motel, the diner, the general store, the laundromat, the gas station. This is a long patient investigation."

"And the store that sells nothing but rubber aprons and rubber boots."

"Yeah, I planted that."

"A seed?"

"Maybe it will develop, maybe it won't. We'll see. But the game is small. Maybe there is even an ethical debate at the heart of it. It could be not a hundred percent evil. This is not SMERSH. This is not a plot to blow up the world. I'm seeing it small. It's a small-town plot, something organic and spontaneous and not really all that well thought out."

It was what he tended to say about his own style of writing, his methodology, to the extent that he even had one. He didn't like to "think too much," he relied a lot on "instinct," the writing had to be fresh and "spontaneous." He didn't really have a "plot" in mind. It was a small-town criminal approach to writing. But, like Reacher, he is trying to figure out what the hell is going on. Is it something or nothing? And Reacher runs into the same kind of problems that Lee has, in trying to make sense of the narrative.

"*They* don't understand *him,* of course. They think he [Reacher] really is up to something. They don't get that he is there on a whim. If they didn't suspect him he wouldn't suspect them. But they do. So their fear and anxiety are what sets alarm bells ringing."

He was looking at his screen, scrolling text. "You know what I find I keep asking myself?"

"What?"

"Can I—the storyteller—get away with this?"

Lee was being radically minimalist. At this point everything in the book looked like digression. Lee held on to the idea that it was linear, at some level, "but in the absence of information." How frequently does the reader need some kind of injection of information? It was all about postponement—but how long could he postpone? And what was he postponing anyway?

The town has a name, but where is it? When is it? It's all a little hazy. The "nothingness" is what is emphasized. We know that Kansas City is somewhere not far away—a few hours' drive. But which state? "For once I don't specify time and place: I'm usually a stickler for that."

And then it looks fairly retro, technologically. It's a time warp—cellphones do not work there. People rely on old landline phones. There are no computers. No easy access to information. Many references to the Wild West—Pony Express, wagon trains. It's like a reaction *against* the abundance of data. "This isn't the Wild West anymore," says Reacher—but maybe it is.

The clues are virtually imperceptible. A handshake. A sudden gesture. The size of someone's bag. Small things.

Then Lee said something surprising—especially for anyone so convinced of the existence of Jack Reacher that they know what he ought to look like (or not look like).

"There are only two real people in this transaction."

"You and me?"

He spins his chair around to face me. "The *writer* and the *reader*. Everything else is just a fantasy, a figment of imagination."

"So no Reacher?" Or, as per the double-tap, *No Reacher, no Stashower*?

"The characters are not real, come on, you know that."

He was in that *it's not real* mood (another day it would be, "Hey, Reacher, what have you got for me today, old buddy?"). "So much of writing theory is just airy-fairy to me."

"For example?"

"They say a character is supposed to *want* something on every page."

"Emma Bovary *wants* something—a new hat, a dress, or Paris, another guy."

"No! It's the reader who wants something on every page. Not the character. The character does not exist. It's just a way of mediating the wants of the reader."

"What does the reader want, then? Coffee? Pancakes?"

"The reader wants a sensation of progress—picking up the pieces."

"But it's not easy."

"There have to be *endless* difficulties. That is my job. To make it hard. Think of it the other way around. If Reacher was a really smart guy, he'd figure it all out in a minute. The book would be one paragraph long. He'd work it all out on the first page."

"What would that sound like?"

"God, it would be so easy," he said. "What do they call those summaries at the top of a *Scientific American* article?"

"Abstract?"

"This is the *abstract*: 'Reacher got off the train, saw something bad, fixed it, killed everyone, got back on the train.'"

"The End," I chipped in helpfully.

"And it would have absolutely *no interest*."

"*No eyes* either, I imagine." I was still riffing on his double-tap.

"Whereas this way around I'm perpetually skating on the edge of in-jokes." Lee got up and grabbed one of my printed-out pages. "Look, here is a phone call. Reacher is only hearing one end of it.

He has all sorts of different interpretations running through his head. 'The context was unclear. In the end Reacher gave up on trying to construct a plausible narrative, and just waited.'"

"It's more Samuel Beckett than Reacher."

"Plot is *essential,*" Lee said. "But you're always fighting against it. There are lots of writers who have nonstop plot. It's a hundred miles per hour all the way. But ultimately that's too relentless. It becomes the same thing as flat. It's plodding."

"It's not so much writer and reader," I said. "It's more *story* and *discourse,* as the Russian formalists would say. The more discourse the closer we are to Beckett, the more story the closer to Agatha Christie. It's the fundamental violence in the book; Lee Child is not telling a story, he's fighting *story.*"

This is what I realized, as I was walking down Houston, like Reacher wandering about Mother's Rest, going up and down the streets, quartering the blocks. Reacher really didn't like plots. At some level, neither did Lee. He was a classic anti-narrativist, an anti-Hegelian. Like all good existentialists, he didn't want everything to cohere and be meaningful. He preferred meaningless and incoherent, given a choice. It was always the other guys who were big on narrative: "They're deep in conversation, plotting and scheming, you mark my words," says the diner's counterman, when in reality Reacher and Stashower are only debating the meaning of Mother's Rest. By the end of every book Reacher has negated the narrative and returned the world to its incoherent meaningless default mode. That was the whole point of Reacher. Not justice, not violent retribution. Killing off the plot.

It was right there on page 27 of my printout. "Reacher strolled back down the wide street, thinking: nap or haircut?" This is not a narrative kind of guy, unless he really has to be. It was all about *being* for him, not doing, or having. Pure *Dasein.*

It explained—I now understood—why it was Lee was so attached to the double-tap. It was his way of articulating the nothingness, twice over.

Flaubert said his novel (*Madame Bovary*) was a novel about nothing. Pure form, nothing but style, floating free. And that, oddly enough, was Reacher's whole ethic right there: float free, carry nothing with you (other than a toothbrush). He was pure form—just a rather large pure form. And, as Lee said (sometimes), he didn't exist either. He was nothingness personified. The characters do not exist, only the nothing is real.

Plot is always summoning up something you want—if not hats and dresses then coffee, gallons of hot black coffee, and clues, almost imperceptible ones; but the point of the double-tap is to come up with nothing. As someone once said of *Waiting for Godot*: "Nothing happens—twice."

THE GREAT COFFEE CONTEST

THE CLASH OF THE TITANS. That's how it was billed, anyway.

In one corner: Lee Child, who drinks around twenty cups of coffee on an average day—straight out of a big fat filter machine (Cuisinart) that squats on his kitchen work surface like a garden gnome. His record is thirty-plus.

In the opposing corner: Joel, who drinks only three or four, but using a completely different apparatus (Alessi) and a different technique. We were supposed to be having a blind coffee-tasting contest. But Lee, the great Jack Reacher, chickened out. Backed off. Deferred to Joel's superior coffee wisdom straight off the bat. "I'm a quantity man at heart. I only drink it for the caffeine. I just need regular injections." He drank it black, but not too strong. He had rejected some other old machine because it came out too much like espresso. Couldn't really drink espresso all day long. He preferred the americano that Reacher drinks in huge quantities in every diner in the land (particularly if they have a "bottomless cup" policy). He didn't really want to be able to stand the spoon up in the coffee, à la Balzac (who died of his habit, probably; that and writing like a maniac).

Joel on the other hand was more of a quality man. He had mantras. Theories. "Thou shalt not tamp" and "Aluminum is bad." The coffeemaker has to be stainless steel. Otherwise all you can taste is aluminum. And you have to heat it up over the stove too. "Look— you can't fill the reservoir above the nipple." Obviously the beans have to be fresh and freshly ground. You don't actually have to go to a certain little village in Costa Rica and buy them direct from the grower, as Joel had, but clearly it helps.

We were *chez* Lee, so Joel had brought his own grinder. Lee had respect for the craftsman. For no reason, Joel and I were debating how bad David Baldacci was (morally and aesthetically) for ripping off Reacher in his Puller series. Puller is a military policeman; he is very big; he head butts people; and he is called Puller. No wonder Reacher takes pleasure in breaking the arms of a character called Baldacci in *Never Go Back*.

"You know he has a subtle critique of Reacher in one of his books," I said.

"HE has a critique of ME?" says Lee. "That's a laugh."

"I think Puller tends to steer clear of coffee. More of a tea guy. Herbal, jasmine, whatever. He's lining up to pull the trigger and says if he had been drinking pots of coffee—Jack Reacher–style— then he would be too jittery and wired to make a decent job of the shot. His trigger finger would be all over the place."

"Bastard!" said Lee. "He ripped that off too! In *One Shot* I have a scene in which a guy is being called upon to make a shot but is worried that he has drunk too much coffee to keep the gun steady."

* * *

They both had mugs bearing the legend THINK COFFEE. Which
I had given them, by way of recognition for their services to the
bean. Well, it was almost Christmas. You could see the lights of
the Upper East Side, on the far side of Central Park, through the
windows, glimmering like stars light-years away across the interstellar vacuum. We ended up talking about the war, mostly, while
we drank our coffee, savored it, tested it. Any war. Lee grew up
wondering how he would have behaved in a war environment. He
was too young for the Second World War. And then Harold Wil-
son (the prime minister of the era) kept Britain out of Vietnam.
"Lyndon Johnson was the most persuasive American president
ever," said Lee. "And Britain was still in hock to the U.S. It was a
miracle he managed to keep us out of it."

Joel's father was a real war hero. He was in Italy in '43–44. He
and a bunch of his comrades were holed up in some farmhouse.
Joel senior went out collecting eggs from the chickens. The chickens started clucking. And suddenly they were surrounded by
German tanks. Blasted the bejeezus out of that little old farmhouse. When the smoke cleared, Joel's dad was the last man standing. He saved a comrade who had had his leg blown off by using
his own belt as a tourniquet. Then carrying him several miles to
safety. They met up again decades later and the first thing Joel's
father said was, "Hey, where's my belt?" The guy was a well-heeled
jeweler by this time and paid for the trip.

Joel had a distinguished Vietnam career, mainly protesting as
one of the leaders of the antiwar student movement, organizing
sit-ins and strikes at Columbia.

"Outstanding," said Lee. He pointed out that it was one of
Reacher's favorite words. Apparently they used it in the army all

the time, especially when they didn't know what else to say. "We've just lost half the platoon and a dozen tanks." "Outstanding."

Joel said he wanted to write a book in which every other word was "no."

"Why would you do that?" said Lee.

"It's what you do."

"Really?"

I drew his attention to the double-tap—the no-no. It was probably his most recurrent syntactical move.

Lee was stretched out on one of his sofas. It was a long sofa, but Lee's legs only just about slotted in. "Hmmm, he said, genuinely struck by the news about his habit. He put down the Think Coffee mug. "I guess there are only two interpretations. The first interpretation is I am a burned-out old hack falling back on the same tired old formulas."

"It's a tic," said Joel. "Pure OCD."

"Or, second interpretation, I really am attached to negation and there is some deep underlying philosophical impulse behind it all. Bit of a nihilist or something."

"I prefer the philosophical version," I said. "But I guess it's a bit of both." I hit him with my theory about Reacher being a plot killer. "Reacher obviously gets to decide who lives and who dies. But annihilates only those who have a plot in mind." That cracked him up.

"You stole it from John Lennon," said Joel, knocking back the last of his coffee. "Or Lennon stole it from you. Whatever."

"*No hell, no heaven,*" I said. What with Lee living just up the street from Lennon's old building. "Imagine" was manifestly the source.

"Outstanding," Lee said. "There's always an earlier origin."

"It's probably in Homer," said I. "*No Scylla, no Charybdis.*"

"Or . . . Okay, third interpretation. Just listen to it. Don't read it.

No eyes, no in-te-rest." He concertina'd out the syllables of the word "interest." "You see, it has this cadence to it. I really liked it for the sound of it." It was fundamentally a rhythm thing with Lee. He agreed with the blind woman (and her dog) at Long Beach: it had to sound right or it was no good.

Joel was knocked out by the immense screen Lee had in his dedicated TV room. Fifty-something inches. He felt a definite pang leaving it behind. "That is what I want. It's what I need," he said, hungering after giant baseball and giant boxing and giant American football. "The only thing is I would have to get a divorce. I had to choose between my wife and a giant TV."

We took the elevator down. Lee said that the new screens were almost as good as the old professional cathode-ray monitors he used to use in his days at Granada. "The next generation, the OLED technology, organic LED, will just about wrap it up," he said. "Super-thin screens, no need for backlight. Saves energy too."

We were having dinner amid the red leather and white linen of the Monkey Bar in the Elysée hotel in Midtown with Karen Rinaldi, Joel's wife. She called the place "old New York." The waiters greeted her by name. She was way better than a giant flat screen TV, no matter how thin. He'd made the right decision. She was a surfer and a publisher and she wore $1,500 glasses. Lee and Karen talked about writers paid too much, writers paid too little. How publishers were basically venture capitalists. Sometimes they blow it. She knew even more about the business than Lee. Not so much about Birmingham, England, though—where Lee had been brought up.

"It was the New Jersey of Britain," he said. "Everybody hated the place. It was the most hated place in England." Lee glared at me, the soft Southerner.

"Hey, don't look at me," I said. "Obviously I hate just about everywhere north of London. I think that's fair." It was an ancient divide in England—something to do with climate, geography, religion, history, soccer, and the binary praxis of antagonistic reciprocity.

"Yep, he hates Birmingham, all right," Lee said. "That was probably in part why I left. But they had this great tradition of making stuff. The small old-time artisans were really good at it. You know those IKEA flat packs of furniture?"

"Nightmare," said Joel. Joel was actually a great fixer too, had recently been rolling around on the floor for a day with tools in his hand putting in a new sink.

"One day we had this bed in a box. Probably the box had a hole in it. Anyway we were missing a bolt by the end of it. No bolt, no bed." Joel and I looked at each other.

"We had an identical bolt. But it was metric at a time when everything else in England was the old imperial measurement. You couldn't walk into a shop and buy one. So I go to one of these old-timers under the railway arches. One-man band. Rough-and-ready workshop. And I say to him can you make me another one of these? He has a good look at it and says, sure, come back in half an hour. So I go back in half an hour and he has these two identical bolts in his hand and I say, 'But I only wanted one!' And I'm thinking oh no that's going to be twice the cost and we're broke. The guy grins at me. Turns out one of them is the original bolt. The second one is the one he has made. A perfect *perfect* copy. They really knew how to make stuff back then."

"You'd never get one now," said Joel.

"*Make me* one," I said. "That's where you get your title from. *Poiesis*—the Greeks didn't talk about poets like they were publishing with Faber & Faber. The poet was a *maker*. It was a practical matter. Poetry was all about the craft. Or graft."

"I like that," said Lee.

We were standing around outside in the rain, having a puff, sheltering under umbrellas. Lee was planning to do some Christmas shopping the next day. "Don't worry," said Lee, as the rest of us pulled a face or talked about *goofing off*. "I can still hear the music in my head. It won't go away. I've got it now."

He headed uptown. We went down. "He is truly touched," said Joel, shaking his head with something akin to awe. "How does he do it? No, don't tell me."

Joel meant something to do with the Muse, the Force, a mysterious source of inspiration, something that couldn't really be explained without killing it. One thing Lee had said at dinner stuck in my mind. It was the exact opposite of something he'd said forty-eight hours before, when he argued that characters don't exist and only the writer and the reader are real. There was talk of movies and deals and certain actors playing the part of Reacher, and Lee was saying that none of the above really impinged on him too much when it came to the actual writing. "You have got to remember: REACHER IS REAL. HE EXISTS. THIS IS WHAT HE DOES."

All Lee had to do was fashion the duplicate bolt.

ONE THOUSAND WORDS

IT WAS THE DAY of the thousand words. I was back on the couch, looking over Lee's shoulder while occasionally a photographer looked over my shoulder. So I think I knew how he felt. Actually, it felt fine and so long as you were focused on the job you could just about bracket it out.

Lee was sitting in front of his desk rubbing his hands. "Down to work, then," he said. "I'm done with prevaricating."

We'd already gone for a pizza. Drunk lots of coffee. We were fully fueled. No more excuses. It was shortly before two, the afternoon of December 19, 2014. Leather jacket, denims, zip-up black boots.

"No, I'm not," he said. "Where's my pack of cigarettes? Blimey, that was a close one." He came back from the kitchen with a fresh pack of Camels in his hand, noticed the photographer wedging herself into a cupboard, trying to get an angle. "You know when they took that author's photograph of me, the woman took two hours with the makeup—German she was—and even then she says, 'Don't worry, Photoshop works wonders.'" And you know what, I really don't worry!"

"Au naturel," I said.

"I'm not wearing shorts though," he said. Firmly. Just in case there was any notion of him wearing shorts. "My legs are too thin. I look like Olive Oyl in short pants."

"There must be some pictures of you as a kid in shorts though."

"I'll tell you a funny thing about my father." Lee was flexing his long fingers, looking at the screen, a bit like a pianist warming up for the Tchaikovsky piano concerto. "This was a few years ago, on Facebook, it was Father's Day, and there was one of those feel-good messages: 'Just think of one afternoon you spent with your father when you had a lot of fun and good times and now just *relive* that afternoon. As a homage and testament to the old man.' And you know what, *I couldn't think of one!* Not a single bloody afternoon. Not an hour. Nothing. Blank. He was like a Martian."

I started reminiscing about all the good times I'd had with my dad, playing soccer, learning to drive, etc., and some of his funny lines, and then I thought, *hold on a sec, don't keep going on about what a nice guy your own father was.* "So," says I, taking refuge in my more clinical quasi-Freudian style, "could Reacher be seen as a kind of substitute father? A bit like Captain Nemo, the *père sublime.*"

"I reckon all writers are trying to compensate for their unhappy childhoods. Or being sick all the time. Lack of affection. They're all basket cases of emotional insecurity."

"Neurotics."

"And my mother was a monster of martyrdom too, so no help

on that side either. I was totally . . . disliked. My mother said I was dog shit brought in the house on someone's shoe. Obviously I'm writing with an idea of getting people to love me."

He was looking back at the end of his last paragraph. *I felt like a normal person. But I got over it.* Mulling it over. "What car are they driving?" he pondered. "It's crucial. You know Birmingham used to be dominated by the auto industry. Not Ford but everyone else. You know when Ford brought out the new Cortina in the early 60s?"

"My older brother had one."

"It was supposed to be the first 'modern car.' That's the way it was marketed. Everyone in Birmingham was panicking. You could get deluxe. GT. Radio. Optional extras. It was said that they had redesigned the steering wheel over and over again—to shave a single penny off the cost. We were divided about it. In Birmingham, I mean. Assuming it was true. The steering wheel was such an important part of the whole thing. The most intimate part of the car, really. And some people were annoyed that commerce was trumping art. The art people hated the commerce. The engineers hated the art people. But I realized even then that *art was commerce*. They're one and the same thing. It's not either-or."

"How old were you then?"

"I would have been seven or eight. I remember that because it was the year I went to watch Villa for the first time. They won 8–3 against Ipswich. Or possibly Leicester." He was peering intently at the screen. "'Westwood.' The *L.A. Times* journalist [in *Make Me*]. Got his name from the Villa midfielder. Injured at the moment."

He put his reading glasses back on. He'd been fiddling around with them. "Here. Look at this. Reacher hears the sound of the plastic chair scraping outside when he's going to sleep. But it's nothing. It's an absence of something. What did you call it? The *Book of No*? It's something, but it's nothing, nothing to worry about. No big deal. One whole page in the paperback edition. Nothing happens, but it dramatizes Reacher. So it's nothing and something."

"It's a nothing that might, maybe, become something. So you're anticipating."

"It's a characteristic of all the Reacher books. We skate past something that will turn out to be super-significant later on. Reacher will be kicking himself for missing it. Or the reader will."

On the shelf on the right-hand side, next to where I was sitting on the couch, there was a mini-model typewriter, with a mini sheet of paper in it, bearing the words, "Reacher said nothing."

Lee lit a fresh cigarette. Focused. Fingers on the keys. Poised. Like an organist about to kick off a Bach fugue.

"Dieter Rams shelving!" gasped the photographer. Jené leBlanc. She knew a lot about interior design. The shelves were holding hundreds of CDs behind me and the same shelves ran along the whole of the wall on the left-hand side of the room, covered with Reachers, hardcovers mostly, first editions.

"*Vitsoe,*" said Lee. "I always admired it. 50s. No real room for wiring of course. But I've never been one to let practicality get in the way of looks."

"Are we putting you off?" I said.

"Okay, we're doing it," said Lee, swerving back to his screen. "We're started."

"*The morning after . . .*" he wrote.

Then he sank into a kind of trance. I didn't hear from him for a while (or from Jené). He smoked only two cigarettes. Coffee, none. He sighed from time to time, or maybe it was just the sound of smoking. Rubbed his thumb against the palm of his right hand. Typed with two fingers. Scrolled back. A line, a puff. Held his chin. Rubbed it. Ran his hand through his hair. Twice. Folded his arms.

The second cigarette had gone out. The smoke still hanging in the air was enough for him. He went back a few lines to add more material. Went forwards again. Sat back. Breathed out audibly.

"Day's work is done," he said. "We're there."

It was 3:05 in the afternoon. He hadn't looked out the window once, that I noticed. Hadn't jumped up and paced around. It was short but it was solid, practically unpunctuated.

"Why did you stop there?"

"It was the end of a chapter."

"I could see the name *Maloney* coming up a lot."

"They're looking for Maloney. They found the name in Keever's room. Remember, it's on the bookmark. Here's what happens. First we have Reacher observing nothing happening. Then he is observing nothing happening *except* the woman in the white dress. So Reacher and Stashower go to the receiving office at the grain silos. A lot of grain but no Maloney. The guy doesn't know any Maloney. He is enchanted and annoyed with them at the same time. He sends them to the Western Union store. We go to the Western Union—Reacher's already been past it once—and the guy who is sitting in there is the Cadillac driver."

"What's he doing there?"

"I have to nudge the reader into the next chapter. That's what he's doing there."

"Word count today?"

"Round about seven hundred."

"Huh. Seven hundred."

"It's not a thousand, but it got me over the next thousand mark."

"Interesting ambiguity."

"Okay, okay," he confessed, as the Inquisition continued to turn the screw, "I really have no idea what the Cadillac driver is doing there. That's why I have to stop. Anyway I'm ahead of where I was at this point last year. Then I was shamefully behind. So I had to speed up towards the end."

"Only two cigarettes."

"I'm having another one right now," he said.

He was conscious of where he was in the greater scheme of things on account of flying out to join his wife in England the day after. He was already packing in his mind, with a reasonably clear conscience. And Aston Villa was playing Man U too. "And then there's this party I have to go to tonight."

Lee had been invited to a party at the U.N. building on the East Side. By Samantha Power, American ambassador to the U.N. and author of the book *A Problem from Hell*, all about genocide.

"Jack Reacher joins the United Nations," I said.

"Her husband is a fan."

"Another night on the tiles."

"If I keep this up it'll kill me stone dead in a week."

"You're looking pretty hale and hearty," I said. "Considering."

He swiveled around to his keyboard to Google the word "hale." I was a bit uncertain about the etymology. Cognate with healthy? "Hmmm Old English, Middle English, ah 'whole.' That's what it means." He was pleased with the discovery. "Leaving nothing out. Funny. I'm leaving nothing in. I'm *un*hale."

Which set him off, riffing on words. "I want to use *ept*. I've had it with *inept*."

"*Ort* is a good one," said Jené. "O-r-t."

"Yeah, it's always popping up in *The New York Times* crossword."

Lee recalled a brilliant crossword the day after the Clinton-Dole election. When the compiler could not have known the answer to one of his own questions: "The winner of the election." It was seven letters. Lee had written down "CLINTON." It fit. Then it occurred to him to try "BOBDOLE." "That fit too. With a whole bunch of different words hooked up to it that also fit. Amazing. I really admired that one."

He had once completed the highly cryptic (London) *Times* crossword on the train in world-record speed. "There was this bunch of businessmen sitting there. All suited up. And they were all working on it. Conferring, muttering, scratching their heads, struggling a bit. "I got out my *Times* and a handy pencil. Pretended to think for a moment. Then started scribbling down the answers. I was putting down any old rubbish. But they didn't know that. Looked fairly pleased with myself. Paused and pondered once or twice, a modest concession to difficulty. But 'finished' it, folded my paper, and put it away. Left them open-mouthed."

He didn't mind faking it. In fact he loved faking it. It was actually better than the real thing. The illusion of reality. The reality of illusion.

"So," I said, "what are you wearing to the party?"

"Leather jacket. Boots. Jeans. No tie. Unshaven. Hard man look." He set his face into a scowl. "I have to put the wind up all these old ambassador types who do nothing but sit around talking all day."

"Whereas you, on the other hand . . . ?"

"Yeah . . . I know. *Times* crossword all over again."

I was getting my stuff together to leave with Jené when I noticed the small white china plate imprinted with the faces of the young John, Paul, George, and Ringo. It was poised on a wooden stand on a shelf, next to the mini-typewriter. "I met Paul McCartney once. PETA party. We're both big supporters."

"I chip in a few quid to those guys," I said, enthusing. It was my only link to McCartney, except for the nice letter he and Linda had once written thanking me for an article about chickens.

"I said to him, 'I used to eat toast off a plate with your face on.'"

"Where'd you get it?" I said.

"Mother," he said.

"The mother who treated you so heinously?"

"Her high point," he said.

26.

CHRISTMAS GOODWILL

NEWS ITEM in the *Sussex Express:*

> Best-selling thriller writer Lee Child and his wife Jane
> Grant have donated £50,000 to an animal shelter in the
> Sussex countryside, the Raystede Centre for Animal
> Welfare.

Mr. Child: "My wife and I are both animal lovers because animals
are always the most defenseless and the most vulnerable and
the most in need of help and we were so impressed with what
they (Raystede) do that we became really enthusiastic and
wanted to support it in whatever way we could."

27.

LEE CHILD'S NEW YEAR'S RESOLUTION

"KEEP ON SMOKING."

28.

HALF A BOTTLE OF BOURBON

"**IS IT A BOOK?** I don't know." Lee was talking about *Make Me*. It was the middle of January and we were having a telephone conversation. He had spent Christmas and New Year in Sussex. With his wife and daughter. So I called him up. He'd done some writing, he said, not a lot, but he wasn't convinced it was all going to fall into place. Reacher 20 . . . maybe it wasn't meant to be. Maybe Reacher 19 was the end. *Make Me* would make "a decent short story," he thought.

Ultimate nightmare. I'm writing a book about his book and he doesn't even finish?

"I'm counting on a massive burst back in New York," he said, with his usual optimism. "I'm not dead yet."

Phew.

"Or maybe I'll go back to working for TV," he said. "It's improved a lot since my day."

Fuck.

When I put the phone down, numbly, I couldn't help but think of Bourbon John and the conversation I'd had with him a few weeks before in New York.

Flakes of snow were swirling around us as we tramped through the West Village to the restaurant. Maybe that explained why John needed to drink half a bottle of bourbon. Just to stay warm. Or maybe there was some other reason. He was a young writer, mid-twenties, from the South, in New York on a year's fellowship. Everyone said he was talented. But he was starting to feel the pressure. Or maybe it was just the Northern chill, getting into his South Carolina bones.

Anyway he had knocked back the half bottle before we'd even gotten out of the door, just standing around waiting for the other guys to turn up. I was sipping, and it was mainly water.

I think it was a Greek restaurant. Somewhere around 6th. I had a Greek salad. There were about ten other people at the table. It was pleasantly warm in there, after the dark midwinter outside. But I can really only remember the conversation with John, sitting on the other side of the table. He kept trying to pour me another drink. Wine this time. I think I had annoyed him by not drinking enough bourbon.

"So what is it you're doing?" John tried to focus his gaze on me. "Exactly?" He was all wound up by the idea of the Reacher project. He'd read only a couple of Lee's books, but Lee was the kind of successful writer he half despised and was half jealous of. John was a serious writer. An artist. He didn't really think Lee was that much of an artist. But at least he was a writer. Whereas I: I was more of a parasite, a sidekick hanger-on, and an academic to boot. He didn't like academics too much, having dropped out of grad school to write. They weren't *all* stories about lonely alienated loser alcoholics desperate to make it and slowly destroying themselves in the big city.

I explained it to him. Looking over the master's shoulder, try-ing to figure out what he was getting up to, and where it all came from, and how he did it. That sort of thing. "Not psychoanalysis. Just analysis. The psycho is strictly optional."

He had been nodding encouragingly, as if getting it. Now he threw back the contents of a bottle of Coors and slammed the bottle down on the table. "Man, I still don't get it. Tell me that again." He was really mystified. He probably would have been mystified even without the bourbon. He was a good-looking guy, with a mop of brown hair flopping down over his forehead. Heavy stubble.

I explained it to him a second time. Think of it, I said, as a kind of review—but before the book is even written. While it's still work-in-progress. Real-time. Going right back to the source and following it all the way down to the sea.

"Now I get it!" he said. John's apparent delight lasted all of a tenth of a second. He leaned across the table, glared at me, and wagged his finger in my face.

"You are KILLING Jack Reacher!"

I wish I could have said, "I have no idea what you are talking about, you drunken prick!" But the reality was I knew exactly what he was talking about. I said nothing.

"You're like that guy. The Person from . . ."

"Porlock?"

"Yeah, that's the one. You want to fuck him UP, don't you?" For some reason he put all the emphasis on "up," which made it sound a lot worse.

John was referring of course to Samuel Taylor Coleridge. Coleridge started writing "Kubla Khan" one day towards the end of the eighteenth century. I could remember the bit about Xanadu and the "stately pleasure dome" and a sacred river and something "measureless to man." It was a great short poem. Much shorter, for example, than "The Ancient Mariner." But it wasn't supposed to be that short. Coleridge reckoned it had all come to him in an opium-fueled dream and the poem was pouring out of him, just like the sacred river. But then it stopped. At precisely the time that, in Coleridge's subsequent account, a "person from Porlock" knocked at the door. Porlock really existed—it was a small town in Somerset, a few miles from where Coleridge was living. The man arrived, they talked, he left again, perhaps returning to Porlock. But—this was the point of the story—he had taken all of Coleridge's inspiration with him. When Coleridge sat down again at his desk to write and pick up where he left off he found that his muse had deserted him. His wonderful vision of Xanadu had curled up and died. He never finished the poem, at least not in the way he originally intended. He just stopped.

I was that man from Porlock, to John's way of thinking. I was going to take *Make Me,* and *unmake* it, suffocate and annihilate the Lee Child muse.

This was all after half a bottle of bourbon, and a couple of beers. And an unspecified amount of Scotch he'd been drinking earlier, so I was told. *What does he know anyway? Wanker.* At the same time, I felt a guilty stab of conscience. Could I really be putting Lee off his stroke? John wasn't the first to denounce me as *toxic.*

"It's like one of those time travel stories," he was saying. "You've gone back in time. And you're changing everything. That picture in your pocket—the beautiful picture of a book—it's like it's disappearing. The more you look at it the less you see of it."

He flipped the top of another bottle off with his thumb.

"It's gone, man. It's all gone!"

I carried on eating Greek salad. Drank some wine. Talked to people. In the end, I had to surrender. The hazy gaze was drilling into me again. The finger was waving.

"Who was that dude with the cat?"

"T. S. Eliot."

"No. Quantum guy."

"Schrödinger?"

"Yeah. Alive or dead? That was the question, wasn't it. Shove the cat in a box with a 50-50 bomb attached. Dead or alive?"

"Dead *and* alive, Niels Bohr would say. The states are superposed. Until the wave function collapses."

"Yeah, well, in Lee Child's case, he's definitely dead. How could he not be with you watching him all the time? Like a pervert. Like a voyeur."

Sometime later I heard Bourbon John had gone back to South Carolina. He couldn't take the chill in New York.

29.

THE STITCH-UP

CONVERSATION ON SKYPE.

LEE: I don't want to get framed.

ME: I don't know how to frame. Why would I want to frame you?

LEE: Are you going to dig up some dirt on me?

ME: Hold on a second. There's dirt? What am I missing?

LEE: Nothing.

ME: I'm going to have to do some serious research.

LEE: It's all myth. Mostly.

ME: Mostly?

LEE: Gossip and rumor.

ME: So . . . is it true what they're saying about you?

LEE: Bastard.

30.

NEVER GO BACK

IT WAS A RULE with him. *Never go back.* It was even the title of his last but one novel. Child was Reacher and Reacher was Child. Of course he *had* gone back—to slip in a comma. Take out the *shit* and the *piss*. Now he was going back again.

He was up to 32,000 words. "It's acceptable at this point," he said. It was the last day of January. Subzero in Manhattan. Central Park all white icing. I had to dress up like some kind of spaceman to survive the rigors of walking down to the C train at Spring Street and coming back up again on 86th. Two hats (one borrowed from Joel: "Handmade Persian—DO NOT LOSE IT!").

He reiterated his rule. "As you know, my method is not to touch what I've done." I had an inkling what his next word was going to be. *"Unless . . ."* Me and my prophetic soul. "Unless I really need to."

Turned out he really really needed to.

Rewrite No. I: Kansas City

Lee just erased Kansas City. Sorry Kansans! He went back and rubbed it right out. You will look in vain for Kansas City in the pages of *Make Me*. As if Kansas City had never existed. *Adiós* sentences like, "It was five hours to Kansas City." *Hola* five hours (or something) to . . . Oklahoma! No KC; OK OKC!

It had a completely different ring to it. No more of the Old West and gunslingers and the Wizard of Oz. We were going to the land of Rodgers and Hammerstein. As high as an elephant's eye.

"Reacher and Stashower have to go to Los Angeles now. To see the journalist. It's all a question of triangulation. We still don't have a clue where Mother's Rest is. But I have to have some kind of plausible geography. Mother's Rest makes a triangle with the other two."

There was a definite tinge of regret in his voice, at losing Kansas City. "I guess it doesn't matter too much," Lee said. "But there is a great tradition of music and barbecue in Kansas City." The idea was that, after all the immense nothingness of Mother's Rest, Kansas City represented a holiday in the metropolis, full of diversion and bright lights. "With Oklahoma," Lee said politely, "the contrast is not so great."

"You mean Oklahoma is dullsville too?" I had never been to Oklahoma. "What about the surrey with a fringe on top and all that?" I wasn't entirely sure what a "surrey" was, but I had a feeling it was fairly fun.

"Don't get me wrong," he said. "You could probably go to Oklahoma and have a good time for a day. Or two. But in terms of world perception, Kansas City is going to have more dive bars and nightclubs. Pity. Oklahoma is going to have to do."

It was a classic structuralist move. It wasn't that Lee was uninterested in how the pieces of his puzzle hooked up to the world beyond the book. For example, he had to take geography into account, even if he was being deliberately hazy. But it was more important to him how the pieces all fit together: Mother's Rest had to sit squarely between Oklahoma and the City of the Angels. Poised, like some kind of fulcrum. Maybe it would be better that way anyhow. Oklahoma would provide more of a counterpoint to the bright lights of Sunset Boulevard.

Rewrite No. 2: Stashower

Something similar applied in the case of Stashower. Lee was going back to fiddle around with her too. Second transgression against the rule. "I punched up a couple of lines," he said. "I only do that once in a while." Or twice.

"So are your women based on some kind of precursor? Or any actual women?"

I recalled conversations I had had in the past with other male writers writing about women. Saul Bellow has two types of women characters: one is gorgeous, sensual, funny, loving, sensational; the second is not—more of a Harpy than an angel. "It's the same woman," he said (on a Boston campus). "Only after I married her." Norman Mailer (in a pub in London) didn't want to talk about Marilyn Monroe; he secretly fantasized about Brigitte Bardot. "I knew I couldn't have her," he said. "Whereas the whole of America had Monroe."

"It's funny," Lee said (sitting in his back office, not looking out over snowy Central Park). "I like to think I'm more realistic. I try to make my women characters real and almost ordinary."

Lee had won a prize in bygone days from a Texas newspaper

for The Most Realistic Dialogue in a Novel. "Ha! It isn't," he said. Ruth, his daughter, had tape-recorded and transcribed some real conversation when she was studying linguistics. "If you look at what we really say, it's hilarious," said Lee. "It's full of contradiction, stumbles, abandoned sentences, placeholders, fragments, nonsense, pauses. If you wrote like that you'd end up with a thousand pages and no one could read more than half of it."

So you had to be unrealistic in order to achieve realism—or what the French called *vraisemblance,* true-seemingness, rather than truth itself. "It passes for realistic even though it isn't." And the same is true of the brief encounters in *Make Me*. "The reality is that if you bump into a random stranger on the street and start having a conversation with her, the chances are that she will tell you to piss off and walk away. The story ends right there, on page one. The probability that you are going to end up spending the next two weeks together, in increasing intimacy, in situations of dire peril, is practically nil. And yet that is just what I am writing. *Staggering* artificiality! Statistically, it's like winning the lottery. But still it has to be believable."

The crux of it all was the relationship with Reacher. "I wanted her to be uncomfortable with what was going on. Whereas Reacher is okay with violence and killing people. She has to be more civilized. Only a patrol cop in a small town by training. She says, 'I never even drew my weapon.'

" 'No shooting, please, I'm a cop!' "

"Obviously in Detroit it's lawless all the time. Apparently Albuquerque has the worst record for police shootings. They shoot people there fairly regularly. Their force was provided with an additional hundred officers. Some political thing. But it was hard to find enough decent guys. In the end they took just about anyone, thugs, madmen, anyone, now they're shooting all the civilians.

But still, statistically, overall, it's rare to even remove your weapon from your holster. It's not like the movies, generally. You ever see a policeman with a gun in his hand, pointing it at you?"

"Nope."

"Exactly. It's a rarity. Stashower needs to be a fish out of water when it comes to violence. You have to have the contrast with Reacher. An argument. One of the strange things about popular literature—a lot of it is like science fiction. Or fantasy. Most women are *not* like that."

"No Pussy Galore?"

"No Ursula Andress either, popping up out of the sea in her bikini. I'm not going to have a *thriller woman* in my novel. I want to be more realistic, restart the clock."

"So she's just like the girl-next-door, then?"

"On the other hand," Lee said, trying to get the picture straight, "the reader can't be bored with her. Neither can I! I have to spend months in her company. She has to have *something* going on."

I wandered back downtown through Central Park, remembering *61 Hours* and winter in South Dakota and even Reacher feeling the cold. Crunching over the snow. Colorless, odorless, I thought, then instantly translating, *No colors, no odors,* realizing that I was starting to think in terms of four-word no-no sentences all the time. One strange thing: Lee hadn't lit up the entire time. Not once. No cigarette, no smoke. He was looking pretty damn healthy too. Don't tell me he'd given up on his New Year's resolution already.

Make it strange! The old slogan of the Russian formalists applied to the Reacher oeuvre too. Rather like Central Park itself in fact. All the old familiar features of the terrain were there—the Dakota building to the west, the reservoir in the center, the skyscrapers around 59th, and that new tall thin one, still unfinished, that looked like an overextended steeple or spire. But the landscape had also been defamiliarized, transformed by the blizzard of a couple of days before into a fantasy of frozen fountains and silver trees festooned with crystal and diamonds beneath a dazzling sky. That night I even got spun around somewhere between Sixth Avenue and Vandam on account of a snowstorm. I didn't know where I was anymore.

T. S. Eliot said we couldn't stand "very much reality," thinking of the skull beneath the skin. Maybe, it occurred to me, trudging across the Manhattan steppes, the opposite was true. We could stand too much—the monstrous, the horrific, the excessive, and we could stand too little as well—emptiness, lack, absence, "no hills, no dales" [*61 Hours*]: *Look at everything that is NOT here!* Reacher seems to say. What we found unbearable was just the steady state, the unvarying quotidian, the flat recapitulation of the same. Reacher 20 was never realism. It was a cunning cocktail of the hyperreal and the hyporeal, the extraordinary and the infraordinary, a cornucopia of violence shot through with great shafts of nothingness. It was a form of aesthetic extremism. Lee, like the snow that enshrouded Central Park, was effecting a purification of the real. Hence Reacher: the purifier.

And he shall purify.

MY LIFE OF CRIME

"THEY'RE ASSHOLES. But no more than any other assholes."

I thought I had worked out what it was Lee had against farmers. He said it was all to do with having read this book on the history of farming in the U.S. in the twentieth century. How farmers had basically screwed up from the Dust Bowl right through to BSE. I reckoned it was something to do with Mesopotamia.

I had been reading an essay on the history of Mesopotamian agriculture. By an archaeologist.* He distinguished between "archival" and "sacrificial" societies. The archival guys started keeping records, mainly about how many bags of grain they had or could sell. It was the origin of paperwork, albeit on tablets, in

---

* David Wengrow, "'Archival' and 'Sacrificial' Economies in Bronze Age Eurasia: An Interactionist Approach to the Hoarding of Metals," *Interweaving Worlds: Systemic Interactions in Eurasia, 7th to the 1st Millennia BC,* edited by Toby C. Wilkinson, Susan Sherratt, and John Bennet (Oxford: Oxbow Books, 2011).

cuneiform (and the grain even gets into the Rosetta Stone, for example, along with gold, silver, high priests, and manifest gods). The sacrificial guys put the emphasis on warrior types to defend them in conflict. The whole point was to produce a better (bigger, braver, more lethal) warrior, equipped with a lot of metal, some of which would be buried with him. But naturally there was a convergence between the two. The archivists needed warriors so nobody would steal their grain and the sacrificers needed archives to record all their great sacrifices (from the Latin, "to make sacred"). The very possibility of there being an archive tended to ramp up the warrior side of things. The archive came up with the idea of the hero. Hence, in some sense, agriculture produces heroes. Farmers and Reacher-types were inherently linked (think, for example, of Clint Eastwood in assorted spaghetti westerns coming to the aid of farming folk; or Shane; or the Lone Ranger). No archive, no hero.

But here was the irony. The archive set them up in some kind of rivalry or conflict or *agon*. Farmers basically hated heroes and vice versa, according to the archive. The opposition was all over Rousseau, for example. The noble savage, living in the state of nature (Jean-JACK Rousseau), versus the decadent civilization of the city and the theater and the arts and sciences. And this was the other irony. The archive—the stela or text that would ultimately morph into the novel—was fundamentally nostalgic. It looked back to the state of nature as a golden age, before everything got screwed up. And guess what screwed it all up in the first place? Yep—farmers, agriculture, and therefore the archive. Thus the book, any book, is neurotically riven, constantly driven to deny what it is (the product of the shift towards agriculture and industry) and harking back mistily in the direction of a pre-agricultural, pre-industrial, pre-literary paradise (with sex dangling tantalizingly in front of your eyes, moreover).

The archive rehearsed its own birth, in a mood of elegy, in the shift from the nomadic hunter-gatherer phase of human existence to the settled, agricultural phase, tilling the earth rather than running around all over it, killing anything that looked edible. It was already right there in the Book of Genesis. The regret, the loss, the recollection of a sublime state of being. And the fall. "Cursed is the ground for thy sake, in sorrow shalt thou eat of it all the days of thy life. Thorns also and thistles shall it bring forth to thee; and thou shall eat the herb of the field. In the sweat of thy face shalt thou eat bread . . ." Doesn't sound like much fun, does it? The times we used to have BEFORE all this farming lark!

Thus, Lee. He would hate farmers, it was built into the great tradition of writing that grew out of . . . farming. He was a farmer who had to deny that he was a farmer.

"It also explains why you hate bureaucrats." I had just about finished spouting my latest theory.

"Do I hate bureaucrats?"

"It's right there in *The Enemy*. Reacher kills the bureaucrat at the end. The Big Shot who doesn't himself kill anyone but sponsors a lot of killing. Reacher pulls out a gun and says it's okay I'm not going to shoot you. The guy breathes a sigh of relief. And then Reacher says, 'I was just kidding,' and shoots him in the head."

Lee chuckled at the memory. "Yeah, I really enjoyed writing that scene."

"You, the glorified pen-pusher, have to kill the pen-pusher. And it probably explains why you're 'goofing off' all the time. You can't afford to be too disciplined. Too much like some kind of bureaucrat."

Lee gave the theory serious consideration. "I only hate the bad bureaucrats. The incompetent and corrupt ones. The cowardly bureaucrat. Not all of them." He had a theory—a sort of revised

Rousseau, latter-day Book of Genesis golden-age thinking—that British civil servants used to be fair-minded intellectuals. Spreading the great British Empire far and wide, administering India, that sort of thing. But that they went into a massive decline in the 1970s, and especially under cost-cutting Thatcher. Which is what led Lee into his life of crime. Or rather the denial of crime. In a spirit of preserving justice. I had almost forgotten: his original specialization was not writing, and not television either, but law. And therefore *lawlessness*.

Back in England he was always picking up tickets, for parking illegally, or speeding. And he would never pay the fine. Not once. "I approach it from a civil liberties perspective. If you ever let the mere accusation of crime become synonymous with a conviction, you have East Germany and a totalitarian state. Everybody is automatically guilty."

"Yeah, but you were actually guilty, right?"

"Of course," he snorted. "Probably everyone really is guilty of something, let's face it. But that's not the point. You have to test and challenge the prosecutors. Citizens should put them through their paces. It's a fundamental principle of jurisprudence."

So whenever he picked up a ticket he would just ignore it. Rip it up and toss it. Then the follow-up letters started arriving. And he would ignore them too, rip them up into tiny little pieces in a spirit of high jurisprudence. Once in a while he would actually get dragged into court. And the formal charge was not the parking infraction, but not responding to an official letter. Lee Child, how do you plead? Not guilty, Your Honor!

His basic strategy can be summed up in two words: WHAT LETTER? "I would make them walk through it in a forensically responsible way. You know, who wrote this letter? Do you have any proof it was actually delivered? No? Your Honor, I beg to have this case dismissed. *For want of evidence.*" He pulled it off six or seven times in Manchester. It was always thrown out for lack of hard evidence.

Lee went out into the kitchen and poured two cups of coffee and brought them back in. "After that I decided to up the ante a little. I started appealing for expenses. You know, a day off work: £300. On account of having my time wasted by a frivolous, vexatious prosecution. And I won too. Which really wound up this woman who was running the whole ticket-issuing business."

Her name was Ms. Bracegirdle. The next time "Mr. James Grant" was brought before the bench, she brought her entire office staff along with her. Reinforcements. To demonstrate the existence of the letter and make the charge stick. Lee had to cross-examine the typist who had typed the original letter accusing him of speeding. And who had been coached in what to say.

LEE: You can recall writing this letter?

SHE: Yes. On May 5.

LEE: Even though this was over a year ago.

SHE: I recall it clearly.

LEE: So you will remember what day of the week it was.

SHE: How do you expect me to remember that?—this was over a year ago! Oops . . .

Case dismissed! [Sound of gavel being brought down]

"It's the duty of the citizen to stand up to the state," said Lee, rather heroically. The same applied in the United States. Where, of course, he had been caught speeding. They didn't know who they were up against. In the U.S. the traffic cop has to make out an affidavit, a report about exactly what took place. "If you ask for the paperwork, it's invariably got a mistake in it. This is my point about bad bureaucrats. They can't get anything right. And they shouldn't be allowed to get away with a faulty affidavit."

Cut to: Lee Child versus the United States or at least the State of New York. There are a load of other people outside the courtroom, all plea-bargaining. "You were doing fifty-one. Will you plead to forty-eight?" That sort of thing. A lesser penalty. A cop comes up to Lee.

COP: You were doing well over fifty, more like sixty. Will you plead forty-five?

LEE: I want dismissal.

COP: Come on, be reasonable. How about thirty-five? Will you plead to that?

LEE: Dismissal.

COP: What about not wearing a seatbelt?

They thought he was bluffing. They were right, he was bluffing, but he would bluff all the way and never give up. Especially when he had an ace up his sleeve. They go into court. Lee is standing in the dock. "Not guilty!" His invariable plea. The cop can't believe it. But we've got this dufus! He is so guilty. He's never going to wriggle out of this one. The cop goes up to Lee in the dock. "What do you think you're doing?" he whispers to him. Lee shows him the affidavit, drawing attention to the "Infiniti" in the first paragraph (which he really was driving) and the "Saab" in the second paragraph (the product, no doubt, of cutting and pasting some prior template). The cop raises his eyes to heaven. Like a helpful go-between he goes back to the judge and mutters something to him. The judge, wasting no further time, bangs his gavel. "Case dismissed!" Again.

"It's partly fun and mischief," said Lee. "But it's part serious.

They've got to do the job properly. It's trivial, but it's the visible end of the spectrum. If we allow an accusation to stand as a conviction, unchallenged, then . . ."

"You should have been a lawyer."

Lee allowed he had had a legal education, which caused him to ask of all office-holders, "What is your jurisdiction?" Flying back to London one time, he had reached passport control and showed his passport to the inspector.

SHE: Where have you been?
LEE: None of your business.

He had the right to go more or less anywhere he pleased, without interrogation. And bureaucrats had to be taught not to overstep the boundaries of their authority. "I wouldn't do it here!" (landing at JFK), he added. Mainly on account of not being a citizen.

"One day I'd like to try not presenting my passport, just to see what happens." He was talking about returning to the U.K. again. "In terms of sheer jurisprudence, they shouldn't need to see it. You're either a citizen or you're not."

He thought the passport was a mere symbol or token that you should be able to do without. But Lee also wanted to push his luck to the limit. Just to see when it would run out. "One of these days they're going to nail my ass."

32.

SHANE: A FOOTNOTE

LEE HAD WRITTEN an introduction to a new edition of Jack Schaefer's *Shane*. He kind of had to. So many people went around comparing Reacher to Shane. And quoting the kid's line at the end, "Shane! Shane! Come back, Shane!" Which is only in the movie, not the book. Come back, Alan Ladd! It was just about as annoying as the allusions to Tom Cruise.

Lee had to have a comeback.

It was a great book and it wasn't. Lee was clinical in his analysis. He pointed out that Schaefer had never been farther west than Cleveland, Ohio, where he was born. If you had a map of America a foot and a half wide unfolded in front of you, then Cleveland would be less than three inches in from the right. A long way from Wyoming, where there was the classic encounter between homesteaders and ranchers, mediated and resolved by the mysterious stranger, Shane. It was on a par, Lee suggested, with writing about William Wallace and the highlands of Scotland when you had never been further north than Luton. And Schaefer knew nothing about fighting either. All his fights, "right down to the balsawood chairs and the spun-sugar glass," were based on radically misleading Hollywood movies. Lee laughed at the quote on the cover of his old coffee-stained copy: "If you're only going to read one western in your life, read this one."

"Don't," he said.

And yet this short first-person narrative (seen from the point of view of the boy throughout) retained its grand mythic status. Lee's concept of the eight-hundred-year-old "knight errant" was too recent for me. This narrative was fully Mesopotamian in outlook, pre-feudal, going all the way back to *Gilgamesh*. It restaged the clash between the archival and the sacrificial societies. It nostalgically summoned up the ghost of the old nomadic hunter-gatherer, who was Shane, who had been Enkidu and Theseus, who would become Reacher.

But when we were talking about it, Lee pointed out something else *Shane* had, or rather didn't have, which made it into the great work of art it was. An information deficit. Realist fiction tended to be bureaucratic: it filled in all the forms, checked the boxes about identity, sexual orientation, ethnicity, chronology, etc. Some writers like to deploy spreadsheets and graphs. They over-explain. Lee, in contrast, preferred to "under-explain." It was like the "Devil's Bridge"—when you lacked a fully articulated historical narrative, then myth took over.

What Lee really appreciated about Schaefer's story was everything he hadn't written rather than what actually made it onto the page. His aesthetics of omission. Shane was a mysterious stranger with no past and no future. Reacher, it was true, was a little like that, even though Lee had been forced to fill in a few of the gaps along the way. But at some level, nobody could really know anything about Reacher. He was a blank. A very large blank. "What I'm doing," Lee explained, "is artificially managing information scarcity."

This is what both Jack Schaefer and Lee Child were good at: all the stuff they left out. And this is the natural habitat of myth—not Mount Olympus or the Black Forest, but the voids, the dark interstellar spaces, and the undiscovered country.

33.

THE THAW

HE WAS MAKING TOAST. This was about as far as his cooking skills went. Even the toast was a bit overdone. His toast was as black as his coffee. But I didn't mind black.

The Independent (London) had published an article about Lee and Reacher in the New Year, one I'd written. Apparently it had swung some people around. The paranoid ones who basically agreed with Bourbon John that I was killing Reacher. Now even they were saying maybe it couldn't do any harm. Perhaps (looked at from a brazenly commercial point of view, rather than the scientific-aesthetic one I preferred to adopt) it could even be a positive for the brand.

"Unless," said Lee, "you come to the conclusion, at the end of all your pondering and analysis, that it's all complete shit."

"I don't want to anticipate my conclusions," I said. Man in white coat. "That would be premature."

"Oh well, you know what they say—so long as you spell the name right, it's cool."

There was a paradox about the Reacher novels. They were immensely popular, published in their millions around the world, with a fan roster that included Antonia Fraser, Malcolm Gladwell, Kate Atkinson, and Haruki Murakami. They were also immensely unpopular among certain readers of Julian Barnes and Jonathan Franzen, frowned upon by Harold Pinter, eliciting frosty nose-wrinkling from such as Edward Docx. Now, I had the impression, maybe there was a faint thaw setting in. For example, a Cambridge postgrad, trying to set up some interdisciplinary seminar series on work-in-progress, had wondered aloud if Lee and I could be interested in participating.*

"Reacher remains a little outside the pale," Lee said. "There are barriers. You can see it from their point of view. They need an exclusion principle. I'm too *low-falutin* for them." It was an axis that stretched, as Lee put it, from the *Radio Times* to *The Sunday Times*. Colin Dexter and Morse had broken through (thanks to Oxford and the opera); then, when he stopped writing, it was Ian Rankin and Rebus. They were the anointed ones, the axis had permission to read them. Reacher remained a guilty pleasure—something you only indulged in behind closed doors. When Reacher came up on some literary panel show on Radio 2 (BBC London), one of the "artsy women panelists" introduced her comments by saying, "I would never have thought of picking up this book if not for the show . . ." It was sheer naked prejudice, but to her surprise she liked it.

"I'm like one of those obscure 60s bands," said Lee. "You know,

---

* Credit to David Winters. A conference, "Books in the Making," will take place in April 2016, in Cambridge, England, courtesy of the Centre for Research in the Arts, Social Sciences and Humanities.

some kind of import, someone's brother has the only album in the country. It still feels like that."

"You're probably never going to crowd-surf. Or fill the O2 Arena." Lee had this fantasy of being a rock star, even though he couldn't play a note.

"I guess it goes to the secret personal business of reading. You're on your own, you're not grooving with the masses. There really are sound waves on the air. Whereas reading—it's weird. There's just these tiny little squiggles on the page. The reader's imagination is humming all the time. In music, you're consuming without creating. It's the hysteria of crowds. Euphoric. When you're reading, you're really creating the text as you go along. It's just you and Reacher."

Or maybe it was a bit like being a member of a club. A week or two earlier I had met Steven Poole, the *Guardian* columnist. He had written a funny pastiche of the Lee Child style in his review of *Personal*. But he was still a fan. Even amid a crowded table in a café in Shoreditch, London, we were soon down to comparing notes, like some kind of secret handshake.

ME: Do you remember the fight to the death with Paulie? The guy who is bigger than Reacher? [*Persuader*]

HE: Never should have tried the flying karate kick.

ME: "He got fancy, and I saw I was going to win after all."

HE: Yeah. Never get fancy.

Maybe it was time to convene that Lee Child seminar after all.

34.

ONLY A MATTER OF TIME

ENGLISH TRIPOS
Part II
[specimen paper]

Date: Thursday, June 4, 2020
Time: 1:30 to 4:30

Paper 12

Lee Child Studies

Answer three questions, one from each section

Do not use the same material twice, either in this paper or in the examination as a whole. Irrelevant answers, or answers only tenu-

ously related to the question, will be penalized. Illegible handwriting may place candidates at a disadvantage.

Write your number, not your name, on the cover sheet of each Section booklet.

Stationery requirements   **Special requirements**

20-page Answer book x 1   None

Rough work page

You may not start to read the questions printed on the subsequent pages of this question paper until instructed you may do so by the proctor.

SECTION A

Discuss **ONE** of the following. Candidates must draw on the oeuvre of Lee Child in the context of other writers and forms of culture.

1. "Literature does not exist. Or if it does, it's a hoax or a delusion."
2. "Writing is insignificant in comparison with the voice."
3. "The history of Western literature is essentially a history of the knight errant."
4. EITHER: "Narrative provides human beings with a tool for survival—or a weapon." OR: "All narrative is a sign of primordial failure and disappointment."
5. "Every book exists in order to be made into a film."
6. "The writer is a neurotic sociopath in need of psychoanalysis."

SECTION B

Candidates should draw on **ONE OR MORE** texts by Lee Child.

7. "*Killing Floor* is not just the first book by Lee Child, it provides the archetype of all his subsequent works."
8. "Reacher is a liberal humanist intellectual with arms the size of Popeye's."
9. "Reacher does not simply eliminate 'bad guys': his mission is to eradicate the very possibility of narrative."
10. "Superficially logocentric, the classic Lee Child narrative is naturally self-deconstructing."
11. "In the work of Lee Child, discourse is invariably privileged over story and character."

12. "The Childean text is an exercise in the aesthetics of omission."

13. "I cannot understand the mentality of one who is awaiting the next Lee Child."

SECTION C

Comment in detail on any **TWO** of the following extracts. You may answer on the extracts separately, or in the form of one continuous answer.

(a)

First thing out of the barrel of Reacher's Barrett was a blast of hot gas. The powder in the cartridge exploded in a fraction of a millionth of a second and expanded to a superheated bubble. That bubble of gas hurled the bullet down the barrel and forced ahead of it and around it to explode out into the atmosphere. Most of it was smashed sideways by the muzzle brake in a perfectly balanced radial pattern, like a donut, so that the recoil moved the barrel straight back against Reacher's shoulder without deflecting it either sideways up or down. Meanwhile, behind it, the bullet was starting to spin inside the barrel as the rifling grooves grabbed at it.

Then the gas ahead of the bullet was heating the oxygen in the air to the point where the air caught fire. There was a brief flash of flame and the bullet burst out through the exact center of it, spearing through the burned air at nineteen hundred miles an hour. A thousandth of a second later, it was a yard away, followed by a cone of gunpowder particles and a puff of soot. Another thousandth of a second later, it was six feet away, and its sound was gravely chasing after it, three times slower.

(DIE TRYING)

(b)

He had always been fit and strong, but the last three months had brought him to a new peak. He was six foot five, and he had weighed 220 when he left the Army. A month after joining the swimming pool gang, the work and the heat had burned him down to 210. Then the next two months, he had built back all the way to about 250, all of it pure hard muscle. His workload was prodigious. He figured to shift about four tons of earth and rock and sand every day. He had developed a technique of digging and scooping and twisting and throwing the dirt with his shovel so that every part of his body was working out all day long. The result was spectacular. He was burned a deep brown by the sun and he was in the best shape of his life. Like a condom crammed with walnuts, is what some girl had said.

(TRIPWIRE)

(c)

No eyes, no interest.

(MAKE ME)

END OF PAPER

REACHER IN TRANSLATION

I WAS GOING TO do some serious research. Like a proper literary scholar (my day job, after all). Maybe it was something to do with the subzero temperature in New York.

I was going to go back to his old school in England, I was going to track down some of his old schoolmates, the ones who used to call him "Grievous"; I was going to interview the current headmaster, maybe even speak to one or two of the teachers of the young James Grant—if there were any still left alive—and get their insights. And, finally—the pièce de résistance—I was going to retrieve some of Lee's old school reports. I was going to be archaeologist rather than analyst for a change. I was sure it would be solid gold. I remember an examiner's dismissive remark, for example, on the young Napoleon's essay on happiness: "A most pronounced dream." Which had tipped the balance in favor of becoming emperor rather than essayist. Imagine, then, if Lee's old

English teacher had scribbled some abusive remark on one of his great early works: "Not another four-word sentence! James needs to work harder and try his hand at five words or even six. And could he please stop all the scrapping in the schoolyard?" Or this, from one of the classmates: "Ah, Grievous—what a lad he was!" Or better still: "I hated the bastard!"

"Nah," Lee said, between spoonfuls of lobster bisque. "Fuck all that."

"It would be like a serious biography."

"Serious bollocks, you mean."

"It could be funny."

"Come on, who cares? It's too Julian Barnes."

We were having lunch in Balthazar on Spring Street, the glowing French-style bistro that makes you feel like you're on the Boulevard Saint-Germain, with a riot of red leather, giant mirrors,* and croissants. There was a new snowstorm forecast for the following day.

Anyway, I tried. On the other hand, I did find out about the Latin translation.

In a very small way, seen over a long period, the genre of Latin translations of popular books has been enjoying a surge. I once read (fragments of) *Winnie ille Pu*, for example. *Alice Through the Looking-Glass* was another modest hit (*Aliciae Per Speculum Transitus*). And, more recently, *Harrius Potter*. Meanwhile, there is a garden in Sussex bearing the legend of Reacher, Latinized. At least of a single recurrent phrase. A three-word sentence. And even that took the best part of a year to complete. The original line was, "Reacher said nothing." But it turned out that Latin translators had rather a lot to say about it.

This is where Lee's old school—King Edward's in Edgbaston,

---

* Exactly one week later, according to the *New York Post*, "A giant mirror crashed onto diners at the hip SoHo hotspot."

Birmingham—finally got into the story. A stonemason in Kent, who also happened to be a fan, offered to make Lee a sundial. Lee said okay. But what about the inscription? Of course, it would have to be in Latin. I know, says Lee, what about "Reacher said nothing"? That can't be too hard to translate, can it? Reacher + *dixit* + *nihil*, not necessarily in that order. Or something like that. Just to be on the safe side, he consulted John Claughton, the new chief master at King Edward's. He was a highly regarded classicist and still taught Greek and Latin. He had studied Greats at Oxford and played cricket for the university (he was a Blue). And he'd written a book about the Persian Wars. Surely he would know? Claughton was glad to be asked (having already tapped Lee for a few quid for the old alma mater) and had a pretty good idea of how to translate it, but, just to be on the safe side, decided to consult a couple of other Oxford Latinists and compare notes. They ended up kicking it around for an age, chewing over alternatives, turning it into a regular forum.

The essential problem, they all agreed, was *Reacher*. They dithered for months over the name alone. You can't just leave it as "Reacher," they argued (unlike *Winnie ille Pu*, for example). But the problem was that, in Latin, the verb can't just morph seamlessly into a noun (*to reach* > *Reacher*). So they came up with "Extensor." Which was cool insofar as it meant something to do with reaching and stretching and straining and aspiring. But apparently sometime in the Middle Ages, notably in connection with the Inquisition, it became associated with being stretched on the rack. So it became a synonym for sadism and torture. And therefore uncool, even for Reacher. They agreed instead on "Adeptus," which had more positive connotations and originally meant not just skillful, having knowledge, but, more specifically, "one who has attained the art of transmuting metal into gold."

Then one of them had a notion that it had to be six syllables, as a kind of nod in the direction of the hexameter. It would sound more Latinate that way. So *nihil* had to be contracted to *nil*. Hence the final form of Reacher saying nothing, as inscribed on the sundial sitting in Lee Child's back garden in Sussex, facing south:

NIL DIXIT ADEPTUS

As a tribute Lee gave the name Claughton to one of the more simple-minded country bumpkin bad guys in *Never Go Back*. The dreaded Claughton clan.

"I love the intensity," said Lee. "That real enthusiasts can spend so much time and energy and intellectual power and passion over something so seemingly trivial and pointless."

A THEORY OF EVERYTHING

LEE CHILD SAID, "Reacher said nothing." Lee Child doesn't often say nothing himself.

On this occasion he listened to me sketching out my own dark theory about why we write. Something to do with lack, failure, an evolutionary pathology, an asymmetry between being and doing, boredom and death. And then, just to wind him up, I mentioned that someone had said to me that the only way Lee could write was to have a "chip on his shoulder." Reacher, in other words, was channeling the author's own anger and bitterness and resentment. Or at best (going back to Virgil), *furor.* Which could be divine, depending on how you looked at it (Aeneas, for example, is frequently inspired by it).

He nodded, patient, and gave the question careful thought. "Any sonofabitch that says I have a chip on my shoulder—he is a fuckin' liar and I am going to hunt that bastard down and . . ."

He cracked up, spluttering. He had me going for a moment. He probably scared the bejeezus out of the two women at the table next to us. He didn't care either.

"Never forgive, never forget," I said, quoting Reacher.

"It's true that Reacher is vengeful. He bears grudges. I'm probably the same. But . . ." He smiled at the ladies. I think they were reassured. Charming psycho with a smile. "I don't begin with the writer: I begin with the reader."

The waiter came up and poured us both some more coffee. I was having the roasted eggplant sandwich.

"You have to ask yourself why it is people love the form of the story," Lee continued. "Whether it's Reacher, or Homer, or a thirty-second commercial on TV."

"Okay, why?"

"You're right about the failure thing," he said. "We were basically crap as animals. We still are. Neanderthals were better than us. They were stronger, faster, better animals. More muscular, probably more virile. Then around two hundred thousand years ago, our brains got bigger and we got language. Maybe it was a random mutation or maybe the development of language increased the size of the brain. Of course plenty of other animals had language. Look at the prairie dog, for example. Their cries can distinguish between a ground-based predator and an air-based one."

"So what's the difference?"

"The difference is we had syntax. It permitted speculation. Hypotheticals. A bigger vocabulary put us right ahead of the game. Therefore we could plan and organize. Thirty or forty people together makes a powerful animal. The power of the mob. We were automatically on top of all the competition. Language was not harmless: we wiped out an entire species with it. But it was fact-based communication to begin with. All reportage. Stuff to do with woolly mammoths and saber-tooths."

"Variations on mimesis, then. Mirroring. The picture theory of language."

"Also comparing notes on killing techniques, I imagine," said Lee. "But then, maybe a hundred thousand years later, we started talking about stuff that *hadn't* happened. We were talking about people that *didn't* exist. Parables, fairy tales, myths. It was a radical shift. A way of killing leisure time? Ha! There was no leisure."

I didn't suggest the thing about leisure. He just came up with that himself. Maybe because it seemed like a bit of a put-down of the whole business. "It was a fundamental insight about cave painting too," I said. "All those great animals—they weren't saying: *Here they are; they are good to eat; go and hunt them down!* It was more: *Look, they don't exist anymore; this is what they used to look like; what have we done?* It was an expression of regret or nostalgia for everything that had been lost."

Lee was impatient with my dark view of everything. O dark dark dark, they all go into the dark. The bare ruin'd choirs where late the sweet birds sang kind of line. He was much more upbeat. "Nothing happened, nothing advanced, *unless* it was helpful to our survival. The stories were either consoling or encouraging. The heroic story would inspire you to be heroic. If you're in a cave with a whole bunch of other people inside, some of them injured or sick with howling predators outside baying for your blood, and someone tells you a story about the guy who got away from the saber-tooth, how you're not going to lose every time, it gave people fortitude, the courage to endure. The guy who turns around and kills the saber-tooth: it makes people feel stronger. So the story must have given people a boost, a psychological edge, a small evolutionary advantage. We must have adapted to be good listeners. We self-selected for those who respond to stories."

I liked Lee's theory. Hope of a hero coming to save you. Hope of *becoming* a hero. It would explain why the Reacher stories were so popular. I was more accustomed to French narratives about sorrowful losers who developed some kind of self-justifying philosophical twist to keep them going. But I guess it was similar. "There's only one problem with your theory," I said. "Obviously if there were truth conditions, then there were *untruth* conditions too. The possibility of deception had to be there from the very beginning." I was far more noir than Lee Child. Everyone was always already a liar, potentially. Cain not Abel.

"But why would you want to tell someone there's a woolly mammoth on the other side of the hill if there isn't one?"

"So you can kill them," I said. "Creep up behind them with a rock in your hand while they're looking for the woolly mammoth. Or send them into a trap."

"The lie." Lee looked thoughtful.

"The con."

"Is that me?"

"Is it?"

"I think I will have that refill after all," he said to the waiter, tapping the empty mug.

"You don't need language to lie," I said. "Sartre says that the garçon in the Café de Flore is faking it—pretending to be a waiter." The waiter had shoved off again by then, but still I kept my voice down. "This whole restaurant is pretending to be a French restaurant. In the middle of Manhattan."

"The whole of Las Vegas is like that," said Lee.

"*Las Vegas*—the fields, the meadows . . ."

"It's like you're always somewhere else—Italy or Egypt or wherever. Never Las Vegas."

"And stories are like that too?"

"Look, if you see a beautiful woman in here . . ." I looked

around. There was no "if" about it. Balthazar was stacked with beautiful women. "You're not going to fly off to the Caribbean and have sex with her all weekend, are you? Well, in a story you can."

I was reminded that Lee was just about to hop on a plane to Bermuda, with his wife. For a week. They were fleeing the New York winter. "Or maybe if you just *write* the story?"

Which definitely did something to the old chip on his shoulder. "Or, say your brother-in-law is pissing you off."

"Do you have a brother-in-law?"

"Okay the bank manager, then. Or a traffic cop. You want to smash them right in the face. You can't, can you? Well, in a story you can. Or someone can. Reacher can. You get your revenge *vicariously*. You can live another life. An imaginary life."

He was rushing to get out the door to light up. Sticking to his resolution after all. I hardly had time to get on my ten layers, two hats, and a double scarf. As he headed off to the subway on Sixth, and thence to the airport and Bermuda, I called out to him, "Hey, don't forget to write!"

37.

MORPHEUS

LEE CHILD WAS BEING HUNTED. He was the quarry, the prey. Everyone was after him, at different times, like paparazzi, like Furies, like hungry wolves. Someone, anyone, party or parties unknown. His bank manager for one. His publishers, his editors. A lot of readers, especially after the mass revolt against casting Tom Cruise as Reacher. Tom Cruise. Me. And Lee Child was running away, as fast as he could go.

Every now and then he would hop in a car, or a train, or a plane. It didn't help. His pursuers were relentless, they would never give up. If one of them dropped out there was always someone else bringing up the rear. Whereas Lee was on his own. He was all alone and he always would be. No one was helping him. Sometimes they had dogs, bloodhounds, or great salivating bloodthirsty rottweilers, packs of them, all with the scent of Lee Child up their noses.

He was not unresourceful. He could hide, for a while, or lose them for short periods. He took refuge in houses, a casino in Vegas, a remote farmhouse in Sussex, a mountaintop chalet in the Alps, a gondola in Venice, the rainforests of New Guinea. But sooner or later they would pick up his trail again. Their surveillance was global and infallible. He could disguise himself as someone else but they always knew fundamentally that it was him. And they would never give up. They were unstoppable, inexhaustible, omniscient.

Finally, they close in. Lee vaults over yet another hedge in his desperation to escape. But this time there is no solid footing on the other side. A void opens up in front of him, the abyss. He twists around, throws his hands out in front of him, manages to cling on to the sheer cliff face by his fingertips. He knows that his enemies are not far behind.

In order to extricate himself from this peril, he would need superhuman reserves of skill and strength and acrobatic agility. But having run halfway around the world, it is all he can do to hold on. He realizes, with total clarity, that there are now only two possibilities. Most likely, his pursuers will loom up over him, malevolently cackling in his face, before stomping on his fingers and booting him down to his doom. Or, improbable though it is, some forgotten ally, having somehow dispatched all his adversaries, would kindly stick his face over the edge and—almost like a miracle, like grace from heaven—a hand would reach down and he would grab on and be whisked up and away to safety. Maybe a savior in a helicopter could throw him a rope ladder, but it amounted to the same thing.

It is at this exact point, having weighed up his last remaining options, that he says, "Fuck it," lets go of his tenuous handhold, and lets gravity do its work, sucking him down into the great nothingness below, which swallows him. And he dies. He has decided that he prefers dying to the other alternatives. Then he wakes up.

This is his most recurrent dream. It's a classic, virtually an oneiric cliché. At one time or another, everyone everywhere is being chased. Most of us would probably wait, while clinging to that cliff face, to find out whether we are going to be saved or damned. Lee, on the other hand, chooses oblivion. "It's the cheesiest narrative ever," he said. "Like a bad movie. The worst movie ever. And it's as if my critical faculty kicks in, even when I'm asleep, and says, 'This is too ridiculous,' and I have to reject both of the narrative solutions on offer. They're both too obvious. Even my subconscious is skeptical."

The interpretation of dreams is not a science. The biblical Joseph was good at it, so was Freud. Perhaps dreams are not even a window into the soul or the unconscious or the fate of nations. They could be just the accumulation and expulsion of mental debris. They nocturnally exorcise our ghosts or toss all the rubbish that threatens to pollute or clutter up our diurnal brain. Perhaps the dream is a delete button. But if it is, then its functionality is limited since certain dreams return to haunt us again and again. Like Lee's.

One of his dreams actually made it into hardcovers. This was in *Without Fail,* the one about the attempt to assassinate the vice president. In his dream Lee is living in a neat house in the suburbs. The mailbox is a metal box on a pole at the end of the driveway. A bunch of kids drives by and smashes the mailbox. The phenomenon is so recurrent it even has a name: "mailbox baseball." In his dream Lee is furious: he comes running out, clenching his fists, and he knows that if he ever manages to catch up with the kids there will be blood on the floor. *Without Fail* incorporates the story into the deep background of the vice president and his pursuers.

But the obsessive dream, the one about being hunted down, also gets into his novels, every one of them. Reacher is looking for something or someone, then someone starts looking for him. It will end badly for one or the other. Maybe it's not so much a bad movie as the story of everyone's life. It's paranoia, but they really are after you.

My own interpretation of Lee's dream was bound to be tilted by all the simultaneous talk of his "big push" towards finishing *Make Me,* what he was starting to call his "marathon sprint," in March and April. "I've goofed off long enough," he said. Not one thousand a day, more like two. He wanted me there every day to keep tabs on him.

Lee had told me often enough his major issue, once he had gone past the beginning, was how *not* to shut down the narrative prematurely. Reacher gets off the train, takes one look at Mother's Rest, changes his mind, and gets right back on. The End. Or Stashower says, "Get lost, hobo!" Reacher beats a retreat. The End. It's the off button. You have to find a way around it. Surely all those drooling beasts baying for his blood are forms of the ending overcoming him too soon, thus killing off him and Reacher in one fell swoop. All those readers—which included me—asking if Reacher was done yet, or dead yet, or dying, it was another version of the same struggle, to keep Reacher alive and still on his feet. And to keep Lee Child in the game.

What is happening when Lee is dangling over the abyss, his own version of the Reichenbach Falls, and he actively chooses to let go and fall to his doom? Was this conceivably the luxury of success? He could surely afford to let go and die, job done, mission accomplished. It was certainly another form of elegant minimalism. *No hand [rescue], no boot [annihilation].* Another translation of "Reacher said nothing." And it was an assertion of his own self-determination.

But it suggested to me a sublime confidence in the ending, a sense that he could come up with a fond farewell of his own, neither happy nor unhappy, and not Hollywood either. Only another approximately fifty thousand words to go. And then aaaaaaaagh! THE END.

BIOGRAPHEME

IT WAS NOT A DREAM, nor a nightmare. He was living in Coventry at the time. About three and a half years old. They had a house with an outside lavatory. It was inevitable that he would get locked in there at some point. When it finally happened, he assumed he would have to stay there forever and ever. There was no way out, none. This was it. That lock was never going to budge. No exit.

Having contemplated a future in a vertical box with a toilet in it, he thought it wouldn't be too bad. But there was one thing that played on his mind. He could surely stick it out indefinitely because they could slip his food to him under the door. It was one of those wooden doors with a gap at the top and a gap at the bottom for the purpose of ventilation. A tray of food would fit under. He could live there perfectly well. Except for one thing.

And it was this that he couldn't get out of his head and which, in the end, persuaded him that a life spent in the privy in his backyard would quickly pall. The question was: What were you going to do with the mashed potato? The whole point of mashed potato (he knew this from the *Beano* and the *Dandy*) was that it was served up in the form of an approximate pyramid, a small mountain (possibly with a sausage sticking out of it). The young Lee grasped at once that it would be impossible for the great mound of mashed potato, an integral part of any decent meal, to fit under the door. The gap was not big enough for the huge dollop of mash.

This was the thought that plagued him: *It will all get scraped onto the floor!*

The idea still haunts him even now.

39.

METAMORPHOSIS

I WAS SITTING in Biff's diner when they came for me. Having coffee. Black. About a gallon or so. Biff's had a perpetual refill system, which suited me fine. I was bottomless, where coffee was concerned. I was staying in some riffraff-only motel, which suited me fine. I had even freshly pressed my hardware store chinos, shoving them under the mattress for the night. And brushed my teeth. I was looking about as spruce and soigné as I'd ever look. I was ready and primed for the showdown.

I knew they'd be coming. I'd been in Biff's the day before. My first day in town. Little place called Cambridge, Mass. Leafy, quiet, classy, full of old stuff. Biff was this okay old guy behind the counter who would break into snatches of song between frying eggs and flipping pancakes. I was reading a newspaper at the time. In a booth. Some story about a few dead guys in Jersey. Which I had left a couple of days before, on a bus going north. (If you want to know, they were roaches, I'm pest control.)

When I looked up from the paper there were these couple of guys looking back at me. Fairly intently, checking me out. Young fit-looking guys. Clocking me, registering my existence, comparing it with some mental database. They looked kind of excited about something, then they left. I knew they'd be back. It was all in the look. Like we were arranging a date, same place, same time, tomorrow? Yeah? Yeah. No retreat, no regret.

So I came back and they came back. I was still sitting there, in my booth, drinking another gallon of coffee. Only difference, this time there were five of them. They were all young and fit-looking. Not big but sinewy. One of the two guys I'd seen the first time came up to my booth. He reminded me of some Hollywood guy I'd seen in a film once—sort of small but packing a big punch. They were all wearing these rust-colored sweatshirts that said "HARVARD" on them. Like if they were lost they could be taken back there.

I have to hand it to the kid—he was only twenty or so—he was polite anyway. "My name is Tom Cruise," he said. "Over here are my friends Bruce Lee, Arnie, Bruce Willis (sorry if that is a bit confusing, with the two Bruces), and, finally, Puller. *Noms de guerre,* of course." They all gave a small bow.

I said nothing.

"Reacher said nothing," he said. "I like that. I assume you are Jack (none) Reacher. You don't have to say anything."

I still said nothing. I wasn't about to stand up and take a bow. He kept on talking.

"I'll take that as a yes," the kid said. Pushing his luck. "The thing is, we are great fans of yours. Admirers. Not everyone is, of course."

I didn't know I had any fans. Not sure I really wanted them either.

"Our professors, for example, really look down their noses at you. But they're just snobs. We like your style. It is sooo primitive. We call it the 'caveman style.' Obviously it works for you. But we are a little more progressive in approach. What with being members of the Harvard Tae Kwon Do team. It's a bit more sophisticated and Zen. The way we look at it, you don't have to be huge and muscular. Like a big, bumbling grizzly bear. You can be slim and fine and still be effective. We appreciate you probably need to drink more black coffee, but, on the other hand, we would like to challenge you to a fight. *Now*. We know you like odds of five to one. But we think we can take you out, Mr. Reacher. We have the skills."

There was something about the way he said *now*. Made me put my coffee cup down. "Outside," I said, in my best grizzly bear voice.

I was lying of course. They all walked politely ahead of me towards the door. Like they were trooping into class. That was their first big mistake. I took out Mr. Puller with a huge and muscular boot to the rectum. Always hated the name Puller for some reason. Bruce Willis went down with an elbow to his head. He'd live. Leaving just the three of them. Game over. They were light on their feet, I'll give them that, like they had air-filled shoes. They danced around a lot. But I steamrollered Bruce Lee up against a door and planted a meaty fist in his solar plexus. That took some of the air out of him. Arnie was a real butterfly. I pinned him to the wall with a tabletop.

Which left only the blabbermouth Cruise. He was still bobbing and weaving. Me and him. I like it simple. Also, I wanted to prove to him just how *primitive* I can be. I'm not an abnormally sensitive guy but still. So naturally I went for the head butt. His head was right there in front of me. And he was smiling. I was snarling. I was expecting to hear the satisfying sound of bone and gristle as it collapsed under the impact of my massive forehead. But it was as if his head just wasn't there anymore. I connected with air and stumbled forwards. Which is when the foot caught me. I never even saw it coming. The foot ended up roughly where his face had been a moment before. I'm fast, but he was faster. Twinkletoes caught me square on the nose.

The head butt was my best move. Never been known to fail. Until now. Old joke: *I hit his foot with my face.* There was blood on the floor, and for once some of it was mine. I was stunned. But not so much for the kick in the head, more because of something he said next.

"I'm not going for the two-footed flyer," he said. "Not like Paulie. He was an idiot."

Paulie had been twice the size of the kid. Then something clicked in my brain. "You know about Paulie?"

"Of course. And Hook Hobie. And the Romford Boys. Not to mention that army bureaucrat you shot in cold blood."

It was like the karate kid knew everything about me. "Who told you?" I looked over my shoulder, like a complete idiot.

"You mean you don't know?"

"Tell me and maybe I won't grind you up into tiny little pieces with my bare teeth."

There was something in his face then. Something I hadn't seen a whole lot of before. I think it was pity. Which sort of stopped me in my tracks.

"Can you even read?" he said.

"I only look like a gorilla," I said.

"Sesquipedalian?"

"Long-winded Harvard types." Okay it took me a second or two to compute. Come on, I've read Proust (it was my brother's and it was only a few pages and I didn't really get it, but still).

"Oxymoron?"

"The intelligent idiot."

His hand went towards his back pocket. "Hold it!" I said, tensing.

He turned around, showed me what the hand was up to. It was hoisting out a book. A cheap paperback. The kind of thing you can pick up at an airport bookstand if you have the time and the inclination. This one was dog-eared and much thumbed, with coffee stains on the cover too.

"Here," he said. "A present."

I took it in my hand. *Killing Floor* by Lee Child. "Outstanding debut novel!" said one of the quotes on the cover. But it was the name mentioned in the blurb on the back that really caught my eye. Jack Reacher. Coincidence? Whatever it was, all the fight had gone out of me. I helped all the members of the Harvard Tae Kwon Do team back on their feet. They weren't too badly hurt. In fact, less badly than I had intended. And Cruise remained unscarred. Which I wasn't too happy about, particularly considering that my nose had been knocked halfway around my face.

I dabbed at my face gingerly with a paper towel in Biff's bathroom. I looked in the mirror. It wasn't a pretty sight. It never had been, but it was looking less appealing than ever. For some reason, something that one or two of my teachers had said to me several decades before drifted back to mind: "One of these fine days, Reacher, you're going to have to stop scrapping and grow up!" Or words to that effect. I was starting to think maybe they had a point. Was I getting too old for all this? I mean, the endless roaming around, the inevitable punch-ups.

I sat down in my booth again. Poured myself another cup of coffee, pumped my caffeine level back up again.

The diner hadn't been too badly trashed with all the fighting.

The karate kid put down a cool $100 note in front of Biff and I offered to mop up the blood or wash the dishes or something. He said he wouldn't call the cops this time. "This is Jack Reacher," said Cruise. "What?!" says Biff. "*The* Jack Reacher? And you kicked his butt into next week too!"

I wouldn't have put it quite like that. But I signed the napkin the way he asked me to and went and sat down. It was like I was under surveillance and everybody else had been tuning in. How the hell was I supposed to fly under the radar anymore? It was like Father Christmas just blew into town. Or John Lennon. Everybody knew about it. Except me apparently.

I picked up the book and started reading. "I was arrested in Eno's diner. At twelve o'clock. I was eating eggs and drinking coffee. A late breakfast, not lunch. I was wet and tired after a long walk in heavy rain. All the way from the highway to the edge of town."

If I recall, it was more like one o'clock. The book was full of little mistakes like that. The author kept making things up. And I was having pancakes. With maple syrup. He missed that. But you want to know the thing that really got to me? Like a kick in the teeth. It was the stupid short sentences. Some of them only four words long. Only four words long! For crying out loud. *No this, no that.* Whatever happened to decent complex sentences, the large, sweeping kind, broad as the Mississippi, with twists and turns and little creeks and coves and subordinate clauses and semicolons? The kind we used to write back in the day, when writers were writers.

A barely literate high school dropout could do better than that. *I* could do better.

Ever since the kid had landed the kick on my conk, I had been thinking: I need to do something else with my life. Maybe this was it. If this was writing, any third-rate punk could do it. I had to put right everything this snooping hack Child had got wrong. It was a matter of truth and justice.

And then I knew there was one last thing on my to-do list before I could pick up a pen (or maybe a pencil?) and start writing. I put down a note and walked out of the door and went to the bus station. I got on a bus going south. The cover of *Killing Floor* had told me something of interest: *Lee Child lives in New York.*

I found myself wondering how that would sound in the past tense.

Then I thought: that would make a better narrative. And that's for damn sure.

40.

THE BIG REVEAL

44,695 WORDS and five and a half months after he wrote "Moving a guy as big as Keever..." Lee was finally starting to work out what the hell was going on in Mother's Rest. It was bad but also good, very good. In a way, it was all already there, in your face, right on the first page. Especially in the word "nothingness." At the same time, the secret to the Child methodology was emerging.

In his previous incarnation, in television, Lee used to oversee one of the original cooking competitions. It was an early exercise in reality TV. But like every "reality" show, the set was a setup. There were in fact two sets in one. Two kitchens. With two fridges. Each fridge contained a different assortment of potential ingredients. In fridge 1, for example, there might be a bunch of grapes, some mushrooms, a tomato or two, an avocado, and a tub of ice cream. In fridge 2, we find arugula, spaghetti, a lobster, and a

packet of M&M's. The challenge to the two competing chefs: obviously, to cook up the best possible dish given the constraints of
the fridge. But there was an imperative to use up everything that
was in the fridge and leave nothing behind. The grape that was left
sitting there, unused, meant that points would be deducted.
Somehow, no matter how disparate the parts, they had to be
merged into a whole.

"What I do is I start by planting all these picturesque details—
the Western Union office, the store selling rubber goods, the
woman in white in the Cadillac—and just like the grape and the
tomato and the mushroom, I try to stir them all together into
some kind of intelligible stew." All through January the stew was
starting to take shape in his mind, and then in the middle of Feb-
ruary, almost halfway into the cook, he started setting out his vision for me. The big picture. The secret.

I had been reading fragments. A chapter here and there. A few
characteristic sentences. Rereading the same pages again and
again. But I had no sense of where the narrative was going. Nor
did Lee. Now, suddenly, he was sitting at his desk and twisting
around in his chair and waving a hand out ahead of him and saying, "I can see a through-line, some kind of a plot." The idea was
electrifying. "I don't know if it will endure." The hand drooped
again.

I was trying not to sound overexcited, like some plot virgin.
Stay calm, no stupid leaping up from the couch. "So . . . can you
give me the gist? I mean, you know, just a feel for what's coming
up."

Part of it was to do with the "deep web." A natural habitat for
criminal conspiracies. The obvious point about the World Wide
Web is that a search engine can find things on it—you can track
down websites, find fridges, toasters, cars, obscure vinyl records
owned by obsessive collectors, and people. People who, by and

large, don't mind being found and who are often advertising their presence. They want to be noticed. The *deep web* is different: here there are no tags, no hooks, no easy-to-remember addresses, nothing searchable. A website on the deep web can only be found by people who know a specific rather recondite URL address. These people desperately don't want to be found, they don't want to be traced, not unless you are buying their particular service (which may well be illegal). This is one of the stories written up by the science editor on the *L.A. Times* (the one Reacher and Stashower were after). "Instead of andymartinink," says Lee, "it would be am3589xyz23 or whatever."

"Okay," says I, nodding, scribbling away, and basically none the wiser. "What kind of conspiracy are we talking about here?"

He had just got back from Bermuda (while New York had been in the grip of the dreaded "polar vortex"). Now he was all focus. With a bit of a tan. No coffee, no cigarettes.

"Remember what happened to Sylvia Plath?"

"Head in the oven."

"You can't do it now."

"Gas is not toxic."

"Natural gas. You can sit around sniffing gas all day long, won't do you a whole lot of harm. Pointless sticking your head in the oven."

"Unless you want to cook it of course."

"Same with cars. The old hosepipe attached to the exhaust routine."

I was shocked. "You mean that doesn't work anymore? It always worked in the movies."

"Catalytic converters," said Lee, in a tone of regret. "They've filtered out all the carbon monoxide."

"I never much fancied the hosepipe anyway."

"Oh, it was one of the best ways to go," says Lee, nostalgically.

"I love the smell of automobile exhaust. And gasoline. I like to sniff the benzene when I'm filling the car. The hosepipe was great. You fall asleep, you don't even know it's happening, and then you just stay asleep. Forever. It was perfect—now it's gone."

"Too bad."

"And what about Monroe?"

"Kennedy killed her. So they say. But he didn't need to."

"So if not Kennedy?"

"Drugs, sedatives, overdose."

"The so-called sleeping pill. It was either Nembutal or Seconal. One or the other. Maybe both. They were good. They really knocked you out. So it was dead easy to OD on them."

"Was . . . ?"

"Can't get them anymore—precisely because of the safety considerations. Unless," he added, "you're a vet. If you'd rather not shoot the horse, then you use Nembutal."

I was starting to get an inkling of what he was on about. The big old vet store in Mother's Rest.

"You mean . . . ?"

"Yeah."

"Oh my God."

"It's like you're in a bazaar in Istanbul, in the Casbah, and there are stalls and loads of people milling about and it's all visible, out in the open—and then you slip through a door and suddenly you're underground, it's hidden. They offer a service: they make it nice and easy. An old V8 engine, unconverted, the hosepipe, pumping into the room. As advertised. Come on in! There is a beautiful boudoir. Nembutal. Comfortable, painless, you're on velvet. But what if . . ."

"Fuck! That's it," I said, leaping up, stupidly, losing self-control.

"What?"

"You have fucking cracked it."

On the whole, I try not to sound like too much of a fan, but this wasn't one of those times.

"You evil mastermind bastard." I was holding my head in my hand, as though it were about to explode.

He cackled, leaning back in his chair, like the evil mastermind bastard that he is.

The Child method was paying off yet again. I had recommended it to a woman called Pali in Think Coffee just the night before when she expressed a degree of nervousness regarding her future. I summarized it in two words: *sublime confidence*. You just assume everything will sort itself out, and it does (unless you "come unstuck").

But there was something else to it. Something I was apt to forget. Lee was not just Reacher: he was every single bad guy he had ever dreamed up; he was the author of all their evil schemes. Good and bad, they are all his alter egos.

"People who want to commit suicide—they are desperate. They want to believe, even though they basically know they are going to be ripped off."

"Reacher is indignant?"

"Indignation," said Lee. "It's a good word. Yes, he begins with indignant, then he goes beyond indignation . . ."

"Righteous fury?"

"Yep. And then it's *kill-everyone* mode."

We were sitting in his office. I gazed out of the window, looking west, as if I could see Mother's Rest in the distance, beyond the rooftops, all the way to the silos.

"Was that in the back of your mind all along?"

"At a certain age it comes to the front of your mind."

I should have seen it coming. He should have seen it coming. We had been talking about it right on the very first day of writing, way back in September. Jump off a mountain somewhere in Austria, one of Lee's mates had suggested. Rubbish! says Lee. Far better: a Mexican veterinary store, with an unregulated supply of horse tranquilizer. And now . . .

"But the main man, the mastermind behind it all, has now ordered Reacher's execution. An assassin is trailing Reacher and Stashower. So they are in mortal danger, but they don't know it yet. I'll try to have them avoid the assassin through chance and luck—without it becoming too slapstick."

At this point I was stalking about the room, kind of groaning. I had unbuttoned my waistcoat. He was just leaning back in his chair, feet on desk, hands steepled on his lap, looking up at the ceiling, a grin on his face. I was too wired to sit down, as if someone had just shot me full of the exact opposite to Nembutal, more like a dose of the great amphetamine stash from *61 Hours*.

"This is huge," I said. For once I should really write "I exclaimed" and maybe throw in an exclamation mark too. Was I talking about a book or, rather like Lee when he goes into one of his trances, thinking more about a very real and badly screwed-up town? I no longer knew.

"I wanted it local. None of that taking-over-the-world bollocks, or it becomes too Tom Clancy."

"It's local," I said. "But it's global, it's universal, in the sense that it taps into our deepest anxieties."

"They're exploiting the difference between Washington and Oregon [where assisted suicide has been legalized] and the rest. Even in Washington and Oregon it's so bureaucratic, it's hard to get all the signatures you need." Lee paused to consider the options. "Of course, you can still blow your brains out."

"Messy though."

"It's more macho. But the 'falling asleep' method—more 'feminine' in some way—it's just not available."

There was a "logical problem" of course. There generally is

somewhere. "It's been bothering me," said Lee. "It's right back at the beginning. Keever. Why would they need to go to all that trouble?"

"With the backhoe. And the hogs." I sat back down on the couch, having finally got a bit of a grip.

Which is when we started talking about the rubber aprons and rubber waders on sale at the rubber store in Mother's Rest. They were like the grape in the fridge. Lee didn't want to just leave them there, doing nothing in particular. He was pleased because now he had found a use for them.

"They won't have to deduct points, then?"

"You want to know the great thing about being a writer? If it hadn't worked out, I could always have gone back and deleted the grape in the fridge. No one would ever have known it was there. Except for you, of course."

THE NAMING OF NAMES

"**YOU KNOW HOW** you think you're influencing me?"

"Do I think that?"

"You said it in that article of yours."

"Oh yeah that. I was just kidding around. Quantum theory."

"Well, here's your big chance. To stick your oar in."

"Really? I don't know. Maybe I should keep out of it."

He had been thinking about it all the time he was in Bermuda. Not writing, just thinking about it. A reader had paid for the right to get him thinking about it. When you got right down to it, probably just about everyone was trying to influence him one way or another. Umberto Eco (and others) used to speak of how the reader must be "constructing" the book, not just the writer. It was a fair comment: every reading was a reinterpretation which skewed the text in the direction of a different culture, a time, a psychology, a specific existence, whatever was happening on that particular afternoon. So it was all collaborative. But everything was in someone's head. Whatever Roland Barthes said, nobody was actually rewriting the text (no matter how "scriptible" it was) in any visible way. You could chop it up and quote it and deconstruct it and reconstruct it in *another* text—academics did it all the time—but the original text remained intact. As Socrates says, "Written words . . . go on telling you the same thing over and over again forever."

Now readers weren't satisfied with that purely theoretical semiotic relationship with the author anymore, they really wanted to get right in there, to leave their stamp on the text, to alter it in some way, to give it a swerve. Readers are no longer satisfied with good old-fashioned reading. They want to be part of the action, not just the reaction. More interventionist, like surrogate authors, or *scriptors*. But how can you let everyone else—the future—know that "X was here"? You can do it, but (you knew this was coming, didn't you?) it's going to cost you. You can buy a character's name, at an auction (online or otherwise). Or rather, it's *your* name, superglued to a character, irremovably. Lydia Lair wrote a fat check for the privilege.

The money was going to a good cause, not into Lee's back pocket. A charity. It was all kosher and aboveboard. I had a feeling Flaubert wouldn't put up with it; on the other hand, even he got "Madame Bovary" from *someone*.

The burning question was: should Lydia Lair replace Michelle Stashower? Lee was torn. On the one hand, Stashower had already established herself, her name was woven into the text. On the other hand, it was not too late, Lee could always press the "re-place" button. *Replace all!* There was a potential stand-in waiting in the wings.

"I like Lydia Lair," I said. "Reminds me of Lois Lane."

"Yeah."

"Then there is that song about Lydia."

"Song?"

"You know the Marx Brothers: 'Oh Lydia oh Lydia that encyclo-pydia . . .'"

"Yeah."

"So it's cartoony."

"Sounds like someone invented it even though it's real."

"A bit like Blair without the B."

"Unfortunate."

"How is it going to be when you write, '. . . Lair said . . . Lair said' and so on? It's a bit short, isn't it. Same number of letters as *said*. Assonance. Another monosyllable. Could be a bit monoto-nous?"

"Hmm."

"I don't want to influence you."

"Ha!"

"Okay, if you really want to nail me down, I do like Lydia Lair, it's a good, catchy name. But Stashower has more . . . power."

"Yeah."

"It's longer, weirder. More Germanic. Or Eastern European possibly. So it suggests more of a deep background of some kind. More substance. More heft."

"Yeah."

"And then there's *Stash* of course. Her nickname. Nice. Crimi-nal associations. Mind you, *Lair* is not bad either in terms of con-notations."

"Fuck it, then! I'm going to stick with Stashower. I'm too in-vested in the name. I've got a whole paragraph of her going on about her nickname. And I've already changed *Janice* to *Michelle*. *No going back!*"

"What are you going to do with oh Lydia oh Lydia, then?"

"She can have a bit part. Something poignant. And then she dies. Short but sweet."

"So . . . was that an influence? Did I influence you or what?"

"Nah, I was already thinking all that anyway. You're just bouncing it back at me."

"Yeah."

THE QUILLER MEMORANDUM

WE HAD TO MEET in secret. Like lovers. Which in a way we were. Or *junkies*. Or maybe undercover agents pretending to collaborate with Mr. Big in order to prise his secrets from him. We did the Poe *Purloined Letter* thing of hiding in plain sight. Having a conversation where everyone else was already conversing at high volume. So high we could hardly hear each other. Like trying to hold on to your hat or umbrella in a howling wind.

The pub was one of those old Victorian classics, the kind you feel Dickens and Mr. Pickwick would have been at home in, with barrels and kegs and purple doors and gleaming brass. It was across the street from the British Museum, in Bloomsbury. It was dark and cold outside but warm and bright and crowded within.

Quiller is an Oxford man. I'm calling him Quiller because I don't want to jeopardize his academic career by mentioning his true name, so I'm using a fictional character instead. He teaches

American literature at a college in London. He has wide interests. Most of which I can't actually mention either. Samuel Beckett, for example. He has worked a lot on contemporary writers, English and American, writes reviews for all and sundry, and he has an endearing weakness for French philosophers, going so far as to produce an online concordance to one of them, with indispensable references to certain key concepts that cannot be named. He has a crew cut and a crew-cut-equivalent beard.

But the other thing about Quiller (and the main reason for our meeting at the pub) is that he is a Reacher fan. "I like Lee Child," he had originally written to me. Adding, "I'm probably not supposed to." Reacher was his secret passion. He was "saving up *Personal*" but he had read all of the previous eighteen, "some of them twice." And he was desperate for news of the twentieth. We were conducting an information exchange: he was giving me tips on text analysis software and I was giving him a few hints and a couple of key lines from the work-in-progress, which left him begging for more.

The aspect of the Child oeuvre that he found so "fascinating" was his "unique style." The four-word sentence killed him ("One of his longer ones then, eh?"). And Quiller yearned to do with Lee Child what he was doing with X and had already done with Y, namely to feed the collected works into a machine and get it all chewed up and spat out again in the shape of word frequencies and collocations. "What do you think the most frequent word will turn out to be?" he said. "Other than 'the,' of course. And 'a.'"

"'Coffee,'" I said. "Or 'diner.'"

"Or 'gun,'" he said. "What about recurrent phrases?"

"*Reacher said nothing.* Or possibly *That's for damn sure,* but I think he's eased back on that one."

"Of course you'll have to check the *least frequent* terms too."

"'Whom'?"

" 'Phallogocentrism'?"

"Come on—that's all over them!"

We looked over our shoulders from time to time. We didn't want to be overheard, not by academics anyway, sharing our thoughts on Lee Child. He was the dark side, the noncanonical, uncertified, unregulated, not quite kosher, a fugitive from justice who had holed up on the bookshelves of the airport lounge.

There were only four writers (at least in the twentieth century and beyond), Quiller said, whose works had sounded an entirely "new note" to his ear, a "voice" distinct from all others: Ernest Hemingway, Raymond Chandler, J. G. Ballard, and . . . Lee Child.

We buttoned up and went out into the night and parted outside the gates of the British Museum. I was heading back to New York the following day. "Convey my respects," Quiller said. "And you can tell him that comes from a stuck-up Christ Church literary snob."

43.

ON THE COUCH

I WAS TRYING TO EXPLAIN to Lee Child why it was he needed me.

It had something to do with Kant and Newton and Homer. Kant reckoned that Newton could show anyone step by step how he worked out gravitation and the whole logic of the solar system in the *Principia Mathematica,* whereas, in contrast, Homer really had no idea what he was doing, how his thoughts connected up one with another. "He himself does not know" was the phrase that stuck with me. Lee/Homer did not know either, thus needed me to explain it to him.

"I need you?" he said. There was a definite note of something in his voice.

"Well, okay, not *need* exactly. You don't in fact need me as such. But in that not-knowing there is the possibility of an interpretive intervention."

We were sitting in his office, he at the big old desk, me perched on the couch, as per usual. He was just back from Florida, spring break with thirty-three other guys (no women), watching the Yankees. He raised an eyebrow. "This is the psychoanalysis thing, right?"

"You okay with that?"

"Let's do it."

I was a Jungian at heart, obviously. Everything cohabited in some vast all-encompassing primordial web of religion, alchemy, and flying saucers, all channeled through the collected works of Lee Child. I fully embraced the totality. But the macro had to include the micro. In a word, Lee. It was time to get Freudian. "Time to get Freudian," I said. "To get in here."

I tapped the side of my head. But it was supposed to be his head.

He got up from his desk.

Martin had finally turned the tables on Child. I had Jack Reacher in some kind of choke hold. The Grand Inquisitor (me) had strapped this heretic (Lee) to the rack. I was going to sit at his great steel desk and he was going to lie down on the couch and reveal his deepest, darkest, innermost secrets.

"Just to get you started with a bit of free association," says I. "*Keever . . .*"

"Yep."

"Kiefer . . . or Keanu?"

"Not Keanu. But Kiefer yes could be. On account of his father wanting to play Reacher, remember." Donald Sutherland and Lee had had quite a correspondence in the past, when Sutherland senior revealed his desire to be Reacher.

"So you *off* the star of *24* in the first sentence. Interesting." Come to think of it, it was more *before* the first sentence.

Lee wandered towards the couch.

I had my list of questions ready. Oedipal instinct? Death wish/

drive/instinct (*thanatos*)? Sublimation? Lacanian mirror crisis? Infantile trauma? Sadomasochistic dreams? I was trying to cover the bases. After that it was pure gravy, the satanism and the Nazi-themed orgies and all that. In my mind, I already had my pipe in my mouth, the knees crossed, the notebook with the insights on my lap, pen in hand.

"You know," he says, ruminatively, "we could do this, or we could catch the second half of Barcelona–Man City. What do you think?"

ON THE COUCH (II)

SO HE WAS ON *a* couch. But he was half watching television at the same time, marveling at Messi, tut-tutting at Man City, especially when they missed a penalty (his own team, Villa, was having a revival and looked as if they might yet escape jeopardy). Also, he was worrying quite a lot about the size of Mars (which strict Freudians might regard as allegorical).

"It just doesn't make sense that it's that small," he said. "Not according to our conventional conception. What is it doing right there, in that orbit? My theory is ... Oh fucking Agüero, nine times out of ten he'd put those away!" He was also concerned that we had not yet figured out what happened in the first nillionth of a nanosecond after the Big Bang.

Technically, at this point, I was on the couch too. It was a huge great brown thing, so there was room for Barcelona on there. Lee's legs still had their own sofa in front of our sofa.

"So this screwed-up childhood of yours . . . ?"

"It's mostly about the lacks and the lacunae," he said. "I've seen it in other writers. And performers. We're in it for the love and approval we never got enough of as children."

"Freud was right, then?"

"Freud was basically right. If you're messed up as a kid, you stay messed up, at some level. You bear the scars. But the real question is, what do you do about it? The analysis is fine.* But *what do you do*? Does Freud have any answers?"

"He says stop kidding yourself that psychoanalysis is going to help, you're on your own."

"So it's pointless. Which is why the American psychiatric movement has become a branch of the pharmaceutical industry. They just offer you a witches' brew, some alchemical cocktail."

"Coffee, cigarettes, marijuana . . ."

"Yeah," he said. He waved a Snickers bar at me. That was "lunch." For breakfast he had had a bowl of Sugar Smacks, which are now called Honey Smacks. As he put it, "I'm eating crap till this book is done." His only rule at the moment was that I had to go and get my own lunch so I wouldn't have to eat the same garbage he was eating.

"You want to know what the real problem is?"

"Of course."

"We're looking at it."

---

* For the strict Freudians, under the heading of analysis, Lee allowed the following:
Oedipal instinct?
"No, evenhanded revulsion."
"You sure you want me to mention that?"
"They won't read it. Sorry."
Death wish (*thanatos*)? "Yes to that. I've been told I'm dying since the age of seven (after the rheumatic fever). Dead boy walking. So I feel, come on, hurry up, don't blow their expectations."
Anything else? "Don't sleep with people you know. Better yet, don't sleep with anyone you've actually met."

"Television?"

"Tribalism. Look at that crowd. Perfectly normal Spaniards. But some of them are fanatical supporters of Barcelona and others, equally fanatical, of Real Madrid."

"Or West Ham. Or Aston Villa, for example."

"They all have this desperation to belong to some tribe or other."

"Which explains sectarianism and genocide?"

"It explains everything!"

It was Freud, but applied on a larger historical scale, to the whole of humanity rather than specific individuals. It was our species childhood that screwed us all up. Nobody wanted to wander the African savannah lonely as a cloud. "Back then it made sense to be part of the tribe. Now it doesn't. But we're stuck with it."

Somehow we got to talking about Wayne Rooney, the Manchester United player. He'd recently been knocked out sparring in his own home. Apparently he used to be known as "the spud-faced nipper" when he started out. "We all have seven million years of evolutionary behavior behind us. Swinging around in the trees. The caveman. It's just with Rooney the neural pathways are more open. You can see right in."

"Reacher likewise?"

Lee said it was like the Empire State Building. You're standing on top of it, right up on the roof, looking down. Like King Kong. "The stuff that is on your level, on the roof, that's modernity. Everything else, all those floors going all the way down, that's history, that is antiquity, that is us."

45.

WHY THE WORKS OF LEE CHILD ARE REALLY QUITE USEFUL

THE JACK REACHER series goes down well with dyslexics and victims of Alzheimer's, Lee was saying.

There was once a woman who used to work as a development officer for the U.S. Tennis Association. She was not only a diagnosed dyslexic, but she also had a terrible fear of flying. It was in the nature of her job, however, that she (a) had to read stuff and (b) get on a lot of planes. Double jeopardy. One fine day she happened to pick up a Jack Reacher volume at the airport. *Running Blind* [*The Visitor* in the U.K.]. She found to her amazement that she could actually read it, several pages at a time, and make sense of it, more or less. She bought the book, got on her flight, and kept on reading so avidly that she completely forgot about her fear of flying. Thus killing two birds with one finely crafted stone. Reacher to the rescue.

She wrote to the author thanking him for his miracle double-barreled cure. "I finished your book!" she wrote. It wasn't so much a backhanded compliment, more a straight forehand drive down the line. Ever after that she would send him a handful of free tickets for the U.S. Open at Flushing Meadows. Lee was indifferent to tennis, but he was glad to have saved a lost soul.

"They use my books for illiterate prisoners too," Lee said. "Or semiliterate, you know, late learners. It gives them a sense of achievement. *You can do it!*"

They weren't "crime" books—they served to prevent future crimes.

46.

A DEAL'S A DEAL

" 'A DEAL'S A DEAL.' " Said Stashower to Reacher. It was the last line of *Make Me,* as of twelve noon on March 19. The book was up to 67,188 words.

At 12:10 on that Thursday afternoon, Lee set out for me what he (vaguely) had in mind, for the next thousand or two words. Reacher and Stashower had been looking for Keever's client, the guy who got him killed. But they couldn't find him because he was already dead. But they track down his neighbor, then his sister, in Phoenix, Arizona. "But we are building the suspense. They are getting information, but at the same time we have to re-up the danger."

"The *agon.*"

"Reacher fixed Hackett, the hired gun. But they're not out of the woods yet. And we need the bad guy point of view."

"The parallel narrative."

"Do you know how Pluto was discovered?"

"Vaguely. Nineteen hundred and—something, wasn't it? Still a planet in my book."

"You couldn't see it, it was too small. But you could see the other bigger planets weaving around. So there had to be something there. It's the Pluto trope. All over crime novels."

"Is this what this is?"

He was already tapping at the keyboard. I let myself out.

He was still there at 6:30 that evening. The word count was up to 68,626 (he was now officially ahead of me). He had produced a grand total of 1,438 words in the intervening period: say six hours, roughly 250 words per hour. He had to get to two thousand words in the day. That was his regular schedule from here on in. Two thousand every day. Eight-hour day. Intense.

He was getting up promptly and getting down to work earlier than before. Putting on the old leather jacket with lots of zips, the one he liked to write in, as if he was hopping on a Harley with the rest of his biker buddies. Around 10:30 or 11 in the morning. "It's the first thing I think of in the morning. I'm already starting to reread yesterday's work over breakfast. It feels good."

But what I was really checking on was how the theory fit with the practice, whether what he thought would happen had in fact happened. "You'd think," he said, "that mysteries would be getting stupider, logically. You'd think all the reasonable plots were used up right at the beginning and now all we'd have left is surrealist fantasies. But, you know, it's the other way around. We're getting more reasonable. Look at "Murders in the Rue Morgue" for example—the fucking pet chimp* did it! And do you know *The Nine Tailors*?

"Dorothy L. Sayers—Lord Peter Wimsey?"

---

* Technically, an orangutan.

"The bells done it."

"I liked that one."

"Or *Gaudy Night*?"

"The Oxford College one."

"Some don gets her manuscript trashed. No worse crime, for Dorothy Sayers."

Lee was calling it a "cubist narrative": sometimes he would narrate one set of events, and then renarrate it from a different point of view. Alternate angles on the same—a little like Raymond Queneau's *Exercises in Style* in which the same seemingly insubstantial story gets retold a hundred times over. But something had happened he hadn't anticipated. A swerve in the narrative line.

"Reacher has this bright idea of not just contacting Westwood in L.A. but telling him to come on over to Phoenix. It will really tighten up the story."

"How does he persuade him to come?"

"Book deal."

"Oh yeah, the Pulitzer and all that."

"But this is the thing—Westwood is sucked in by the notion of doing a great book on the subject of Reacher's investigations. But the reader will therefore be wondering—could *this* be *that* book? Is *Make Me* the story as told by Westwood? Some kind of meta-book?"

"Or a book-within-the-book. So you've got a writer in the story. And Reacher is talking him into writing it. Holmes and Watson. Reacher is admitting he needs someone to record events. An archivist. A troubadour."

He had an atlas open on the floor and he was punching the keyboard with a certain vehemence. "What about this line: *Michael McCann's disappearance began with a desire to visit Oklahoma.* I was thinking—that could almost be one of those bullshitty literary novels. You know like . . ."

Lee mentioned one or two titles. Whatever they were, he had to be *against* them. All his writing was a form of retaliation. It was the Reacher model, applied to literature: one man against the world. "Yeah," he agreed, "there's a perpetual threat of violence or there's nothing. It's like DON'T MESS WITH THIS BOOK!"

There was one word that kept cropping up. "Revenge." Lee had a revenge theory of literature. He was following on from *Hamlet* and Kyd's *Spanish Tragedy* and, before them, Agamemnon and Phaedra. He thought that what most people wanted was revenge for all the injustice in the world—and he was providing it.

I happened to be rereading *Bad Luck and Trouble* at the time. Middle-order Child. Reacher 11. It starts with some very bad people tipping a guy out of a helicopter. At three thousand feet. It ends (look away now if you don't want to know how it ends) with those very same guys getting tipped out of the same helicopter. This time at over five thousand feet—a mile high. Over the same spot. The novel read like a palindrome, the same backwards as forwards.

Karma might be a better word than revenge. It is a rebalancing of some temporary imbalance in the universe. Of course, the revised equilibrium might never be achieved without the intervention of Jack Reacher. This is his function in the novel: to rectify bad karma. For every *action* there must be a *re-action*. It's the aesthetics of symmetry.

47.

END OF THE THIRD MOVEMENT

Friday, March 20. Snowing again on Central Park. Chapter 39.

"HERE'S A QUESTION for you. If someone was going to Oklahoma, where would they be going to exactly?"

"No idea."

"Could be Tulsa. Could be Muskogee—home of the Muskogee tribe. Or it could be Lawton of course, you know, because of Fort Sill nearby."

"I vote Tulsa. It's got the song going for it: '24 Hours from.'"*

"And Route 66."

There was one other matter Lee had finally resolved. The question of Lydia Lair. Lydia, it was worth it. You are now the sister of the missing Michael McCann, married to a doctor, Evan Lair.

---

* We both listened to the song later. Gene Pitney, "24 Hours from Tulsa." This is what Lee wrote to me: ". . . notice how it's a very plain told story, all telling not showing, but genuinely suspenseful—and atmospheric. See what plain can do?"

And your daughter is about to get married. I just pray it doesn't all blow up in your face, that's all.

"You're not going to kill her off, are you?" I felt some kind of responsibility for Lydia. If only I'd tried harder.

"Haven't made my mind up yet," Lee said.

"So she lives in this nice house and she has a daughter and they're having tea and cake . . . hold on, don't tell me."

"Yep. *Home invasion*. Utterly terrifying. It was bound to happen."

"Does Reacher see it coming?"

"He has a premonition." Lee had only just thought of it himself. Something to do with having a party and then the idea of gate-crashers and then postponing it till the house has gone quiet again.

"From here on in, you're heading inexorably towards a climax. A collision. The final movement."

Lee parsed and dissected my two metaphors. He liked the symphonic idea. He thought that the home invasion was like the end of the third movement, "a major restatement." But there was no collision as such. "It's all in the first sentence, isn't it?"

"Keever, the grave, the dead body."

"You know everyone is going to get dragged back to Mother's Rest. Whether they like it or not. We start there. We end there."

"They're all trying to get away. To Chicago, L.A., Phoenix. But there is no escape. Black hole narrative."

Naive critics fondly imagine that Lee Child is sitting around all day working on plots. He isn't. Quite what he *is* working on, I hesitate to say. Maybe nothing. Especially in this book. "Listen to this," he says. He'd just written it. " 'No one came back to the shuttered study . . . Nothing doing . . . An interior hallway, empty . . . There was no sound. No voices, no footsteps . . . No voices, no footsteps . . . No sound.' "

"The Book of No," I said. "I'm doing a word count: No, nothing, nothingness. It's a leitmotif. And it's creepy."

"Seems like a stronger backbone. The description . . . ," he says, pensive. "Sometimes what is *not* there is more important than what is."

I'm not going to call it an epiphany. More a coincidence, really. But his freestanding touch pad (on the right of his keyboard) flashed up a warning message on his screen. It was running low on battery. Irritating. Lee used to have a wireless keyboard too. "Not anymore," he stressed. "Look at that—a nice fat wire!" It connected up the keyboard to a power source in the computer. Once he had been tapping away at a novel on his wireless keyboard. He wasn't a great typist. He used two fingers and had to look at what he was doing mostly. When he finally got around to looking up he discovered that the last immortal paragraph did not exist. Instead there was a message:

CONNECTION LOST!

"God, I hate that," he said. "A whole paragraph up in smoke. Not even smoke."

This was what he was doing all day (when not feasting on Snickers and Sugar Smacks). *Making connections*. It didn't have to be cause and effect. Who is doing what to whom? All that stage business that can be classified under the prosaic heading of the "metonymic" (following Roman Jakobson's classic essay "Two Aspects of Language and Two Types of Aphasic Disturbances"). Which, in Raymond Chandler's terms, is having a guy walk through the door with a gun in his hand. Lee Child was more preoccupied by the *metaphoric* (or the "poetic function" as Jakobson would say). Which didn't mean he was coming up with improbable metaphors all the time (remember the waterbed of the second sentence); no, the point was to connect up stuff that wasn't obviously adjacent or contiguous, but linked at some dark symbolic level. Adjacent ideas, obscure but harmonious images, resonances, affinities, recurrent phrases/words/refrains, syntactical echoes, the whole vast realm of the intransitive, governed only by association and similitude, all singing out to one another across the deeps, like blue whales miles apart in the ocean, like the distant rhymes of a lyric poem or song. (Example: consider the backhoe in *Make Me*—it's function but it's also form; or the four-word structure; or the frequency of "coffee.")

Reacher was doing what Lee Child was doing, trying to stitch disparate fragments together. But, having in mind that since the author was also all of the evil geniuses he had ever summoned up out of the darkness, perhaps it was not so surprising that one of the key themes of the book is the clandestine "deep web"—and all its connections that are invisible to the average search engine. If you want to find out what they are, you just need to build a better *search engine*, i.e., Reacher.

QUOTH HE

I KNOW, it looks like slow progress here.

From here to here.

But, look, you can't just write: AND NOW FOR SOMETHING COMPLETELY DIFFERENT. There is a subtle, seemingly self-determined momentum towards a new direction. In a naturalistic way.

You know what you said about the black hole. It's like they're circling a drain. The plughole. Mother's Rest itself is inert. It's *at rest*. We know they're going back. They're going to be sucked down it.

I'm building up to the home invasion. That'll be two whole days' work.

Without wanting to overshadow anything in the fourth movement.

We've got Reacher and Stashower in the house. They're talking to Lydia. She's interrupted. She comes back. Then we cut to the bad guys. The determination to nail Reacher and Stashower before it's too late. And the sister, of course, who knows too much. While they have them all in their sights. "They could be talking right now." Then we go back to the talking, precisely, in a nice domestic environment. The cubist thing. The first time we see anything of the bad guys is . . . their arrival. In the house.

This is going to sound pretentious, but it's a bit like playing chess. You're always looking several moves ahead, four or five. You have a feel for what is coming up, and you have to leave a space . . . into which it can fall.

Reacher has to have a premonition. It's an observational thing, leading to mental leaps . . . Now we're into the first stirrings of his premonition. He asks, "Do you mind if I ask you a personal question?"

It's an exercise in optimism. You want to use as few words as possible. The optimism is that it will be enough. You can't go back. But then maybe it's too few. So you have to. "Dr. Lair . . . paused a *quizzical* beat." Yeah, it needed an adjective there. The optimism is that the meaning will cling to the word. But it doesn't always. So you have to force it a little. It's not so much sinister, although that might be in the reader's mind, it's just this social situation. Reacher is tentatively trying to prepare for something that could happen. Without wanting to panic everyone. "Do you keep a gun in the house?"

Sometimes it's frustrating. You have this nice idea—and it will take up only three lines. But you can't milk it too much. Keep it small.

On the other hand, the fight scene is going to be a monster.

THE OLD CEMETERY

HER NAME WAS CORRENA. She pronounced it with a long "e": almost like Karina.

"Are you a novelist?" she said. She was sitting on the stool next to me one evening at Think Coffee. I was tapping at my laptop, writing up some notes. "Is that a novel? It looks like one."

"Nope," I said, looking up from the screen and swiveling to take her in. "Book about a novel. Not in itself a novel. At least I hope not. It's supposed to be nonfiction."

"What is the novel?"

"There's this writer, Lee Child. I've been watching him write his latest book. It's not out yet. *Make Me.*"

"Oh my God," she said, looking at me with a degree of collateral respect. I can imagine Stendhal must occasionally have had, "Wow, you're working with Napoleon. *Mon Dieu,* what is that like?" If I recall, he met Napoleon only three times and only once had a two-way conversation, but he must have been tempted to play it up. "Bonaparte? Oh he's not a bad sort, you know, a bit driven, but really quite *sympa* when not actually in the midst of battle . . ." That sort of thing.

She was young (twenty-something), dressed mostly in black, with red lips. The red and the black. A winning combination. So naturally I would say, "Oh yeah, Lee, good friend of mine, nice guy in fact, etc., etc." Bit of reflected glory.

Bollocks. No way was I succumbing to that sort of bullshit. "I'm just a spectator," I said. "An academic." There, that ought to kill any potential enthusiasm or surplus emotion of any kind. Guaranteed buzzkill. "Sort of taking notes while he does the serious writing. So I guess that would make this a meta-novel."

"I have handled hundreds of his books," she said.

"You are kidding me!" Now she really got my attention. "You're a fan?"

"I work in the Cincinnati Public Library." One of the biggest circulation libraries in the country, maybe the biggest.

"What are you doing in New York?"

I should have offered to get her a drink at this point. Obviously. It was the evening. The bar was open and we were sitting right in front of it, at the counter. I completely forgot to do that. I was impressed by her story. She was here on Spring Break. She was also taking creative writing classes at the University of Cincinnati. Said she found New York inspiring (which I guess is true of Lee too). Not that there was anything wrong with Cincinnati, she said, and she was really fond of her own neighborhood.

"Well, maybe there are a few things wrong with it. Dumb name, for example."

"Yeah, Cincinnatus. What did an ancient Roman have to do with anything?"

"I much prefer 'Losantiville'—the earlier name, even if it is a mishmash."

She wrote poetry but was an aspiring novelist. She knew she had a novel in her, she just didn't feel she had a big enough idea yet to sustain it. She said she was thinking of trying the coming-of-age novel but was anxious that maybe she hadn't really come of age yet.

"What do you think of Jack Reacher?"

"I feel bad about it now, sitting next to you and all, but in fact I haven't actually read any. Yet. Lee Child and James Patterson—we have so *many* of their books." There was a kind of weariness in her voice. "People are always wanting them. I swear about half the people who come up to me in the library say, 'Can you tell me where I can find the Lee Childs?' Or the Pattersons, whichever. They are the two most popular. So . . . I don't know, I didn't bother."

"Okay, here is the thing, I'm not in the least evangelical and I don't want to twist your arm. But you might be inspired by *Killing Floor*. That's the first one. Written when he was out of a job. Just a hopeful would-be writer, starting out. Like you." So far as I could work out, he had no big idea either, maybe just an idea of bigness.

"Really? That sounds great, I definitely want to read it."

"He has this technique. A way of getting started. Ask a question—and then don't answer it."

"Hold on." She tapped that into her phone.

"And the other thing is: he is nothing like Patterson. Patterson is a franchise. The McDonald's of writing. Lee Child is a serious writer, with a degree of artistic integrity, like him or like him not."

The fact was, oddly enough, I had been having dinner with Lee and a woman writer and her husband in some Upper West Side French restaurant (in which the waitress really spoke French and in fact burst into song à la Edith Piaf) only a couple of nights before. When he was not gracefully signing napkins for the people at the neighboring table, Lee was saying he had nothing against what Patterson was doing. "He just figured out that there was this huge demand and he set out to satisfy it. Like a factory. The books come off an assembly line." Lee, in contrast, had rejected any notion of trying to churn out more than one book a year. And had poured cold water on approaches from the James Bond estate to take over the Bond franchise. Turned them away not once but twice. Lee had turned down Bond. "You can't write a modern Bond," he said. "It's impossible. You want to know why? It's because of Bond. Bond changed everything and now you can't go back and write Bond again. Plus, they don't pay you enough. They take half. It's pitiful."

When I relayed all this to Correna from Cincinnati I skipped the bit about not getting paid enough. "Lee exists and he writes his own books. I can testify to that much. He doesn't have anyone to help him. And he eats garbage while he's working at full tilt." The end of the third movement. The Sugar Smacks phase.

She was impressed by this last detail in particular. He wasn't looking after himself. Like a true artist. "He has some kind of death wish," I added for good measure. "And he's tormented, even though successful. Unhappy childhood probably. Lack of self-esteem on account of bad parenting."

"Now I really want to read *Killing Floor*," she said. She wasn't a full-on Goth, so far as I could work out. No spiderweb tattoos and whatnot. But she respected the death wish anyway.

"If we have three 'holds,'" she told me, "then we have to order one copy of the book. For Lee Child there are always hundreds of holds. So we buy a lot, believe me." But she had realized now that, at least where Lee was concerned, it wasn't all about the quantity.

She dropped me a line when she got back to Cincinnati. The

weather was "lovely" there, she told me. She said she was feeling inspired by our conversation, and added, "I'm going to go to the old cemetery near my house and try to make a start on this novel."

I guess that makes sense. Peaceful sort of place. Good for concentrating the mind. Maybe all the best writing is done when poised on the edge of the grave. When Keever—or anyone else for that matter—has been freshly buried.

50.

HOME INVASION

"LYDIA IS STILL ALIVE," Lee said. He knew I took a protective, almost paternal interest in her well-being. "So far," he added, with a sadistic chuckle.

It was the day of the Home Invasion. Reacher had become increasingly absurd. Following his clumsy attempt to find out about the gun in the house, he invites everyone out to dinner. Anything to get them out of the house. But it's too late. The bad guys get *into* the house instead. Three of them, armed with the same guns that Hackett had. Three Rugers, fitted with suppressors. Reacher has a gun, but he can't use it because Stashower has been taken prisoner. So he poses as just another victim. At last this semi-autistic socially dysfunctional drifter is in his natural habitat. Surrounded by people who wish him harm.

It comes almost as a relief to Reacher. Hence he has time for the under-pressure bitter joke, which is also a gesture of provocation.

The gunmen are trying to sort out who is who so they know which three to kill out of Reacher, Stashower, Lydia, her doctor husband, and Emily the daughter. "You got a sister, wise guy?" says one of them to Reacher. "Maybe you should tell me where she lives." Reacher says: "If I had a sister, I would. Save me kicking your ass myself."

"I'm *building* here," says Lee. "In a way postponing. Most fights are over incredibly quickly. Reacher's fights are typically over in a second. But at the same time we can crank it up some more. We're unashamedly jacking up the testosterone."

The murder threat goes off at an angle and becomes amalgamated with a rape threat. In a home invasion it's always a strong possibility. "Help me out here!" says the gunman, ironically. In principle in command. "What could provide us with recompense?" (for having to kill a couple more people not originally on the menu). Oh I know . . . your wife, your daughter, or your lover.

"Obviously," says Lee, "Reacher has got to do something about it. How exactly I don't know yet. But I'll figure it out. Maybe I need to go back and strengthen the beginning of the scene."

Chin rubbing. "Now what word would a criminologist use here?"

"Sociopath?" I floated.

"Yes, that works," says Lee. "And it segues nicely into the next word too . . ."

He didn't mind me slipping in the occasional word. Not so much because he was totally in control. He wasn't. *Au contraire.* He welcomed random input, as if it was some kind of extra grape in the fridge. All grist to the great mill of the *bricoleur.*

The housemaid was hoovering the apartment and shoving a bucket around and turning taps on and off in the background. The word "bucket" appeared in the text. To be exact, a "bucket of chicken."

Somewhere in the distance, typical New York, a new building was going up, or a major revision to an old one. Muted, but still audible, sounds of hammering and drilling registered on the sense data horizon. Suddenly Reacher is uttering the word "nail": verb, sexual connotation. It was like a dream in which alarm clocks inside the room or hooting owls outside would subtly edit and alter the oneiric discourse.

"We're at 74,378," Lee said. "It was four thousand words ago that Reacher had his premonition."

But there was something bothering him. The spell checker. He'd bought the computer in the summer and he'd had to download Word. But the spell checker was faulty and ran so slowly, it might take an hour to scroll through a long text. "I might as well do it myself."

He was fiddling around with the software. "Having had a traditional English school education, I'm a good speller, but I feel a little insecure." *Silhouette,* for example, stumped him. Or, hold on, should it be *silouhette*? Where did the "h" go? He couldn't make his mind up. He was okay on *yoghurt* though. "Yog-*hurt,*" he said confidently. "Except here, of course, where they drop the 'h' completely." *Weird* was another one. "Ruth had to teach me: *We* are *We*-ird. Now I've got it. I used to get the 'i' and the 'e' the wrong way round."

I suggested he flip on the spell checker so it corrected as he went along. "Okay," says he, "let's try that for a while." He clicked on one of the options.

"Your only problem is going to be words it doesn't recognize."

"What happens then?"

"It changes them."

"I hate that."

Lee said he admired the immortal sticklers of the Académie

française (forever issuing edicts about spellings and the *mot juste* and the correct use of the circumflex) mainly because they were "so tenacious. I'm more descriptive than prescriptive though: I don't want to get too far away from what the majority [of people] think."

This is the thing that struck me. Lee is 100 percent verbal. And he is 100 percent visual. At the same time. When he is describing the home invasion house he is setting up the stage so that his characters can enter and exit smoothly. He saw the room on an analogy with a baseball field, with the three runners on three bases. On a diamond.

He had been sitting there for a while in silence. Arms folded. Sneezed a couple of times. Finally he shoved his head forwards and shrugged, as if readying himself for action. He flipped up the lapels of his black leather jacket. "Time for Reacher to get going. We are doing the takedown."

Typing. "The spell checker just corrected 'funneling.' Only one 'l,' according to the American style police. It's always fascinated me—those halfhearted efforts to reform English—the 'x' for example in 'connexion.' American optimism—it's something that can be fixed. Everything should be made better."

Still typing, still talking. "Like illness. In Europe you just get ill. You accept. Here it's like an affront—an injustice—not to be tolerated."

Tap tap. "What is a four-letter word, anyway?" He had written: *Their smart play at that point would have been to start blasting away, there and then, no hesitation, recognizing that the situation was turning to shit right in front of their eyes.*

"You vetoed *shit* on page one."

"Funnily enough it was the *piss* more than the *shit* that worried me. . . . Here it's clearly metaphorical. Whereas back on page one it was literal. The language can morph now. In the fight scene. It's more no-holds-barred. We're in combat mode."

As I was leaving, Lee nicely said he would like to do this again one day, the book and the meta-book. "Maybe on the fiftieth," he added.

KNOWLEDGE BY DESCRIPTION

LEE WAS DOING ME out of a job. He had taken to commentating on himself. He was writing and commentating at the same time. "The Reacher seminar," he said, announcing his next topic. "He bends down and picks up the weapon. So naturally it's time for the scholarly digression. *There were many factors that made a handgun either accurate or not accurate* . . . blah blah blah all about the theory and history. But then he'll always bring it back to the vernacular and the pragmatic. *The human head was a big enough target, generally hard to miss at close quarters, and the man-on-first's was no exception* . . . He starts academic, but then he gets specific and hardcore."

There were two things Lee talked about that afternoon, while writing. One was the influence of cinema, the other was Bertrand Russell's distinction between knowledge by acquaintance and knowledge by description. But in some sense it was all one.

I've gone on about how metaphoric the Child text can be (with its network of symbols and echoes). But it is also quintessentially metonymic. Every cause has its effect, every action its inevitable reaction: the house has become a mini–Newtonian universe. An immense piece of clockwork in which all the cogs and the gears are grinding away in harmony (e.g., "Reacher eased the trigger home, and he felt the mechanism turn, gears and cams and levers, effortless . . ."). A mechanism, a solar system with all the planets orbiting according to their iron laws.

"We are all competing with one another. Filmmakers and writers. So naturally you have to see the bullet and its whole trajectory ('exploding a pile of wedding presents on the table in the yard outside, in a cloud of paper fragments, white and silver, like confetti a few days early'). It's slowed right down and examined, analyzed. I love doing that. It's video porn in a way."

He was saying how he needed meticulous detail. *"Wet slap!"* he said vehemently. "Isn't that great? I love the onomatopoeia of that." ("Twenty feet behind the guy's head the wall instantly cratered, the size of a punch bowl, and a ghastly split second after that the contents of the guy's brain pan arrived to fill it, with a wet slap . . .")

"Maybe it's the plosives," I said. "Sound effects."

"It's third-person, but it's very tight to Reacher. The rambling stream-of-consciousness—it's almost more intimate than the first-person narration. Reacher has already shot two people. But there is a third. He has to swing his weapon around but the other guy is simultaneously bringing his weapon to bear on Reacher. It's a slow-motion race."

"Like *Killing Floor*?"

"I love doing that. Again it's cinematic. He's moving the gun, feeling the levers. It's been relatively unlyrical. But still flowing. I wanted to pull it back to Reacher brutalism. Like this. *A red chunk came out of his neck.*"

"That is fairly blunt."

"He doesn't have to be precise at this point. All he cares about is whether the guy is dead or not. I loved that passage in *Personal* where she says, 'Reacher! He's not breathing!' and he replies, 'What am I? A doctor?'"

Lee was pleased with the way the scene was developing. "It's a nice sequence this. People are going to like some of this. It's picturesque."

"And the shooting in the face. Is that like a close-up?"

"Better to shoot someone in the face. It's more cinematic. And Reacher is annoyed. So is the reader by then. The reader wants to see the guy's individuality eradicated. Hence the face."

But he was thinking all the time, making micro judgment calls, about what to put in and what to leave out. "You don't want to be lazy. But you don't want to be laborious either. I don't want it to be like one of those old ballroom dancing charts—you know where you lay out the steps in front of you on the floor. One foot here, another foot there."

There was a great passage about Reacher having the gun in his hand, with some quasi-erotic talk of him grasping the *butt:* "He snugged the butt in his palm, solid and reassuring, and he fit his finger in the guard, against the trigger, hard and substantial, and he brought the gun up." I had to ask about the research. "Are you actually going about firing guns to see what it feels like? Do you have to go to the gun range?"

"The thing about the gun . . . you don't really need to have the gun in your hand. It's better because you're forced to imagine. If you go to the gun range and shoot, it's a lose-lose situation. It's either exactly what you thought to begin with and you've wasted your time . . ."

"Or?"

"Or it's different—and then you want to say, hey this is so different to what you think. And then you become a boring and proselytizing writer who likes to say how different everything is in reality to what you thought it was."

I mentioned Correna going to the cemetery in search of inspiration. He had some firm advice: "Don't *go* to the cemetery: *imagine* the cemetery—and then see what happens. We already know what the spooky cemetery feels like. We have a common collective pool of knowledge. The thing is, you don't want to step too far outside the consensus. You need to deepen it maybe."

Lee, like Roland Barthes, thought we were all governed by the *doxa,* the "cultural code." We talked about the difference between, in Bertrand Russell's formulation, "knowledge by description" (say, Stephen King's *Pet Sematary,* a case in point of the *doxa* at work) and "knowledge by experience" (actually going to one particular cemetery, reading the inscriptions on the gravestones).

"It doesn't matter if you copy a movie—they copy us. You're not in search of the ineffable. Knowledge by experience sounds plausible enough. But . . . I was talking to a writer about her scene where she'd discovered a body underwater. In order to write that scene she had actually taken up scuba diving. To give it more authenticity. Which sounds reasonable. But then I pick up her next book and there on the first page is her heroine who has been shot in the leg. Are you going to 'experience' that too? And what about people dying in your books. You're going to do that too?"

"Maybe that's why Plato says the true philosopher has to die. To attain knowledge of death. Hard to send back reports, of course."

"I'm going to stop here," he said, peering at the screen suspiciously, "because I've got to decide what to do next. Where to go. I feel worn out by the sheer imagining."

I got up to leave. "End of third movement?" I said.

"You might as well say it's a bloodbath from here on in."

It was only when I was walking along Central Park West, heading downtown, that I realized something:

There was a *we-ird* echo in his novel of what had been happening between Lee and me—had I not invaded his home (his Manhattan apartment), for all intents and purposes? I was just a lone guy and I was not threatening rape and murder, but still I had somehow managed to smuggle myself in, unsolicited, and I was tracking if not his every move then as many moves as I could cope with. But you didn't have to shoot me to get rid of me: all you would have to do is write a strong scene about, for example, killing a bunch of home invaders: yes, that would do it.

52.

THEY THINK IT'S ALL OVER

"**DOCTOR CHILD!**" Lee was holding open the door. I'd recently discovered he was a "doctor of letters" (hon.) somewhere or other.

"Professor Martin!"

"Only in the States. That's why I come here, so people will call me 'Professor.'"

"You mean you're not a professor?"

"Mere lecturer."

"An inferior rank? Why am I even speaking to you?"

"I'm the lowest of the low. That's why you're speaking to me. I remind you of you."

"I'm going to get one of those serious academics next time."

"I'm going to get a serious writer to write about next time. Martin Amis maybe. Or Jonathan Franzen."

"Sit down and read this."

I read it. Chapter 42. It completely killed me. Just as Reacher was killing one of the heavy mob all over again.

"I love that," said Lee. "It's so hard-core. So challenging."

Reacher notices that one of the three guys is not dead yet. So cold-bloodedly finishes him off. This time it's Stashower saying, "Reacher, this one is still breathing."

"But you know the thing I really love about this," Lee was saying. "It addresses the reader directly. It's Reacher talking to the reader."

Reacher has got his fingers pressed on the "carotid arteries" up near the ears of the second guy, the big mouth, who is not exactly talking much anymore, not since he had a big chunk of his neck blown off, but is not quite dead either. The idea is to choke off the blood to the brain and thus a quietus make. Stashower is shocked, indignant even. She thinks he needs a trauma surgeon. "You can't do that," she says.

Lee's idea is that the queasy reader might be saying exactly that. And, again, "It feels wrong."

Reacher responds, while still slowly killing him: "The first time he was a piece of shit who was about to rape you at gunpoint, and now suddenly he's some kind of a saintly martyr we should rush straight to the hospital? When did that part happen?"

Partly won around, she asks a more basic question—how long is this going to take? Thus giving Reacher the opening for a line that made me laugh out loud: "Not long. He wasn't well to begin with."

So, on the one hand, the scene is entirely naturalistic; on the other, the author is addressing the reader over the heads of the characters who are bent over—tending to—the guy stretched out on the floor. "The reader has to deal with it. The reader is saying all this to me. And this is my defense. I'm letting the skeptical reader have their say."

Metaphorically, the iterative homicide scene looks ahead towards revelations to come and, finally, the end of the story. Again, through the figure of Reacher. "'We're doing him a favor. Like a horse with a broken leg.' And, '. . . it's peaceful. Like falling asleep.' The *holy grail* of the suicide community. So this is a fore-shadowing. I would say that was fairly deliberate. And there's more: the heavies have killed the guard at the gate, ruthlessly, without a second thought, and Stashower calls what Reacher did an 'assisted homicide.' Yeah, it's all coming into focus. Every death now is a way of riffing on the conclusion."

Lee was going around strengthening the metaphoric "back-bone." Cutting out anything in the least superfluous. "I don't care how it turns out," Reacher says to Evan Lair, the doctor. "They'll never find me. But I would appreciate a head start."

"That sums up all of Reacher, really," said Lee. But he had originally written "thirty-minute head start." Then he slimmed it down. "It's more resonant like that." More Reacher. More mythic than realist.

"It's all so cold-blooded here," said Lee. But he wasn't in the least apologetic. He was reveling in it. "We can't shy away from the brutal." It was one of the things he felt most strongly about having a recurring hero. "You have to be careful not to fall in love. Some authors get too hagiographic."

He had two main examples. Dorothy L. Sayers. "She falls in love with Lord Peter, doesn't she. After he gets married. The early ones are great. And they are great social documents too. Look at *Murder Must Advertise:* Wimsey quells a riot just with his accent." He adopts a crusty old colonel's voice. "I say, you there, stop it!" Some proletarian East Ender: "Oh, sorry, guv'nor, beggin' your pardon. Won't 'appen again, Your Honor." Brilliant and plausible. But later on he just becomes cloying.

The second was more surprising. Thomas Harris, author of

The Silence of the Lambs. "Obviously Hannibal Lecter is an insane cannibal in the first couple of novels, but believable. *The Silence of the Lambs* made a great movie too—the last one to take all the five main Oscars: film, director, actor, actress, screenplay. But when he comes back again—nine years later—it's ridiculous. Suddenly he's the world's biggest wine expert. He was a psychiatrist to start with—now he can carry out brain surgery on living patients. It could be parody—either that or Harris just fell in love with his own creation."

53.

ALSO SPRACH LEE CHILD

LEE CHILD WAS STRUGGLING.

It wasn't a total block, but the torrent had slowed to a dribble. "I'm spending hours on just a few lines here. The bloody 'positioning scene.' The trouble is, nothing happens, but you have to drop the weight in the right place. Vector everything towards Mother's Rest."

He took out his pipe, filled it with unadulterated marijuana from a pouch, and puffed thoughtfully. "This is just a maintenance dose," he said. "A top-up."

I drifted off to the kitchen, poured myself a glass of water, and went into the living room, with a still bare Central Park through the windows, the East Side in the distance across the lake. There are bookshelves at both ends: fiction south, nonfiction to the north. I pulled a biography of Beethoven off the shelf. Jan Swafford. *Beethoven: Anguish and Triumph.* Hyperbolic title, possibly justified. It was nicely done but at the same time entirely pointless so far as I could make out. Almost everything was unbridled hypothesis. Approximate quote: "Beethoven must surely have been feeling delighted [at some positive review or other]. On the other hand, being Beethoven, maybe not." In other words, the author really had no idea. A void sucking in speculation backed up by hazy rhetoric and lyrical flights. And then the account of the writing of the 9th Symphony: so he *starts* with the "Ode to Joy" (from the last movement) and everything is bent towards that end. Maybe, but it reminded me too much of Sartre's strictures (in *Nausea*) about biography being overly teleological: the end throwing a "radiant light of future passions" over the beginning and "catching time by the tail." We live forwards (and therefore don't know what is going to happen next), but write the symphony backwards?

I knew there was no "Ode to Joy" in *Make Me*. But then again, maybe there was. A joyful affirmation of riot and righteousness as Reacher gradually zeroes in on Mother's Rest. The piece of music Lee had in his mind (I know because he told me when we were heading off somewhere in a cab and he was humming it) was actually the opening section of *Also Sprach Zarathustra,* the Richard Strauss tone poem, paying homage to Nietzsche, his concept of the *Übermensch,* the will to power, and eternal recurrence—and used by Stanley Kubrick as an overture to *2001: A Space Odyssey*. He was saying how, if you listen really carefully, you can pick out not just the visceral rumble of the organ, but the throb of double bass (tuned lower than normal) and a bass clarinet too, and then of course the timpani kicking in. Perhaps the whole opening section of *2001,* in which a primordial ape-man finds a way to smash in the brains of a contending group of ape-men, was just the right accompaniment to the final movement of *Make Me*. The climax of a Reacher is a return to primitivism, a lethal burst of Lévi-Strauss's "savage thought."

"I'm over the hump now," Lee said.

He had just realized something, which helped him a lot. "The more we understand about archaeology, the harder it becomes to acquiesce to the notion of progress."

"True," I said. "Meaning?"

"We always were vicious bastards. And we still are."

54.

TWO FOR THE PRICE OF ONE

"THE BOOK IS FINISHED," said Lee.

"Your book?"

"Generally." Taking the cigarette out of his mouth, he launched into one of his tirades. Mainly about the past, but unusually also about the future. Lee Child in J. G. Ballard mode. "The book is fundamentally a spoken medium. The audiobook is the future. I know, in some ways, that seems lame—like a National Health Service hearing aid. But the iPod has changed all that. We now have a generation that takes downloading for granted. And earbuds."

Lee gestured towards all his books lined up over several shelves, as if looking forward to some imminent bonfire of the vanities. "Print is an aberration. Literacy never really caught on. We are going back to oral. Everything is oral. There is nothing beyond the . . . ?"

"Song," I chipped in. He was riffing on Derrida's "There is nothing beyond the text."

"Yeah, song," he said.

"Rousseau says it was all song to begin with. The song of nature."

Now it was the song of Reacher. Which is why he was planning what he was planning. *The Great Read-Through.* September 1, 2014, felt like a long time ago. Whereas the duration of the narrative itself (t_1 Reacher enters town; t_2 Reacher leaves town) was just a few days. "It's strongly bonded. You can't have: *I took Friday off to do my invoices.* One brick is half on top of the brick below for strength." The "voice" had to be consistent, it couldn't vary according to the author's moods, good days and bad, or whether he had a toothache on a particular afternoon. "I'm in the groove right now. Was I in the same groove then?"

Even on a day-to-day, hour-to-hour basis he worked a little like this: he would go back a page or two, or a paragraph or two, and only then work forwards again, using the previous as a platform, defining the key, or a chord. Backwards and forwards, again and again. Extrapolating. But when he got to around ninety thousand words, then he would normally go right back to the first page and read it all through to himself, sounding the words out in his head, to get a sense of the whole, the flow and trajectory and momentum. He could iron out the wrinkles if he needed to. He could "foreshadow." He could "echo."

"Come and listen to this."

He took me through to the office. "Sentence I've just written. I'm really happy with it."

I sat down on the couch.

He gave voice. "*She touched the screen and the phone made a sound like a shutter.*"

"Nice parataxis," I said. "No subordination. And the simile, of course. Oh yeah and the sibilance."

"It has a *forward-leaning* rhythm. And it's all one syllable."

"Apart from *shutter*."

"Yes, you put that at the end of the line."

"Like a feminine rhyme. The extra syllable. Gives it a cadence."

It was exposition, plain and simple. And yet it had an onomatopoeic feel to it. "*Sound like a shutter* actually sounds like the fake camera noise that phones make." All Lee Child prose aspires to onomatopoeia. It strives to make the meaning *audible*. To synchronize sound and sense. Because it's a song. He gave me another example, another line he'd just written that day.

It's about this very fat guy. He is the capo of the Russian/East European gang that has been harrying Reacher and Stashower ever since they left Mother's Rest. Reacher tracks him down and shoots him, without much ado. Merchenko is colossal and sitting outside his strip club. "The sentence is deliberately *ugly*," Lee said. "See how it dumps all the weight on the last word. It's all shuffly and laborious. The *fatness* is in the rhythm, rather than just saying it."

Lee reckoned you could actually hear all the "excess" syllables. "The sentence is trying to stand up, and it can't."

"*Asynchronous wobbling and shaking*, for example."

"It's a liberty for sure. Over-the-top. Like the guy's waistline."

But the "churning" (his word for the rethinking) meant that he wasn't always happy with what he had just written. In the page that he had shown me only twenty-four hours ago, and originally proclaimed as perfect, he had already made half a dozen changes.

"I got cold feet about 'carotid.' I don't want five thousand med students after me. I went more generic. *Compressing the arteries that feed his brain*."

Stendhal has this trick of weaving alternate micro-narratives into the macro-narrative. Here is a simple example: Julien Sorel comes out of Madame de Rênal's bedroom. *"On eût pu dire,"* writes Stendhal. "You could have said, in the style of a novel, that . . ." Almost as if he is not writing a novel at all himself. So you get the romantic version (all his desires have been fulfilled) and the more downbeat, realistic version (What! Is that all it is?) almost simultaneously, like parallel worlds. There is an indicative mode and then there is a subjunctive, conditional mode. Lee Child has a similarly quantum technique going on.

In the home invasion scene, Reacher rehearses mentally what he is about to do (kill three guys in fairly short order) and then doesn't do it. Or again: we get a decent sketch of what Reacher *might have done* (subjunctive) with the Fat Man: confront him, tell him exactly what he is about to do and why, achieving some kind of justice for McCann and co., and then (indicative) just goes ahead and shoots him in the head, thus circumventing any "tall tales."

Having his cake and eating it. "It's two for the price of one," Lee said. I would call it three for one: (1) what Reacher actually does; (2) what he might have done but doesn't; (3) the ironic meta-layer (just like Stendhal ridiculing novels)—a contemptuous dismissal of any notion of telling tales.

ALLEGORY

THIS REALLY HAPPENED. But it's sort of an allegory of what Lee feels about editing.

It was when he was living in the apartment downtown, the one that looked out on the Empire State Building, the one that made me think of a cartoon with Clark Kent at a window in Metropolis. He was going away for a week or two and he wouldn't really need his housemaid to clean the house while he was gone. On the other hand, he didn't want to put her out of a job either. She needed the money. So he said, "Why don't you do the stuff you don't normally do? Concentrate on cleaning up the paintwork."

He had in mind the kitchen units, which were the kind with push-push cupboard doors. Naturally they would get a little grubby over time. They would benefit from a thorough clean with some kind of fingerprint-removing detergent. All well and good.

Except that maybe he should have been just a little more explicit about exactly what he meant by "paintwork."

He had recently bought a wonderful painting by a certain American artist, then little known, but who went on to become a superstar. A street scene done with bravura and spontaneity, full of wild color, layer upon layer of paint, brushstrokes characterized by a high degree of swashbuckling freedom. Somewhere between impressionist and abstract expressionist. The artist had begun by using pencil to provide him with a rough guideline and he didn't always bother to cover the marks entirely with paint, so there was a glorious rough-hewn feel to the canvas. And Lee really loved those scrappy little pencil marks, the ones that weren't really supposed to be there at all, maybe because they showed the sheer labor that had gone into the work.

Lee returned from his trip. The apartment looked spick-and-span. He went to bed. But there was something amiss he couldn't quite put his finger on that kept him awake. Even in the darkness.

He flipped the light back on. Some instinct guided him to the great work of art. But (a moment of confusion and disbelief) what had become of the beloved pencil marks? Surely there used to be a mark *here* and *here*! But now . . . He saw it all: the housemaid, in pursuit of her mission to improve the "paintwork," had inspected the painting carefully, spotted the pencil marks, and gone out and bought an eraser. It was definitely an improvement. But she was determined to finish the job for Mr. Child. Properly. So she went out again and bought some Wite-Out. And applied that liberally wherever the artist had failed to cover up his own original marks—really, as grubby as any fingerprints you could find on a kitchen cupboard.

The masterpiece had been corrected, erased, Wite-Outed, and rectified and thus deprived of all the brio and creativity and spirit that had gone into it. Lee couldn't live without those pencil marks.

"I couldn't explain to her where she had gone wrong. I think she might have actually committed suicide. At best she would have felt terrible and would have been punishing herself forever. No one ever told her that she was not supposed to 'fix' a work of art."

So he had the room redecorated instead, rearranged all the furniture, and quietly had the "cleaned-up" painting removed and given to someone who didn't know what it was like to start with and would, in all probability, be able to live without the pencil. He hoped.

But ever after he was careful not to leave the maid alone in a room with any "paintwork."

"You seen the play *Art*?" he said. "The one with the all-white canvas." We were having dinner in the Union Square Café.

"I've seen *Red*."

"Nobody much liked it in the play. But I would buy a canvas like that. White on white. In fact I think I may go out and buy some canvases and paint them all white and hang them on a wall. A white wall."

56.

REACHER VISITS A BOOKSTORE

HE IS THE ONLY PERSON I know, other than actual basketball players, who is taller than Lee Child (by a centimeter or so).

"You could play Reacher," I said, "when Tom drops out."

"I'll have to bulk up a bit," he said, shoving back the great mop of chocolate brown hair that threatened to bury his entire face like a giant wave wiping out a surfer or the rainforest swallowing up an ancient Inca city.

Carl Cederström had been reading *Personal* on the plane from Stockholm (where he taught at the business school and had once invited me to speak about the project). He loved the idea of Little Joey's house—the one that was the opposite of a doll's house, a giant's house, where everyone else felt small. Probably because he needed something like that himself.

He put a copy of *Gang Leader for a Day* (Sudhir Venkatesh) in my hand. We were in Book Culture on Columbus. "Read that," he said. A "rogue sociologist" gets to hang with "J.T." in the Chicago projects. A real gang leader, with a network of crack dealers, pimps, thieves, and henchmen at his behest. Carl said it reminded him of me and Lee. I could see some parallels. A certain coarseness of language, the drug taking, the loyal lieutenants. To be fair, I estimate that a greater proportion of what Lee does is on the legal side of the line. But when I read about the college kid, the author, kicking some guy off another guy, I realized I felt a little like that when slipping in the word "sociopath," for example. I was infringing on my subject's own territory. It was participant observation taken to the point of active collaboration. I was involved, I was committed, I was compromised. I was on his side (mostly). Academic or gangster? I was definitely being pulled into the gangster (or, to be fair, creative writer) orbit. "In this world there was no such thing as neutral, as much as the precepts of my academic field might state otherwise" (Venkatesh). I could just about imagine Lee saying, like J.T., "You're either with me, or you're with someone else."

Carl (with coauthor André Spicer) was launching his own book called *The Wellness Syndrome* at the time, dissecting and mocking our increasingly self-destructive drive to be not just well all the time, but happy, prosperous, sexy, and generally wonderful. And feeling guilty about it if we don't quite manage to check all the boxes. There was a *New York Times* journalist in the audience, an editor from Stanford University Press, a bearded philosopher who asked me if I was interested in "barebacking," and an older lady with a big fluffy cat in her arms. I had just gotten back from a new exercise routine, consisting of running up twenty stories (10 stories x 2 in my building in the West Village). I could hardly stand up, suffering as I was from what I called "concussion of the calf muscles." And I wasn't being massively stoical about it either.

"Why don't you just stop?" Lee said. "It's all pointless." He could have been talking about the exercise or the moaning or both.

He bought a copy of Carl's book and pitched in a question in which he quoted the baseball player Mickey Mantle: "If I'd known I was going to live this long I'd have taken better care of myself." He theorized that it was our parents' increasing longevity that had led us to becoming preoccupied with being in better shape than them in our own later years, thus spoiling the short span of years available to us now. He was all for fatalistic insouciance and against regular exercise. He (like Reacher—see *Persuader*, for example, where he mocks muscle-bound workout freaks) never went anywhere near a gym. He totally scorned *wellness*. He and Carl were like kindred spirits. We had to resist the divisive and class-based ideology of wellness, they maintained: which I 100 percent agreed with (while harboring a secret propensity for home baking, safe sex, and hand sanitizers).

Carl was a natural member of the Lee Child gang. He was like his second-in-command or enforcer or at least attack dog, savaging celebrity chefs and lifestyle coaches of every stripe. On the other hand, he was also into the meta-book idea. So much so that he conceived a notion of writing a meta-meta-article, looking over my shoulder while I was looking over Lee's. It was as Sartre says, in *Being and Nothingness:* you're spying through the keyhole and then, all at once, you realize someone else is behind you, spying on you. "Where is this madness going to stop?" I said. "Soon everyone will be watching everyone."

"It's already happening," said Lee. Then to Carl: "If I can stand *him* watching me, I can stand *you* watching him. It'll give him a taste of his own medicine."

The next morning I met Carl in Starbucks.

"Are you starting to write like him?" Carl said.

"I'm his opposite," I said. "He's making stuff up to put in his book. I'm taking his book and leaving stuff out. He's constructing, I'm deconstructing."

"But you're adding as well, aren't you? Not just subtracting. Are you making any of this up?"

Cue outrage. "It's reportage!" I was still just leaving stuff out (more coffee, more cigarettes, more Snickers, pizzas, etc.). But Carl was a better Grand Inquisitor than I am. "Okay, okay, you bastard," I blabbed, surrounded as I was by the typical Starbucks torture instruments of long tall lattes and croissants with jam. "I've been telling myself *I'm* influencing *him*. But it's all the other way round, isn't it? He is getting some kind of stranglehold over me."

"Does he worry you're going to sell more books than him?"

"Yeah. I believe it keeps him awake at night."

We walked the block over to Lee's. Carl slotted right in to those XXL chairs and sofas. Like they were made for him. It really was a template for Little Joey's place. He took the proffered mug of black coffee.

"So it's a home invasion?" said Carl. "Having Andy around."

"Technically," said Lee, pouring himself a mug. "From the Latin. *In-vadere*. It's my home and he's in it. But I'm not that worried."

"Do you ever get sick of him?"

"He generally gets out just before I start feeling physically oppressed."

"How do you see the practical purpose of having him observe you?"

"He serves no actual purpose, as such. The publishers still think he wants to destroy me. But after writing nineteen of these books I thought it would make a bit of a change. He's a . . . wild card."

It was a gang of three. I guess if you added in more obscenities, some guns, bags of coke, prostitutes, and a lot worse interior decor, we could have been back in the Chicago projects. "J.T." always fancied that his sociologist sidekick was going to write a "biography" of him. And Lee optimistically mentioned some book about Jimmy Page, the Led Zeppelin guitarist, that had just come out, with some hazy idea that it might provide me with a how-to manual of sorts.

His default alter ego is always: rock star.

And as for feeling "physically oppressed": all this is coming from a self-toxifier who smokes twenty a day. I was the one who should be feeling oppressed.

Carl helped Lee practice the pronunciation of the name of a Swedish noir author he was due to interview in May, then he headed off to JFK. After he was gone, Lee said, "He's such a healthy-looking bugger, 'course he doesn't need all that wellness crap. You know, if I was choosing a name for myself all over again, I might choose Carl Cederström. To hell with 'Lee Child.' Something cool and Scandi, with umlauts. It sells better. Academics and intellectuals wouldn't mind reading something by Carl Cederström. And it's another 'C.' It's the right place on the bookshelves."

I went back to Lee's at the end of the afternoon. "Stop press," says Lee. "Bookstore scene."

"Bookstore scene? In Mother's Rest?"

"San Francisco. They're killing time and Reacher goes into a bookstore."

"He doesn't pick up a copy of *The Wellness Syndrome* by any chance?"

"He has a concussion. He's rambling on about books. A bit like you."

THURSDAY, MARCH 26, 2015

7:45 Up, straight to work

Coffee 3 (mugs)

Camels 3

9:28 Breakfast. Sugar Smacks.

9:35 Back to work

Coffee 3

Camels 5

1:29 Lunch.

Toast and marmalade and cheese (Swiss)

Coffee 2

New Yorker 1

1:55 Back to work

Coffee 5

Camels 7

7:01 Dinner.

Alpen cereal (original)

Coffee 2

Camels 4

7:34 Evening shift

Coffee 4

Camels 7

10:20 Shut down

Total number of words in the day   2,173

Total mugs of coffee   19

Total Camels   26

no texts, no calls

HAS LEE CHILD
DONE HIS RESEARCH?

HE WAS CONSULTING his daughter, Ruth (thirtyish, slim, dark hair, beanie), on the vexed question of onomatopoeia. At the age of seven she queried a sign in a supermarket saying "10 ITEMS OR LESS": "Daddy, shouldn't that be *FEWER?*" She also appears in *Gone Tomorrow* as "a girl with a rat terrier" going along Broadway near the Flatiron Building. Now she was visiting with a couple of two-legged friends and their dog, an amiable and shaggy variety. They were all standing in the kitchen.

"I've got this scene," he was saying, "in which I blow this guy's brains out. A through-and-through shot. There's a big hole in the wall and 'blah blah the contents of his brain pan arrived to fill it, with a *wet slap*.' Wet slap—why is that onomatopoeic? It is, isn't it? Is it the plosives?"

She was clearly used to having her father blow someone's brains all over the wall, and was coolly analyzing the phrase down into

its phonemic parts: "'T' is a voiceless alveolar stop . . . dental fric-
ative . . . 'p,' a voiceless labial stop." She made various trilling and
chirruping noises to go with it.

I wondered if we might be projecting the sense onto the sound.
For example, would Beethoven's *Pastoral Symphony* sound quite
so pastoral if we didn't have the word "pastoral" attached to it: the
storm scene sounds like a storm because of the word "storm." And
so on. Lee said, "The cuckoo definitely sounds like a cuckoo."

"Does *West Side Story* sound like the West Side? Or only because of the words 'West Side'?"

Lee said, "You know that song, 'Somewhere'?"

"There's—a—place—for—us . . ."

"It's right there in Beethoven's piano concerto. 5th. The Emperor. Top of the second movement, the first violin figure. Ta—
da—dum—ta—da."

Which somehow got us back to talking about suicide. Again,
Ruth and her friends didn't seem to mind. I had been listening to
Philip Glass's 2nd violin concerto once—the slow movement—
when a guy went hurtling past my window. Going down. A slow
movement combined with a very fast movement. Followed by a
voiceless stop.

"What floor was this?" (Lee)

"I was on the third floor. One of those NYU buildings on
Bleecker."

"Not high enough," he said.

"The guy lived on the seventeenth."

"Ninety-three percent probability of mortality."

He snapped this back at me in a nanosecond. His daughter
gave him this look that seemed to say: *trust you to know that!*

"Shotgun to the head, ninety-nine percent," he went on. "Handgun to the mouth, ninety-seven percent. Jumping in front of a
train is right up there at ninety-six percent. Driving into a concrete

bridge support a mere seventy percent, but it goes up to seventy-nine percent *with* a seatbelt, surprisingly. Self-immolation, barely seventy-six percent. You might as well not bother. And it hurts like hell."

"I always wonder about the guy on his way down," I said. "He'd had an argument with his wife apparently. So instead of going out the front door and going to a bar and getting drunk the way he could so easily have done, he goes out the back door, the fast way. But on the way down, do you think he could have had a change of heart? It must have been a good couple of seconds. He could have thought, *Whoa that was dumb.* Or at least *oops.*"

"Eighty-two percent of people who jump off the Golden Gate Bridge and survive say that they changed their minds on the way down."

Still I'm not sure if he actually does "research" as such. Information just sticks to him. "It's almost all trivia," he said. He gave one example, or possibly two. It concerned a Super Bowl some years ago. Britney Spears was singing at halftime. And the show was sponsored by Pepsi-Cola. Lee Child had a sudden insight. He realized two things: that "Britney Spears" was an anagram of "Presbyterians"; and that Pepsi-Cola was an anagram of "Episcopal."

And finally that this was the kind of synchronicity that might come along only once in his lifetime. "Is that not awesome?" He stored it away without even thinking about it. Maybe Reacher would remember it one day.

MAIGRET *ET MOI*

Monday, March 30, 2015

LEE WAS 5K AHEAD of where he expected to be, so he didn't feel too bad about it. He was giving a talk at the 92nd Street Y that evening and it always threw him when he knew he had something coming up, even if he didn't have to leave till six. So he spent the day working on a couple of smaller things, the introduction to an anthology for a diabetes charity, and a short piece about Simenon for a Mystery Writers of America banquet program.

He had always been impressed by Georges Simenon. He seemed to Lee to exemplify a golden age of pulp productivity. They had one thing in common: they were the only two Europeans to have been elected president of the Mystery Writers of America (Simenon in 1955, Lee in 2008). Simenon had Maigret, Lee had Reacher. I thought twenty novels was a big deal and that number partly explained what I was doing there. "By current standards," says Lee, "it's worthy of note. I'm considered a veteran after twenty." But Simenon was on a different plane altogether. He wrote two hundred novels. And he could write twenty thousand words in a day, which made Lee seem like a slouch even when at full steam ahead. Simenon still has 550 million books in print. "By those standards I'm pathetic." The classic paperback writer had to be judged on sheer quantity, like a Brazilian bulldozer mowing down rainforest.

And then there were the ten thousand women he is reputed to have slept with.

"Do you believe that?" I said. I had tried reading his autobiography but got bored with it. "It's a suspiciously round number. I mean when you compare with Warren Beatty, for example. On 12,775 at the last count."

"Journalists make a lot of stuff up."

"So do novelists."

"He clearly had a habit. The zipper-problem."

"Like Camus and Kennedy."

"And Clinton, of course."

"I always liked that phrase in Camus: *un amour sans lendemain*. A love without a next day. I suppose it's just 'one-night stand' in translation."

"Pure Reacher. It's what he does. Maybe more than one night, but not much more."

Simenon had once signed up to sit in a glass cage in a restaurant in Paris, exposed to the public gaze, just him and a typewriter on a table in front of him. And crank out the whole novel then and there. I asked Lee if he would have a go at that. He said he had no "artistic objection" at all. He could probably manage a few hours of productivity in a Manhattan bar. But . . . the age of Simenon was no more. He would be a little self-conscious, probably. Because it wasn't just the people in the bar on that particular day. It was the whole massive audience on YouTube too, since it would inevitably be filmed on somebody's phone, even if it wasn't set up in advance. It was like a football match: every last move scrutinized and subjected to interrogation, rewound and watched again and again.

It was when I went to Starbucks that I realized that most of the people there (me included) were doing a Simenon, tapping away in public. The whole thing was a glass cage.

"You do the writing in private, and the promoting in public," Lee said later. "And never the twain shall meet. That could be confusing. Same with the ten thousand, of course. Those numbers are so made up. I try to be honest about my figures." He was thinking about sales figures suddenly. He had bumped into a fellow writer at a conference somewhere who was talking about his figures and asked the guy what model he followed, in case there was anything to learn. "Oh, we just make them up, my agent and I," the writer had replied cheerfully.

"These figures get bandied around and inflated. Ten thousand—that is one a day for . . . thirty years. Ridiculous! Think about it: you can't get better than the teenage years surely. And if I extrapolate from that, I still wouldn't get close."

"Even with two in the first thirty minutes?"

"You can't keep that up. It's not humanly possible."

60.

NAPOLEONIC

HE HAD TWO more short scenes to complete that day:

1. A bedroom scene.
2. They go to collect weapons.

Then it was all down to *planning*. The difficulty was that Mother's Rest was like an island in an ocean. There was "nothingness" all around it. Any attack was easy to see coming from a long way off. They would be ready for them. Reacher, and therefore Lee Child, had to figure out how to get in there without being spotted. "It really is like a military campaign," he said. I thought it was the closest he came to playing Napoleon.

"It's great," said Lee, "I just sit around drinking coffee and working out how to kill people. This is the fun part of it all."

He reckoned that his skill in this domain went back to the

period he called "the Great Unpleasantness," when staff were being cut at Granada Television and, as union shop steward, he was trying to rally resistance. "You know what it's like. Obviously you want to go out and break some guy's leg. And you don't. But I really thought about *how*. I wanted to know exactly how it would work. I planned it all out. Clearly I couldn't do it myself—I was known to them. So I would go to a particular pub, find some thug willing to do the job. There was a question of timing and financing and so on. I was completely practical about it, not theoretical."

I mentioned my theory about the return to primitivism and savage thought. Lee said I was forgetting the obvious. Reacher, at the end of the novel, has to *penetrate a lair*. "There's something subconscious about it," Lee said. Even though he was now conscious of it. "I just have to have that going on."

So Lee would sit there and plan it out on Reacher's behalf. But this was the twist he was thinking about. *He wouldn't show the planning*. Hitherto we have been close to the inside of Reacher's head all the way through, when not actually keeping track of his adversaries, with their backhoes and hogs and hired henchmen. But there was always a risk of information overload (making the plan and then executing it). So Lee was considering a completely different point of view that he hadn't employed at all yet, at least in this book. He would switch to a more remote omniscient viewpoint. Completely disconnected from Reacher. That way you wouldn't know what Reacher was planning, what he had in mind. You would only see him from afar: "through a telescope."

"Do you know how to get back to Mother's Rest without being spotted?"

"Haven't got a clue. So yes it helps me, not showing the plan. Since I don't really have one."

The next time I saw him, later that same day, he'd already started the read-through.

"Did you do the bedroom scene?"

"Done the . . . 'leaving dinner' scene," he offered tamely. He said he couldn't go on because he knew that he had to set the tone with the next scene, but he didn't know what the tone should be in the final sequence, so he had nothing to work back from. No "Ode to Joy." So he could only work forwards. But in order to do that he would have to go back. Hence the read-through. His method was less teleological (closing in on an end or *telos*), more *archaeological* (springing out of the beginning, the *archē*).

"It's like climbing up the stairs of a ski jump," he said. "A bit of a slog. But then you sail down, effortlessly. It launches the end."

61.

GARDENING TIPS

IT TOOK REACHER a long while to catch up with the Lee Child method. He should have realized sooner it was all there in the opening paragraph. The opening sentence.

But at least Lee had finally answered one of the questions he posed way back in September: Did Reacher see anything from the train? The seven o'clock train that was delayed and goes through Mother's Rest at midnight.

Somewhere around page 250, it all starts to fall into place. Hey, what were they doing with that backhoe? Isn't that a little strange, at midnight, even out here in the sticks? It's like Reacher has had a prolonged concussion (or "cerebral contusion") throughout the novel. And, in the manner of a true Platonist, he at last remembers what he already knew right from the start. To be fair to Reacher, he didn't know then that he was at the beginning of anything. From his point of view, it was pure flux.

"Here is the thing about the first sentence," Lee said. "There are no sentences preceding it." Not strictly true, of course. When he wrote, "Moving a guy as big as Keever wasn't easy," there were no preceding sentences—in *Make Me*. But since this was Reacher's twentieth outing, there were approximately 200,000 preceding sentences to go on. Some of them involving burying people, some specifically using a backhoe.

Reacher ought to have had suspicions. After all, had he not done something remarkably similar himself? Similarly on a remote farm, but in England.

Consider *The Hard Way*. Reacher has just shot or stabbed to death the mercenary leader Lane and several of his henchmen. What to do with the bodies? And, moreover, all their vehicles and attendant hardware? Answer: dig a massive pit, using a backhoe, chuck them all in (preceded as they were by fellow corpses from the Stone Age, the Bronze Age, the Iron Age, Celts, Romans, Saxons, Vikings, Normans, and English) and move the earth back again, plow it over, and plant wheat. Entirely reasonable. But surely when Reacher saw the backhoe at work in the first paragraph of *Make Me* it should have set off alarm bells?

"Yeah, logically," says Lee, sprawling on the sofa, wreathed in smoke, with (at last!) the window open. The fresh air from Central Park was fighting to get in. "I'm reprising a classic Reacher trope. But I hate Reacher having to refer back to his previous adventures. I like him to start with a clean slate."

"*Tabula rasa.*"

"I got that from a true crime story in the U.S. Apparently some guy and his car had completely disappeared. No trace. Nothing could be proved. It was a totally cold case. And then one detective happens to notice that there is a patch of wild hyacinth that is bluer than the rest in a whole meadow of hyacinth. Approximately the size of a car. And he happens to be a keen gardener, who therefore knows that the addition of iron, or ferrous sulfate, will produce higher color in a lot of flowers. It perks them up. They can suffer from iron deficiency, did you know that? Anyway, so they dig down and *voilà*."

"Was the guy still in the car?"

"Makes you wonder, doesn't it? Probably explains my dislike for farms. How many bodies in cars have they got down there? Nobody knows. It reminds me of digging up Roman coins in England. Those Romans must have been incredibly careless with their coins. They're all over the place."

We kept coming back to the question of Keever. He is right there on the first page and it looked likely that he would still be there, one way or another, on the last too. I knew that Lee had been reading or rereading Stephen King's *Pet Sematary* while he was writing *Make Me*. King imagines a cat and then a few humans coming back from the dead, rather deformed and lumpy and lumbering, and exerting their maleficent influence over pitiful nonzombie types. And there is almost a hint of that here. No actual Keever, somewhat the worse for wear, haunting the streets of Mother's Rest, but it's close.

"Yes," said Lee, "I've had Keever in my head all the time. The whole book revolves around him in a way. Reacher and Stashower are surrogate Keevers. They are doing what he was doing, following in his footsteps, potentially risking the same fate. They are him, essentially. And it echoes the structure of *Killing Floor* too, now that I think of it. Joe is dead at the very beginning of the novel. Just like Keever. The dead guy is the *animating* force of the novel." *Make Me* as valediction and eulogy.

And he had a soft spot for the *backhoe* too. The backhoe had never really gone away. Perhaps it would return at the end? The palindrome structure again. "It's a logical but brutalist way of getting rid of evidence." But what really drew Lee to the backhoe was the word itself. *Backhoe.* He loved the economy of the American (preferring it over King's English *digger* or *JCB*). He said the vernacular was part of what drew him to the States in the first place, the elision and the explicitness.

"They used to have this mortgage back in the day. Can't get 'em anymore, of course. All you had to do was *say* what your income was. Didn't have to provide any evidence as such. They called them *liar-loans.* That's beautiful, isn't it?"

WITTGENSTEIN
ON SIXTH AVENUE

ALL OF NEW YORK looked strangely familiar. Of course, I had lived there before. But there was something else. Eventually, I started to realize: I was living *inside* a Jack Reacher novel.

My building was just around the corner from the guy with no hands and no feet. Hobart in *The Hard Way*. He and his sister lived on Hudson. Reacher walked along Charlton Street (where I was staying) to get there. Whenever I got on a subway train I inspected the other passengers carefully, conscious (like Reacher at the beginning of *Gone Tomorrow*) that one of them could be carrying a bomb or about to blow her brains out.

I revisited Sixth Avenue with the beginning of *The Hard Way* in mind. In fact, to be honest, it was right there in my hand. I was rereading it as I walked along the street. Reacher is sitting outside a café on one side of the street (the western side), on the block between Houston and Bleecker, and a guy crosses the street and picks up a car (which turns out to have a ton of money in it, ransom money, but Reacher doesn't know that yet). The car is parked next to a hydrant (or "fireplug"). Like Reacher with Keever, I retraced his steps.

There were differences. In the book it was a warm summer's evening, hence Reacher sitting outside. For me it was morning, the beginning of April, but sunny enough for me to sit outside too. And there really is a café right there, just where Lee Child says there is one. More remarkably still, it is called "JACK'S." I went and got some of Jack's cold-brew coffee. Obviously, I had to ask.

"Is this place named after Jack Reacher by any chance?" I waved the book around.

"Reacher? The big guy."

"He sits at this café right here."

The barista had neatly combed ginger hair and a neatly trimmed ginger beard. *"Quelle coïncidence!"* he said, brightly. "Our Jack actually lives on 10th Street. That's where he opened his first café. We're hoping to expand to the West Coast. L.A. That's where we source most of our supplies."

"So . . . is your Jack anything like Jack Reacher?"

"He's a good-looking guy for sure," said the barista. "But he's more Tom Cruise than Jack Reacher."

And then there was the park near the Flatiron Building, in *Gone Tomorrow,* where the girl is walking her dog. The park reappeared in the short story Lee had written too, "The Picture of the Lonely Diner," where Reacher pops up out of the subway and obstinately keeps on going, major incident or no major incident.

It made me wonder if there really could be a place called Mother's Rest too. Surely somewhere there would turn out to be such a town. But I was mainly thinking about Wittgenstein at this point. Lee had sent me a sentence or two in which Reacher is talking about Keever and is saying that he didn't have to keep on going, he could have backed off: "He could have renamed himself Wittgenstein and chosen to live."

The Wittgenstein was, at one level, like the "bucket" and the "nail": I had been talking about Wittgenstein only the day before and now, alchemically transformed, his name appeared again in *Make Me*. The novel, like the housekeeper, liked to hoover up stray particles.

There is a line right at the end of the *Tractatus Logico-Philosophicus* (proposition 7) which anticipated "Reacher said nothing": "Whereof one cannot speak, thereof one must be silent" (*Wovon man nicht sprechen kann, darüber muss man schweigen,* now retranslated as "What we cannot speak about, we must pass over in silence," ironing out the original grammatical quirkiness). Wittgenstein, so far as I can make out, changed his mind about his "picture" theory of language. He had gotten it, he said, from looking at the diagram of a car's engine, when he was in the trenches in the First World War, where all the parts had arrows with their names attached. Isn't this just what language was doing generally? But in the later *Philosophical Investigations* he swerves around and says that there are many other kinds of "language game" you could be playing: there is ostensive definition, true, pointing and designating, but there is also (for example) asking a question, ordering, joking, praying, cursing, doing a crossword, making up a story, singing a hymn. But what happens to meaning then? Is that now lost? Is everything automatically hazy and impressionistic? With no clear labels and arrows anymore?

Not entirely, says Wittgenstein, for we have the "forms of life" to bind us together. What these *forms of life* are exactly, he never really explains.

Lee was having a decent shot at it though, at the New York Times Building. "If I use the word *car,* for example," he was saying, revisiting the classic Wittgenstein analogy. "It's a *signifier*. But everyone understands broadly what I mean by car. So I don't need to go on about it. Four wheels and so forth. What is the point? Keep it economical." There was, in other words, no need for infinite regress (so what is a *wheel*?). Equally there was no need for X (he named someone specific) to go running off to Tahiti under the heading of research. "That's just a vacation!" he said. "Tax-deductible."

Consider the "morning star" and the "evening star" (as Frege suggested). There would be general consensus that it was the same celestial object (Venus). "Never stray too far from the consensus," Lee had said. Aristotle called it *anagnorisis,* or recognition. Sometimes it's a big drama: your husband goes off to war for years, finally returns—hurrah! (Penelope and Odysseus). The guy who killed his father and married his mother . . . *that was me!* (Oedipus). But it doesn't have to be quite that dramatic. It could be a plain old car. These are the forms of life that we share in common and that a book serves to remind us of constantly.

I think something like this was happening when I sat in Jack's café on Sixth and looked across the street and said to myself: *Aha! The* [Hard Way] *fireplug!* (No Mercedes with a million dollars inside, alas.)

63.

THE PROPOSAL OF
A ROMANTIC NOVELIST

IT WASN'T THE FIRST time Reacher had been under the care of doctors. Look, for example, at the end of *Tripwire,* where he has been shot (while amply reciprocating), and is *hors de combat* for several weeks. And in *Gone Tomorrow* a paramedic is about to administer a painkiller (Reacher warns him off), but this is only after Reacher has been laid out by the kind of anesthetic dart normally used to knock out a gorilla. But this may be the first time that Reacher has walked into a doctor's office *while still conscious.*

On the one hand this shows the seriousness of the injury Reacher has sustained (from the blow to the head). But it also shows how seriously he takes the advice of Stashower. She insists, he—for once—accepts someone else's advice to go and see a doctor. So it's physiological and romantic all at once.

Lee was voicing both parts. It was like listening to Samuel Beckett playing Vladimir and Estragon. In this case it was

Stashower checking on the sanity and cognitive abilities of Reacher. They are in the bathroom at the hotel in San Francisco, where Reacher has been checking to see if he can still walk in a straight line. Soon they will go about acquiring weaponry (mainly from local drug dealers). As a final test, Reacher has to recite the opening of the Gettysburg Address, which he does rather well. The next morning, as they leave the hotel, the journalist Westwood is complaining that some lunatic kept him awake reciting the Gettysburg Address. A shift of point of view, so that we see the full absurdity of Reacher.

Lee laughing at his own hero.

But he mainly had in mind the evolving relationship between Reacher and Stashower. Reacher has never before been quite as vulnerable as he is here, physically and emotionally. As he says, there is a "first time" for everything—as he goes meekly to the clinic. But, more pertinent, is this Reacher falling in love? Is this conceivably a *durable* relationship?

"Now the romance has deepened, logic dictates that Stashower should be shot and killed, so as to liberate Reacher all over again. You know, have someone blow her brains out. So I'm not going to do that. I've made a crucial strategic decision. Stashower gets to live."

Lee admitted he had been sentimentally affected by a woman. He had been out for a drink with her the previous evening and she had been offering him some romantic advice. Made a serious proposal in fact. "Give Reacher a longer relationship," she said.

M. J. Rose was a writer and publicist and specialist in romantic fiction. She and Lee liked to get together from time to time and talk insider talk. But she was also very much a Reacher fan. And she basically loved Reacher. "So she was seeing it all from a Stashower point of view," Lee said. "I gave her a few details. Naturally she wanted to keep it going. Didn't want her killed off just as their relationship is warming up. She would go on a date with Reacher like a shot." What M.J. was loving in particular was that Reacher was "not lonely anymore," that there was someone "taking care" of him for a change, looking after his needs. And he was admitting that he had needs, which was a rarity in itself. And this is what she was voting for. More of that. She argued that readers (women readers in particular) would really appreciate it.

You could call it a cliffhanger of sorts: Reacher's major relationship with Jodie, daughter of General Garber, in *Tripwire*. Which tumbles into the next one (*The Visitor—Running Blind* in the U.S.), before she dumps him, in favor of a career move to London. "The women are too smart for him," said Lee. "That's what happens. Then he takes it out on the bad guys." But at least he gets a temporary stay of relationship execution: in effect, a romantic enjambment overflowing from one book into the next. And maybe something similar could work here, in *Make Me*.

Having admitted to being "influenced" by his romantic publicist, taking her advice just as Reacher was taking Stashower's, Lee argued that you could reasonably draw a parallel between the thriller and romantic fiction. "They both offer the kind of satisfaction you don't get in real life. Not often." There was "a similarity in mechanism," in his phrase. In one genre, you are granted one wish (get rid of anyone who arouses your anger); in the other, you are granted a second (go to bed with someone who arouses your desire). Hypothetical wish-fulfillment. With built-in safe sex. "You finally get to fly to the Caribbean with a beautiful woman," he said. "Or, in your case, Cincinnati."

64.

WHERE IS THE PIPE?

THIS IS WHAT REACHER wanted to know: Where exactly was the exhaust pipe? He was analyzing Google Earth photos of Mother's Rest. According to the website there ought to be an old Chevy with its exhaust pipe all hooked up. The website was very precise and very lyrical about it. That and the Nembutal and the concierge service in a restful ambiance. No way of checking the Nembutal, of course, but from the photographs you could reasonably infer *there was no exhaust pipe.* Therefore, Reacher is justified in concluding: "their website is a lie." As he has been saying for some time: *There has to be more.*

It had been Lee's slogan since before September 1: there has to be more, and more, and more. And there still would be more, in the final sequence. Discoveries must be made as well as justice being seen to be done. No one really knew the awful truth. So there was a twin track to be followed, at once military and epistemological (adversaries decreased, knowledge increased). And then, looking further ahead (another chess move, approaching checkmate), the "wind-down." Lee spoke like a grand master who knew that he had won, even though the game was far from over. "I'm feeling a sense of relief," he said.

He was back in the chair; I was back on the couch. "The great thing is—I managed to miss out the middle again. Just like last time [in *Personal*]. The chorus is belting out the 'Ode to Joy.'" He had adopted my Beethoven's 9th analogy. "We're at the point where the final theme is stated with total conviction." There would be a "pastoral moment" and then "all hell will break loose."

I remembered how much he said he hated the middle phase. Which might kick in around day two. After the "gorgeous feeling" had dissipated and then the hard work began, like Sisyphus, or like Jack Reacher digging yet another swimming pool, by hand, shoveling and sweating. "So you mean you kept the beginning going all the way until it just blended right into the end? It was just a single continuous stream of inquiry?"

"The middle would be like . . . a digression. You're going off at a tangent. You really have to work at it. I didn't have to do that. It was more like . . . going downhill all the way. I didn't feel like I was adding, I was only leaving stuff out." He liked words like *ellipsis, elision, eliding*, which all implied an aesthetics of omission (*leipō* = "I leave").

"It's like, I've left the first trapeze. I'm flying through the air. Are you going to grab hold of the other one swinging towards you? Or are you going to crash? I know now, I'm definitely going to make it." The first trapeze and the second trapeze: the beginning and the ending. Somehow he had managed to swing from one to the other without touching earth in between. A high-wire act. There was no middle. That was the ellipsis.

He was looking back over Chapter 51 with a view to making a

start on 52, swinging from one small trapeze onto another. Enjambment, overflowing into the next line. "One thing I've noticed," he said. "If you polish the dialogue, till it sounds right in your head, if you write it properly, it sounds right in any accent. It can sound like Michael Caine, it can sound like Tony Curtis, it still comes out right."

"So what accent does Reacher have in your mind? Does he have one?"

"Well, he was in the army, which is homogenous, with everyone sounding like everyone else. But I hear it as slightly inarticulate, slightly downbeat . . . a bit like Kevin Costner in *Dances with Wolves*."

"The voiceover. Right, like a diary. Reportage. But naive."

"That was foundational for Reacher, I can't deny. A major influence. But also, speaking of voiceovers: Do you remember *Days of Heaven*? Richard Gere. But the voiceover—it's the point of view of a young girl. Magnificently laconic. Her voice was so sensationally economical—the elision, the nuance—I knew that was what I wanted for Reacher."

"What about Beckett? Talking of laconic. I know you've seen *Godot* thirty-nine times. That must have had an impact?"

"Remember how much I hated that production with Ian McKellen and . . . who was it?"

"Patrick Stewart."

"Yes, those two. They played it like they were end-of-the-pier comedians in Blackpool. But the thing you have to remember is that Beckett was not English. He was an Irishman writing in French. And thinking in French. The key to understanding it is, it's French not English."

Lee, like Beckett, was coming at another language, i.e., American English, from the outside. He spoke it fluently, he inhabited it, or it inhabited him (his accent was somewhere between Michael

Caine and Tony Curtis), but he was always conscious of its strangeness at the same time. He didn't take "backhoe" for granted, for example. Or "elevator." He was also a great fan, oddly enough, of "blacktop." Every now and then he had a problem, for example, with the phrase "Not a problem!" "I ask for a coffee and someone says, 'Not a problem!' and I think, well, in what conceivable universe could selling a paying customer a cup of coffee *be* a problem?" (Although he blamed this phrase mainly on the Australians. Similarly the abbreviation "uni," for university, which he hated.)

I went back to *Days of Heaven*. The young girl's voiceover is oblique, fragmentary, flat, affectless, but at the same time wonderfully evocative of a mood and a life in constant crisis. There is a point towards the end of the film where everything is coming apart (several deaths and a plague of locusts) but the girl and Bill (Richard Gere) and Abby (Brooke Adams) are sailing away from it all down a broad river. "You could see people on the shore," the girl (V.O.) is saying. "But it was far off and you couldn't see what they were doing. Prob'ly calling for help—or trying to bury somebody or something."

Calling for help and *trying to bury somebody*: they were prob'ly the twin themes of *Make Me*. And that scene helped to explain another of Lee's metaphors, when he was talking about how he liked to steal from movies. "We're all in the same river."

But that wasn't really the point. The point was that Lee didn't have a narrative "voice" at all, he had only a narrative *voiceover*. And the point about the voiceover is that it never has to tell you everything. You are relying on the movie to do that. The voiceover is an extra layer of information, going off from the narrative at an angle, with a particular perspective and accent and bias all its own. It had a built-in inadequacy. It left out nearly everything. It was commentary, a form of meta-discourse. You didn't really need it, *à la rigueur,* but I had a soft spot for it myself (try to imagine, for example, *Big Wednesday* without it; or *Stand by Me*).

Setting aside all talk of Tom Cruise, goats ("the book was better"), and that time he got invited to dinner by a movie star and turned her down ("it would have been overly exciting"), I think I had finally worked out a general law as regards the Lee Child philosophy of the relationship of text to film:

Life is a moving picture; the book is a voiceover.

65.

STAIRWAY TO HEAVEN

IN AN IDEAL WORLD, we should have been singing the "Ode to Joy," preferably in the original German. If I were scripting this, it would have been "21st Century Schizoid Man" (King Crimson); if Lee were scripting, I would guess, an old Led Zeppelin song, maybe "Stairway to Heaven." In fact, our duet went like this:

> *"Now hands that do dishes can feel soft as your face . . .*
> *With mild green Fairy Liquid."*

We were rehearsing a bunch of classic TV commercials. No good reason. Unless it was something to do with "a portal on the culture." Lee fondly recalled the old Oxo ads and Hamlet cigars and "a Mars a day helps you work, rest, and play." And "the sweet you *can* eat between meals" (Milky Way). He recalled that the Chesterfields ad had a big impact on him as a kid: "Doctors say, for the sake of your throat, smoke Chesterfields!" He didn't care if it was a total lie. In a way, it was actually true.

Lee (taking a defiant, doctor-certified drag on his Camel): "Doctors, having been paid a generous sum by Chesterfields, really were saying it. Maybe they even believed it. Or was that Lucky Strike? Whatever. Everyone was smoking then. Look at *JFK,* the Oliver Stone movie. Remember those documentary clips? They're all smoking! The entire Warren Commission. Ashtrays all over the desks. It was hard work trying to fit up Oswald for the crime; they needed a fag."

He was supposed to be working on the "pastoral scene," purely descriptive, a tranquil prelude to the final showdown. But he was more critical than Goldilocks. "This has to be exactly right," he was saying. "But is it?" This was the detached, omniscient perspective. He had his feet up on the desk, looking at the screen from afar. Then he sat up. "Am I making the same point twice here?" I noticed that the word "infinite" or "infinitely" was coming up. It's dawn. Lee was describing the transition between night and day. A gradual blossoming of light over Mother's Rest. He had used the word "lumen," which he agreed was a "rarity." There was a celestial or cosmological feel to the writing, with reference to the stratosphere and stars and luminosity. A hint of "Stairway to Heaven" after all. Or Phoebus and his chariot. And a reminiscence of Shakespeare or Chaucer or maybe Wordsworth in the description of the day invading the night. "Okay, I'm taking out a few words here. I hate doing that. But I'm pushing the image too hard."

He lit up another Camel. He was stringing the cigarettes more tightly together, like pearls on a necklace. He said of water (which I was drinking), "What's the point, unless it has been run through a coffee machine?" And he felt something similar about air—what was the point of breathing in air not laced with nicotine?

He hopped up to make coffee. There was a big glass jar of cookies on the table in the kitchen. "Chocolate chip?" I asked.

"Oatmeal raisin," he corrected. "My fruit intake for the day."

"So this chapter is lyrical?"

"But we also have to have the sense of a configuration of forces. Players on the board. It's the calm before the storm. But there is a sense of anxiety: Is it *too* quiet?"

We are back at the desk. The *nothingness* is back. The vastness and emptiness of the open plain. "They're staring out into the nothingness . . . But now it's working against them." Lee was gradually bringing in the point of view of the sentries manning the ramparts of Mother's Rest, specifically the immense grain silos, which are like watch towers or a panopticon.

Lee stared at the screen. "How much nothingness? That is the question." It was a semi-Hamlet-like mini-soliloquy. "Before something starts up." He more or less answered his own question. "I feel it should plow straight ahead now. No artificial delays!"

I couldn't help wondering: "Any chance of the backhoe making a comeback? A *come-backhoe*?" I put my feet up on the couch, hands behind my head. Surveyed all the framed photos of *New York Times* bestseller lists with his name right at the top (*Worth Dying For, 61 Hours, One Shot,* etc., etc.).

Lee nodded as if to say, *of course*. Not taking his eyes off the screen. His Tintin quiff leaned into it like the cornice of a rock face overhang. "That backhoe has definitely been in the back-*hoe* of my mind. It could be something unexpected. For example, here we are at Mother's Rest. But the bad place is twenty miles south of here at an isolated farm. How do you get Reacher from one to the other? What kind of vehicle can he acquire? Maybe he could improvise with all that agricultural equipment. Could he drive a backhoe all the way there? Or a bulldozer?"

I thought that would suit him, physiologically: big, bulky, never going to be elegant, but, yes, very effective.

"It's all beginning now. There's something incoming from the West. Then something else from the East. Train from the South. And then I thought I'd throw in a couple of helicopters. God knows what they are supposed to be doing. This is going to be good. It's exciting. But it's also: *What the fuck is going on?*"

66.

RISEN AGAIN

"**TWO MOMENTOUS** items to report."

That was it. Lee's emails tended to be terse. As always I had to know. So I headed on over to his place. But, unlike his, my narrative was digressive. There was a definite middle phase. It was Easter Sunday after all, it deserved a digression.

Beginning: (gorgeous feeling) I set out from Charlton Street, the sun on my back, caught my usual C train at West 4th. But got out at 59th and backtracked and sidetracked till I hit Fifth Avenue around 49th.

Middle: (digression) Fifth Avenue on Easter Day—it's not a hat party, it's a ritual hat orgy, Dionysian hat revelry, hat frenzy. I was wearing my Orlando Palacios from Worth & Worth (Joel, sick of me borrowing his, had insisted), technically known as a "Belmondo": coffee-colored, with a big brim, and a band. Up against stiff competition from the likes of people wearing wedding cakes, or buckets of eggs, or pink rabbit ears, or bowls of fruit. One guy actually had a black cat on his head, but eventually the cat got tired of all the attention and sloped off.

I was there mainly for the organ recital at St. Thomas Church on 53rd. A Rutter organ *duet* (how rare is that?), some rousing Bach and Duruflé, but also a lovely, lyrical, ethereal piece by Widor, "Choral" from his *Symphonie Romane* (hitherto unknown to me). Everything else cried out "the anguish and the triumph" (to recall the title of that Beethoven biography), but the Widor was toned-down and blissed-out. Obviously we were all resurrected, sublime and shimmering, there was no struggle about it, no pain. It reminded me of Fauré's *Requiem,* gentle and lilting, lots of piccolo, almost like a lullaby: Oh death where is thy sting? No Underworld, no Dantean descent into the inferno, no wrestling with the Minotaur, just an elevator direct to Paradiso. It was tempting. I could understand the customers lining up at Mother's Rest.

End (finally): the second trapeze. Central Park West. Sitting by the window. Sun and air. White mug, black coffee.

"Momentous item one?"

"I've just passed the 100,000-word mark. It's really a thriller now" (Lee counted 60k romance; 80k mystery; 100k thriller). "I think it's even specified in my contract." I was only on eighty-something, he'd gone zooming past me, Porsche Carrera to my Chevy.

"Momentous item two?"

"Stashower is dead."

"What!?" Italics and underline. "What about the romantic enjambment and everything?" I felt obscurely betrayed.

"It's okay. It's still on. Stashower is dead. But long live Chang. I've changed the name."

"Chang. Tintin's best friend. Chinese. Appears first in *The Blue*

Lotus, then decades later in *Tintin in Tibet.* Tintin somehow knows he is lost in the Himalayas and rescues him from the yeti. Boy, not girl." It wasn't until later that the obvious point occurred to me that *Chang* is just *Change* minus the "e." "First name?"

"Still Michelle. Look," he said, "I got it from here." He pointed to an orange spine on the shelf over his head. Another book. Not Daniel Stashower's obviously. *The Rape of Nanking,* by Iris Chang. Japan invading China. Same story Hergé was telling. Massacre. All of history right there.

"There were just too many syllables! *Stash-ow-er.* I was compressing it to two in my head, more like *Sta-shaur* or something, but it's not going to work for the reader. It's that 'sh' in the middle— it's really intrusive. Affects the rhythm. When I think of this character in my head, I think: Great! There is coherence and there is development. But there is something wrong for sure."

"For *shower.*"

"Exactly. It's the name. In my head she is Asian. There's a way she has of talking to Reacher. There is an Asian inflection in her voice."

"Chinese specifically. So she's American Chinese."

"I don't want to generalize. Or stereotype. I'm drawing on several Asian friends here. She's still big, she doesn't have to be small. What I had in my head was not what I had on the page. It was jarring all the time. I'm not doing this for *diversity* in the Reacher world. There was a dissonance, and I finally figured out what it was."

"One syllable. More compact, economical. *Said Chang.* That works."

"And it's something to do with her respect for hierarchy, authority, structure. Which Reacher doesn't have. She didn't like getting dumped out of the FBI. Even owned up about where she'd blown it. Now the name fits the character. It didn't before."

It *was* momentous. The name Stashower will no longer appear in his book (read it and see). I was glad that she would live on, phantasmatically, in mine. I was preserving the heritage, the ancestry, the secret archaeology of Chang. Saving her from total oblivion. She had been through a lot already. She deserved some kind of recognition.

He was lying there on the sofa, looking sphinxlike behind a veil of smoke, satisfied at having all at once annihilated Stashower and yet resurrected her as Chang. "Do you remember those Tintin cartoons on television?"

Hergé's *Adventures of Tintin*! We both put on the booming, melodramatic voiceover voice (halfway towards the big fight introduction).

"Do you know what my mother thought that was?" Lee said. "*Thursday's Adventures of Tintin.*" She could never work out why it would be showing on a Monday or Tuesday."

Lee emailed me the following day:

> *I always heard her voice the same, and when I thought about her without view of the text she seemed of-a-piece and coherent. But when I read what I wrote I kept tripping up on some hidden disconnect. Eventually I realized her manner/cadences/ reactions (and possibly what I saw as her self-image, to get really heavy) were essentially Asian-American, and it was the "Stashower" name that was tripping me up—implying essentially a whole different cultural inheritance that didn't match what I had in my head. Changing (ha!) the name snapped the whole thing into focus, and it feels like a big relief. Like taking a stone out of my shoe.*

67.

THE BALDACCI PROGRAM

THERE WERE ONLY FOUR sequences left to write (as far as Lee could work out, looking ahead):

1. Get down there (south to the isolated farm)
2. Oh my God, look at this!
3. Kill all these guys
4. Wrap it up

"I've definitely got a firm grip on the second trapeze." There were certain matters he was still a little anxious about. *Speed* for one (or "pace management"). The temptation is to go fast: you're approaching the end, let's speed it all up. "But then you run into the reader who complains that the ending feels rushed. They want to savor it, to spin it out." But there was an alternative criticism: *this drags!* Somehow he had to find the right balance between rushing and dragging. The answer, he thought, was to "vary it, so some of these scenes are fast, some slow."

It all made sense. I'd just been rereading *Gone Tomorrow* in which he does just this in a complex fight scene with two women (sadistic al Qaeda ops), three knives and several chairs, a whole blood-spattered choreography, but then followed by a moment in which Reacher, worn out and himself badly cut, simply strangles one of them. It's blunt, emphatic, pulls no punches.

But there was something else that occurred to me only then, for no particular reason. "I was thinking . . . I'm writing all this down."

"So?"

"Do you think it's possible some smart cookie at Google is going to come along and read all this and turn it into a piece of software that can write virtual Lee Child novels from now till kingdom come? Are you giving too much away?"

I mentioned the classic structuralist essay by Claude Lévi-Strauss and Roman Jakobson on Baudelaire's "Les Chats." A gorgeous sonnet about . . . cats? But Lévi-Strauss and Jakobson do not ask themselves the dreaded "about" question at all. No, they focus on the rules: the phonology, the grammar, the syntax, the metrics, and how they intersect one with another. What they are not interested in could be summarized as the "soul of the poet." They don't really care if Baudelaire owned a cat or was having an affair with somebody at the time or had been gloomily pondering his own inescapable fate. It's twenty pages on a fourteen-line poem and at the end of it you have in your hand enough in the way of rules to write a computer program for generating a decent sonnet. It was pure Turing, solving the "enigma" of the poem, reducing it to code.

"Right now," I said, "I can probably take a few words, feed them into a program, and produce an utterly pointless poem of some kind."

"You're wondering if you could do something similar with a novel?"

"One of your novels specifically. Could it all be done by a machine? A 'Reacher engine.' Maybe you could relax and go and lie on a beach or watch the Yankees all day?"

"Logically, it has to be possible," Lee said. "The 'Deep Blue' of fiction."

"Or HAL."

"Whenever anyone asks me where does one of my ideas come from, I always think: from *reading*. Read enough books, you can write anything. You're extrapolating in some way from what already exists. And you can get a machine to read *everything* now. Think of the Gutenberg Project. You can easily imagine, if everything is digitized, you could come up with an algorithm. Just feed it all in and see what pops out."

"Like a Pop-Tart?"

"You could call it the *Baldacci Program*."

"When Barthes predicted the *Death of the Author* he didn't realize Baldacci would be taking over," I said. "It's a bit like *Pet Sematary* again: your pet is brought back to life, it's there, but it's a mess. Death is better."

"You'd get the flats but none of the peaks. No *flair* or spark." None of the madness, or the sublime confidence, or divine *furor,* or the chip-on-the-shoulder aggro. How can a machine have a chip on its shoulder?

Lee mentioned the software he uses for screenplays, "Final Draft." "It's brilliant, you only have to write, 'S' and the name 'Stashower' pops up. It spaces it all out for you. And sometimes I'm tempted, writing this novel, to wonder if there is a bit of software I could use to do something similar here. But then I think—no, I like to have total control over every last keystroke. No auto-correct. And the spaces on the page."

Perhaps this explained why Reacher harked back to the analog age. He didn't really want everything to be reducible to binary bits and bytes. Not long before, Lee had written this line: "He heard the whoosh of her email or text or whatever." He has adapted but he is not really interested in participating. His life of violence is in part a revolt against digitization. He still has the "soul of the poet." Half Rambo, half Rimbaud.

I couldn't help but notice, however, that when Reacher goes into the bookstore in his concussed state and starts "rambling" about books, he adopts a fundamentally binary attitude. He decides he prefers fiction to nonfiction.

And, after due reflection, he comes to the conclusion that there are essentially only two genres: "Either shit happens, or it doesn't."

68.

ON THE SOFA

LEE CHILD WAS LYING on the sofa, shoes off, eyes closed, the smoke from the cigarette between his fingers curling lazily up to the ceiling.

"I know, I'm lying on the sofa with my eyes closed. But—this is going to sound self-serving—this is *work*. It is. *Honest!*"

When he went back to the keyboard he tapped out another couple of paragraphs, then he got up again and paced around. He had reached that stage of the novel where he was as tense as Reacher with a gun in his hand. He had to keep jumping up and making coffee or lighting the nth cigarette of the day (I saw a modest cairn of virgin packs of Camels piled up on a table like backup ammo) or watching the whole of Aston Villa drawing 3–3 with QPR, or going for a working lie-down.

Still, it was disconcerting: like seeing the captain desert the bridge. Or get up and leave the cockpit and stroll around the plane, chatting with passengers, having a drink and a snack, and all along his maniac copilot is at the controls, and possibly sabotaging the autopilot.

I had been reading the Stephen King book *On Writing*. "Stephen King says you have to stay put in that room with the door closed until the two thousand words are done, or you are not serious."

"I like that voice of his. Comfortable. Like he's sitting on a country porch somewhere telling you his tale." In *Under the Dome* King has one of his characters call up Major Jack Reacher for a reference, so the admiration was mutual.

"You have to have loud rock music pounding away too."

"I've never understood how he can do that. Led Zeppelin fan though I am. I'm trying to keep the beat of my own music—and someone else's melody is cutting across it. Not to mention lyrics. It would be such a jarring clash. Dissonant. Or I'd surrender to some other rhythm."

"He says you can have a lie-down afterwards."

He was back on the sofa. Well, it was a different sofa, but still a sofa. Gazing up at the ceiling again. He said he would sometimes stretch out on my couch if the housekeeper was roaming around, but otherwise he liked to change the space too, to get away from the keyboard for a moment. "I think I would say it's almost the opposite. The best thinking is done *horizontally*. It's not a departure, it's part of the writing day. You see, when you're in there *typing*, there's a certain amount of sheer drudgery involved, mere secretarial work, it's technical—I'm *typing* for goodness' sake, doing stupid things like correcting spelling errors and so forth— whereas here it's pure . . . it's pure *something*, anyway, there's no typing. Full-on daydreaming. You're more in the zone lying down with your eyes closed. It's like . . . I'm going to the top row of seats in the stadium: I can see the whole field from here."

All these sofas in the apartment: they weren't sofas, they were *workstations*.

"Do you ever get inspired when you're on the subway or walking down the street?"

"I've written a few sentences on napkins."

"No notebook?"

"Like you, you mean? Constantly jotting? Too weird! My basic rule is, if you can't remember it, it probably wasn't worth remembering."

He was in the middle of Chapter 55. He had changed things around, the way he always did. *Drift* was built into the narrative. Two sequences, "getting down there" (1) and "killing all these guys" (3) had merged somewhat. He wasn't going to kill all of them all at once, but "I couldn't wait," he said. He was confident it would leave more time for (2) "oh my God what the fuck is this!?" The revelation section was very important, he argued. This book was a real exception to the general rule where Reacher was concerned. Normally Reacher would have it all figured out *before* he launched a full-scale assault; in *Make Me* we are about to "breach the walls," but he is still fundamentally baffled or at least puzzled: so Reacher and the reader would make the discovery at the same time.

"It's great: we *still* don't know! The very first question and it's still unanswered."

The POV had swung around again, so that we had shifted away from the Mother's Rest sentries back to Reacher (now in a diner) and his allies (Chang—the artist formerly known as Stashower—and Westwood the journalist).

"Are you going to let the bad guys tell their story?" I thought it would be fair, given that we have had multiple points of view in the narrative. "To explain why they are doing what they are doing.

They have some kind of logic after all." I recalled that Reacher didn't give the obese Merchenko a chance to state his case.

Lee smiled and nodded. "I thought I'd turn that around 180 degrees. You know, Reacher would think about killing him straight out but the guy speaks first. A chance to spin his version."

"Do you know what he's going to say?"

Lee had totally inhabited the mind of evil. "They *paid* for this! They *volunteered*. Didn't they relinquish all rights when they walked in here? And anyway, we have to make a few cents on the deal. It's win-win!" He paused, slipped out of character again. "It's like body disposal, but shifting it up a gear. *Depraved* moral agenda, of course. But it's an attitude. It has to make some kind of sense. You have to find it plausible that someone would think that. Maybe he can finally explain the origin of the name Mother's Rest while he's at it?"

He got up and drifted off again, saying, "I've got to go and think." I had to take a peek at the screen, naturally. There was stuff about a "second exit" and the word "trapdoor" came up at least twice. I had the keyboard in front of me. For a moment I toyed with the idea of slipping in a line from Proust or James Joyce, in a spirit of sheer vandalism, but I let it slide. Child was fine just the way he was. I found him having another lie-down. He had a cigarette between his fingers and an ashtray poised on his chest.

"What are they doing?" he was muttering to himself, smacking ash off the tip of his cigarette. "Who are they? How did they get there?" No wonder he was having to *drift* again: fundamental questions still unanswered.

"So what's all this about trapdoors, then? Sounds like Houdini or something."

"Oh yeah, you know what you were saying about the *Under-world*?" We had been riffing on Theseus and Orpheus and Dante and Reacher's basement scene on Easter Sunday. "It's right. We need to go down again. It's only fair. We start off burying. We have to dig down again. To get right to the bottom." The archaeological mind at work. "And it fits with the idea of the *deep* web. The underground bunker. It's a natural. Something you can't see from a satellite. It has to be invisible from aboveground. It's not going to show up on Google Earth obviously. So it's an allegory. But I don't have to labor the point."

"Don't worry," I said. "I can do that."

THE END IS NIGH

"THE END IS NIGH." I had actually seen a sign saying that on Fifth Avenue. The prophet was also suggesting I might want to consider repenting before it was too late and I was judged and found wanting. And it was true, I was really worried about *the end*.

Lee, just like the Fifth Avenue evangelical, had been anticipating the *Rapture* for some time. As I've said, he is a nonteleological thinker at heart, noneschatological, but as soon as he was over the 100,000-word mark, he automatically started thinking in terms of wrapping it all up. I basically hated for a Reacher novel to come to an end. I was one of those readers who would moan about him *rushing* the ending. *Slow down*, you bastard, I was saying to myself. *There must be more!* (as he/Reacher would say). "King says he can write 150,000 words in three months."

"Workaholic!" he said, with a degree of exasperation. "I'm such a lazybones. But the trapeze is carrying me on. I'm still swinging."

He was over 105,000 now. "But look, what if I have a Reacher novel of 300,000 or 400,000 words. Something massive in your hand. Like *Lord of the Rings.*"

"Or *A la recherche du temps perdu*. About a million or so."

"That's going to look pretty weird, isn't it? *The Enemy* was 140,000. I think the market has gotten slicker. I don't think readers will tolerate something that huge and unwieldy."

But there was another thing. It wasn't just that I didn't really want the novel to come to an end. After having kept track of the text for so long, faithfully following Reacher on his itinerary, getting off the train and then Oklahoma City and L.A. and San Francisco and finally back to Mother's Rest, tracing his steps all the way back to the very beginning, I had a growing anxiety: What if I *missed* the ending? It was nigh, but what if I was at the other end of town or stuck on the subway or sitting in Think Coffee? And missed Lee's final sentence. *What then?*

"You'd better get here early tomorrow," he would say, filling me with alarm. "It could be all over. The contractions are coming thick and fast now."

Then he'd email me. "Who am I kidding? There's still loads of stuff to be done. No rush."

70.

WHAT'S IT ALL ABOUT, THEN?

I WAS EXAMINING some of the books on the shelf: *Dictionary of American Slang; Dictionary of Military Terms*. Lee Child was worrying about tenses. This is what he had written:

"Guess how many files they had . . ." [The answer is 200 . . . and now it had gone up to 209.]

"Does that sound like 'the number of files they *had already accumulated*' or just 'the files they had *on that particular day*'? I can't be too precise. Remember these are two guys talking in conditions of extreme stress."

"Stick with the preterite," I said. "Let the reader work it out."

"Okay," he said. Then he switched to the pluperfect. "It's a ridiculously small nuance. But it's better to get the tense right." It was like he wanted to apologize for being so obsessive about matters of detail. More academic than an academic.

He leaned back and zoomed out. "Today is the Big Reveal."

Even though we both knew it was coming, it was still a magical moment, pure prestidigitation, pulling the rabbit—or something more like an elephant—out of the hat. It had taken Reacher and Co. this long to catch on. It was unbelievable. They had to physically see the evidence to believe it. The horror. "We are finally there. All my efforts, all the reader's efforts, are at an end. But we don't want to pile it on!" Lee hated to overdo anything (he called it *lard* or *larding*). "Less is more here. It's the final *oh-my-God* moment. It only needs a few short pars."

He said he felt "delicate" about it. For two reasons. (1) "You have to be not beating anyone over the head with it"; (2) Yes, the content was extreme. He would let the reader fill in the blanks. "But," says he, swinging around, "you can't afford to be coy about it either. Reacher is never coy."

Lee comes up with a series of movie titles in this passage. "Which are banal but economical" (e.g., McCann and his friend become "Sad Couple with Something to Be Sad About").

"We have arrived at exactly *that*," he said. *That* was the secret at the core of Mother's Rest. We had started discussing it in January. "But the route we have taken could not have been predicted."

Lee was feeling pleased that the various "ideas" that he had "cast out" at the beginning were now "coming together."

I can personally testify, hand on heart, that when Lee Child wrote that first sentence about Keever back in September, he really had no idea what *that* was. *That* emerged spontaneously. "People are going to say it was all cunningly plotted." There was a note of sadness in his voice. He would be unable to convince the die-hard skeptics. "It looks planned, but it totally isn't. I'm really happy with the way it is all tying up. It's vectoring in. It's a good trajectory. But I didn't know what was ahead when I cast off."

His technique of *drifting* could be better thought of as *surfing*: there was a lot of art in just staying on your feet and avoiding the wipe-out, let alone doing it stylishly, but it all depended on the wave; without the wave there was nothing. Lee didn't think it was the unconscious at work ("it could have bubbled up, but that's all unfalsifiable, and it doesn't feel like it"). Nor that his narrative was a "found object," as Stephen King would have it: "You can have *found* scenes, the ones you have no intention of writing at all." But there were too many "strands" to a narrative for it to be *found*. "Imagine a boy dives down into the sea and comes up with a pearl. You'd be impressed, wouldn't you? But now what would you say if you knew that the boy had previously scattered a whole lot of pearls on the seabed? It's not so impressive, is it?"

He was satisfied that now (after the Big Reveal) readers would understand "what the book is all about."

"Do *you* know what it's all about?"

Lee thought the "about" question was fair. He didn't mind answering it, but he would give different answers depending on the occasion. "There used to be this slogan in publishing, there were supposed to be just three words that would govern all the communications between author and editor and printing and publicizing, everyone. And the first two of those words were: *It's about* . . . So I'd say it's about *suicide*."

Lee believed in the right to self-directed death or "assisted dying" (and invoked *Being Mortal,* by Atul Gawande). "It's a calm and ethical argument," he said. "But if you look at it through the lens of thriller requirements, obviously I had to throw in some doubts. There always had to be *more*. It was never going to be *just* suicide. One word, it's ridiculous. Give me forty-five minutes on NPR and I'll give you a better answer."

This is just a voiceover. Or voices. I'm leaving out all the movie. Condensing ("*Dichten = condensare,*" Ezra Pound). Lee was always tapping or hopping up and down and making coffee or going to put his feet up for five minutes and so on. I would go and stand by the window. Across the street the gray bones of Central Park were finally greening up.

And the situation he was describing or unfolding on the page—the *that* was hurting him, even as he was writing it. Lee (lying down on sofa): "You know, I think this is the most . . . affecting thing I've written."

I was lying on the couch, looking up at the model plane that dangled from the light fixture in the middle of the ceiling. I sort of wondered if, although he himself believed in the right to die, he had nevertheless conspired to undermine the case, by showing how it could be exploited. He felt he had covered all sides of the argument, one way and another, but that it always came back in the end to Reacher. "Reacher is a bit like Spock (of *Star Trek* fame), he is crippled by logic. It's like he is actually handicapped by it. No one asks to be born, he realizes."

"It's the Heidegger argument, isn't it? We are *thrown* into the world. The condition of *thrownness* (*Geworfenheit*)."

Lee was back at the keyboard now, so I was probably interfering with the forward momentum of the prose. For which I repent. "Reacher says, 'So it's like taking the sweater back to the store.' You have a right. Of course, Reacher doesn't even own a sweater and has never taken anything back to the store in his life. But readers have, so they will get the point."

"Is there a *point*, then?"

"Nah, where would the point be? It's all particles . . . More of an *agon*. I like that. A conflict. It has to be. This is my NPR version. It's a novel *about* the collision between the ultra-new and the ultra-old. Fighting it out."

"On the ultra-new side, it's the Internet and DIY filmmaking. On the ultra-old, it's . . ."

"Vicious bastards for seven million years."

"And you're saying the ultra-old is still . . ."

"Colonizing the new, yeah it must do."

"So the Google Brave New World mentality? Everyone will behave better with a smartphone."

"Are we making progress? I don't think so. The funny thing is, there are so many references to Google in here, people are going to say it's product placement. They haven't paid me. We can delete that if they do. But it's more a satire if anything."

Lee thought it was part of being a "pro," being able to answer the "about" question. It was like the "elevator pitch." But he knew it was awkward and didn't mind putting other people on the back foot with it. One day he was taking the subway at 34th. And there was a whole bunch of guys selling commentaries to the Bible. He put on his best English accent and pretended to be a tourist, just off the boat. And a particularly ill-read one at that. "Oh a commentary to the Bible, that's nice," he said to one of the pleasant young men manning the stall. "What's this 'Bible' all about, then?"

"You haven't read it, sir?" The kid was flummoxed.

"No," he said. "I've heard the title a lot though. Tell me what it's all about. Maybe I will."

Later that day he switched the pluperfect back to a preterite.

NO EXIT

"WE'RE THROUGH the oh-my-God," Lee said. "It's intricate. Which is why it's been fun."

He was still having to get up and roam around every fifteen minutes or so, trying to work out either what was happening or what might happen next. This was the problem, he said, of making it up as you go along. Even as he approached the end, he still wasn't quite sure how he was going to get there. He wanted it to appear seamless, but it wasn't. It was full of seams, he just hoped nobody would notice too much.

"They get into the farm. They hypothesize the remaining two guys are locked in the tornado shelter. They reason that guys like this—that anyone, really—will always have a *second exit*. They trap them by parking a car in the way. But ... WHAT IS ALL THIS SCRAP METAL? It's lying about the place. In front of the hatch. Is it bits of metal fencing? No, it looks all wrong for that. Oh my God, it's manacles . . ."

"Instruments. Medieval."

"The hardware horror that provides an intro to the software horror."

There was one outstanding *tactical question,* to Lee's way of thinking. How to introduce the real meaning of "Mother's Rest." Who was going to deliver the truth? It could be the main man at Mother's Rest—as he is giving Reacher his spiel. But Lee felt that "seemed wrong." It could be a local FedEx driver, a few chapters back. He might know, local knowledge and all. But Lee didn't want to "shoehorn it in." Lee felt it had to be something fairly left-field; it couldn't be lame. He'd done all the lame explanations. A translation from the Arapaho? Could it come via Twitter? And therefore Westwood. And then Reacher would have to be educated in the way of Twitter.

"So it's like talking, then?" says Reacher (this is the conversation Lee imagined).

"Yes, but it has to be less than 140 characters."

"Works for me!" says Reacher, naturally laconic.

Reacher, meanwhile, in the midst of the "deeply affecting" scene, is still managing some kind of sardonic graveyard humor. He conjures up the title of a film that might be made about Westwood, had he been one of the Mother's Rest customers, as he was purporting to be: "Hack Attack."

Lee was still puzzling over what was going to happen to all his characters. So he went back to see if the previous paragraphs would give him some forward momentum. But then he shook his head and turned away from the screen with a kind of horror. "You know I mentioned *optimism*? You put these things down and you try to keep it crisp and economical and not beat anyone over the head—and then you go back . . . AND IT MAKES NO FUCKING SENSE!"

I mentioned the photograph in *Gone Tomorrow* that is eventually destroyed, unseen. No explanation of what was so embarrassing to Osama bin Laden. "Yes," he said, "people don't mind if you give up on the McGuffin. But they do get upset if you lose track of the minor characters. They really care about them. Do you remember Chester Stone and Marilyn Stone in *Tripwire*?"

"The businessman and his wife who get imprisoned and tormented by Hook Hobie?"

"Some readers wanted to know what really happened to them at the end of the story. Because it wasn't there."

"What did you tell them?"

"I tried to have a rational conversation about it. I tried to be smart. I said, 'You tell me what *you* think happened to them!' You know, your guess is as good as mine."

"They didn't like that, I bet."

"They thought I was pulling their leg. How were *they* supposed to know?"

"*Knowing*—that was your job."

"*Why buy a dog and bark yourself?* as they say in Yorkshire."

Lee spent a few minutes pondering the word "they" in the text. There was an ambiguity over the pronoun. "It's not clear who *they* are anymore," he said. He replaced it in the end with the word "con men." Reacher and his team would pin down the *con men* and get their story, their explanation. They knew where *they* were. Didn't they?

"I feel a terrible need to list caveats all the time," Lee said. "So, for example, there are two guys down there, right . . . UNLESS there are actually three, or maybe four, who knows? Sue Grafton said, 'I know it's true because I made it up myself.' But I'm not so sure: each logical step has about a thousand caveats attached to it. They're there, I just don't spell them all out."

Sometimes he felt he was stretching the "suspension of disbelief" so that it was "as long as the Severn Bridge." But then again, he guessed that something like what he was describing was already happening. He had done this once before that he knew of: in *A Wanted Man* he had dreamed up a camp to house witnesses of undercover operations who had seen more than they should but were guilty of absolutely nothing: a sort of high-security motel. Then an FBI contact told him that they already had something just like this in the back of beyond. "Same thing here," he said. "I'm not making this up at all. I'm probably not making it bad enough, that's all." He felt as though he was somehow intuiting stuff that he had no firm evidence about.

"I think it was Tom Clancy who said the difference between fiction and nonfiction was that fiction had to make sense. You know, cause and effect, culpability, crimes actually get solved, justice is really done."

"It's what Sartre said in *Nausea:* you have to choose, live or narrate, you can't have both. The funny thing is you seem to get away with it. Because you don't have an ending, you're not working back from the ending, you are rolling forwards, not really knowing where you're going, so it's more like life."

Lee was quite struck by this. But he didn't turn around. He wasn't typing but he peered more intently at the screen and everything he had written on it. He scrolled through a few pages. "This whole process is like living for me. I don't want to know what's coming. But also, in a very existential way, I am doing this Walter Mitty thing all day. But it's exactly the same as living, isn't it—it's all just electricity in the brain."

He plowed on for another paragraph or so. "A year from now," he said, "my memory of all this will be about the same as if I had done all this. And it had all really happened."

Then he tapped out a sentence and said (or sang or cried out) "Ta da!," excited about what he had just written. "Look, this has all worked out quite nicely. I really like this passage. It's efficient in so many ways. Descriptive and narrative. They're in the basement, you come at it obliquely. You move the car blocking the second exit. Reacher and Chang take up positions around the hatch. Remember Reacher is still below par with the concussion. Here is the pedantry issue coming up. Look, Westwood flings back the hatch and . . ."

There was no hole.

Those were the last words Lee had written. A four-word sentence. It had only one "no," but the "hole" kind of counted for a second. Like "no-no" almost. It was a double negation, a double bluff. *No Exit.* "This is a dummy exit!" Lee roared, as if to say, *You idiot, Reacher! How could you miss it?*

"He was suckered because he was *not pedantic enough.* He had forgotten about all the *caveats.* Suckered by a lack of pedantry. He should have been asking, hold on—what if there is a third or even a fourth exit? If there are two exits, then logically there can be an infinite number of exits."

There was something Reacher had once said that came back to Lee now. "It was one of his most profound statements: *You can't hit a guy less than once.*"

THE OPPOSITE OF THE CERN LARGE HADRON COLLIDER APPROACH

THE TRUTH WAS I had not read a single page of *Make Me*. I had read pixels of it on the screen. I had dipped into a few scrappy printouts. Not a genuine cast iron page among them. So I couldn't say if it's a "page-turner" or not. And like one of the worst-ever readers, it's taken me between seven and eight months to plow through it (even though "it" did not fully exist for 99.99 percent of this period). Thus probably qualifying as the slowest ever read of a Reacher novel. By and large, people (and I include myself in this baggy category) tend to "gobble" or "devour" the Reacher novel. It is "unputdownable." Other commitments in life tend to get put aside. A baseball manager once texted Lee Child to say that he was glad there was a World Series rainout so he could carry on reading the latest Jack Reacher, just published. In any case it is clear that total and unstinting dedication to rushing through the novel at top speed is the norm, perhaps even a categorical imperative.

I, on the other hand, was limited to authorial speed. A cheetah having to get in step with a snail. I was taking a class in readerly slowness. And the surprising thing is: the "pleasure of the text" (or *jouissance*) was if anything only greater. If Phileas Fogg could go around the world in eighty days, then he could have done it twice in the time it had taken me to read *Make Me*. In fact, come to think of it, I still have not read *Make Me:* as of today, I still do not know how it ends. And there are whole chunks of the text the author has not allowed me to see and that therefore remain mysterious. And he is still going back and "churning" bits of it. So all in all I'm still nowhere near the end. Time for one more lap, Phileas, I should think, before I'm really done with it. If I ever am.

Then again, I have read quite a few of the 100,000+ words that it is made of, many of them more than once. I have read *lines* of text, certain sentences, even whole chapters quite studiously. For once there has been no question of deconstructing anything. It would be like trying to deconstruct one of those New York building sites which consist mainly of a great hole in the ground and a lot of equipment lying around and a few heavy machines, a backhoe perhaps, and only one guy in big boots flapping his arms to keep warm while waiting for the rest of the team to turn up. Deconstruction would presuppose some prior construction worthy of the name. A towering edifice. Solid foundations. Elegant art deco architecture. *Make Me* is nothing like the Chrysler Building or the Empire State. It's more like the Hudson River if anything, when not entirely frozen; or the traffic steaming along the West Side Highway, only to come to a halt at stop lights; or the crowds in funny hats on Fifth Avenue on Easter Day. A form of pre-Socratic flux, equipped with endless cups of coffee.

The only book I can think of that has taken me this long to read is the Bible, and I'm not sure I've read every single word of that. Or maybe Proust's *A la recherche du temps perdu,* where I read the volumes out of order. But *lost time:* yes, perhaps that is the best way of thinking about reading—not in terms of chronology, of sheer duration, but of time that is not counted, not measurable, moments out of time, a Jungian synchronicity that encompasses or transcends mere clockwork. The great thing for me is that I still feel I have yet to begin the book that I have nearly finished. The book itself is virgin, undefiled, in fact inexistent. *Make Me* remains (as of writing) a virtual book, even though many would-be readers have already preordered it. They are confident that it will ultimately exist. But there is room to doubt this naive assumption.

I don't doubt that there will, in due course, be copies of a tome claiming to be Lee Child's *Make Me.* Many of them, indeed. In several languages, scattered around the four corners of the globe. My old blind friend, Terry, and her dog, Eden, will be able to listen to the audiobook. Perhaps Lee Child himself will read extracts to her, like some Latin crooner serenading his sweetheart. It is possible that Tom Cruise or others will think of translating the book into film, largely by virtue of junking most of it, perhaps all of it. But as to the existence of *the* book? Will we ever agree on precisely what *that* (to quote the author) is?

The CERN Large Hadron Collider in Geneva works by speeding up small chunks of matter to the max, spinning it around an underground track to see how it behaves under extreme conditions. I, in contrast, have slowed matter down to the max (constrained, as I say, by the author's habit of goofing off on a regular basis and not slogging constantly like Stephen King). And yet, surprisingly, the Collider and I have come to similar conclusions. I have borne witness to the cataclysmic Big Bang, to the expansion of a fictional universe, which is still growing. And, rather like the ostensibly solid table or chair you are sitting on, it turns out on close inspection to consist very largely of empty space, an interstellar darkness lit up by seemingly random particles flitting this way and that, highly charged, spinning deliriously, like ceaseless roulette wheels. I suppose if I had to obey that onerous three-word rule beloved of publishers and publicists, I would have to say: *It's about . . . nothing.* Flaubert would have been proud of it/ that/whatever.

The origin of the name "Mother's Rest." Maybe that was the text's "God Particle" (or DNA or quiddity or quintessence). Reacher finally gets an answer to his question, from a new girl at the motel. It's a corruption of the original Arapaho name, she explains, meaning: "The empty place where nothing happens." (An etymology destined to morph and warp.)

73.

TIME-LAPSE PHOTOGRAPHY OF THE PENULTIMATE CHAPTER

(**METHODOLOGY: SIT IN ARMCHAIR** by Central Park window and read chapter of *Seduction,* bewitching 2013 romantic novel by M. J. Rose, then amble into office, take snapshot of latest, freshly minted sentence in *Make Me,* then back to next chapter of *Seduction,* and so on, until such point as author runs out of steam or patience or both.)

The guy came hard up against the pig pen fence.

Thirty.

Reacher said, "I don't think they did."

"That wasn't the holy grail."

For a second, he stayed upright, just a guy leaning on a rail, and then everything gave way at once, and he went down like liquid, in a sprawled puddle . . .

The hogs came running.

Not down here.

"What should I tell the cops about how they all ended up dead?"

Easy come, easy go.

Then they walked south through the plaza.

Himself, his photographer, all kinds of interns and staff.

Reacher walked with Chang to the diner where the red Ford was parked.

74.

BOMBSHELL

LEE CHILD IS THE KIND of writer who likes to remove everything from the stone that does not resemble an elephant, as per Michelangelo, but then lop off a few limbs too, or, like *Reservoir Dogs,* an ear. He liked to "subtract," as he put it. Which is how we ended up talking about poetry.

Lee was worried about sounding pretentious, but he had just written this:

The wheat moved in waves, heavy and slow and silent.

"I originally had just 'slow and silent.' But I wanted the wheat to be ripe. And it's ominous too. Pastoral as usual, but ominous. So I went back and put in 'heavy' for its sound and suggestiveness. It's longer and slower and heavier that way. I imagine a poet would do the same. I like *subtracting,* right down to the bare minimum. But then I also like to revel in completely unnecessary luxury. Go back to 'Johnny B. Goode.' Chuck Berry. Seems tight and economical, doesn't it? But he revels in the language too. 'A log cabin *made of earth and wood.*' It's an extra layer of description. He didn't really need the earth and wood. He wanted the rhyme of course. But he gives you an exuberance . . . Yeah, I'm being economical, but I'm also reveling."

He softened me up with the poetry. Then he hit me with the bombshell. "This may well be Reacher's last adventure."

[REACHER'S LAST ADVENTURE!? Time to absorb shock.]

How did he work that out, considering he is contracted to write at least one more? Oh, that will probably be a prequel, says he, indifferently. "So this could be *it* for Reacher."

"Reacher rides into the sunset à la Shane? Or are you going to tip him off the Reichenbach Falls or what?"

"Remember we discussed how to *end* Reacher in Madrid?"

It came back to me then. Sitting in the evening sun on some plaza, not far from the Prado, and Lee was saying, "There is a question in my mind—when is the right time to stop?" But then he was still near the beginning, he had only just started, he had to keep on going; but now he was approaching the end and the "question" had returned with a vengeance.

"You were saying how you wouldn't kill him off in the line of duty, no heroic death, no 'aaaaaagh,' but just leave him turning around at the bus station and saying, *I think I like it here.*"

"This is *not* that," Lee said. "For one thing we have Reacher *reaching out.* That's a first. He's changed. 'I need you with me,' he says to Chang. It's just a hint, but a hint in Reacher is the same as a total collapse. Of course he is still suffering some kind of brain damage."

I still don't know what happens in the final chapter. But I know there are forking paths. Chicago (Reacher's destination) this way, Seattle (Chang's base) that way. Reacher has to choose.

I knew he wasn't going to write THE END. "If there is no more text, it's obviously the end." But the implication was that *the end is nigh*. For him as a writer. At least as author of the Reacher series. "What are you going to do?" I said. "Try long sentences or something?"

"You want short I can do short, you want long I can do long," he said. The thing you couldn't do as writer, he said, was *fake it*. "You have to write what appeals to you instinctively. And if that appeals to a lot of other people then you are a success; if not, then not. But you can't *be* something else. It's just impossible to do it. Especially in a downward direction. William Boyd trying to do a James Bond, for example. It's probably easier to go in the opposite direction, but why would anyone bother?"

"Academics do it all the time," I pointed out.

"I sometimes have people coming up to me and saying, with a note of contempt, 'You write popular bestsellers!' I reply, 'What? You want to write *un*popular *worst*sellers?'"

Sometimes he cracks me up. This was one of those times.

"Don't worry about the end of Reacher," he said. "I always feel like this at this stage of the process."

Then he said, "The hogs have come back. I had no idea they would be so useful."

Hogs, each one the size of a Volkswagen.

75.

CLIFFHANGER

LEE CHILD FINISHED writing the final sentence of the first and only draft of *Make Me* at 12:24 P.M. on April 10, 2015. Which posed an ethical problem for me. Should I know the ending? I had been worrying about missing the end; now I was worrying about not missing it. There remains something sacred about the *telos*. That after which there is only silence. *Nada más.* Maybe I ought to just bear witness, but not actually gaze upon the words. See, but not perceive. It was just a feeling I had.

"Do you want to hear this, or do you not want to hear this?" he said, impatient with my epistemological qualms.

"I'm glad just to have been here."

"I [*aaah* in her Louisiana accent] would like to hear it." Photographer Jené leBlanc was there to record the moment for posterity. Like all good observers she was bound to have an impact on the subject under observation.

So Lee went ahead and read aloud the whole of the last paragraph. There was a definite "Ode to Joy" feel to it.

"I feel like crying," Jené said. "'Get in the car.' That is so powerful."

"It has to land," he said. "It's like a plane landing."

"What are you going to do to celebrate?" I said.

"I'm going out to buy toothpaste and kitchen towels. It's getting ridiculous."

Including the title, *Make Me* weighed in at 111,730 words. The last sentence alone made up sixty-seven of them. He had thought of it during the night, hardly had to change a word of it. It was an echo, a variation on a couple of other earlier sentences about Reacher and Chang driving, and then a line in the Mother's Rest website, all about the "road." Possibly the longest sentence in the book, right at the very end, to make a point (and, not coincidentally, the last word was "needle").

It had taken him 222 days to write, from beginning, through the nonexistent middle, to the end. *Moving . . . needle.* Like an old vinyl record player. The song of Reacher. Pure analog. Or a compass.

"It's like getting out of school." Lee was unfolding himself, pushing away from the desk and getting out of his chair. "I can be normal again. Go out into the world. I'm going to have a different life now. At least until September."

He still had to go back through the text one more time. "You can't have the verbatim transcript of a guy ranting in a pub." He would "keep the contour" but take out a few "maybe's" and "the guy." "It's brought it home to me how intense this is, having you around every day. You come through the door and I think: *Wasn't he just here?* Oh yeah, that was twenty-four hours ago. So a whole day has gone by and *nothing has happened.*"

At last he could go and eat a decent Indian meal. "I've been starving for the last month." He had this lean, mean look, possibly even leaner and meaner than when he started.

Jené was taking pictures of him in the front room, reclining on the sofa. He was saying something about how he'd been "feeling crap since the age of fifty-five" and how there were "more leaves on the ground than on the tree" and "the meaning of life is that it ends" and Jené was saying something about how his books would live on. "People say I'll be *immortalized*." He lit another cigarette. "Ha! It's all moonshine. As soon as I stop writing the front list, the back list will curl up and die."

While she was distracting him, I went and sat down at his great metal desk. It felt like being at the beginning of something. A genesis moment. His text with his final paragraph was still on the screen, so I read it again then I opened up a new file. On his computer. The new blank window completely blotted out *Make Me*. I had my fingers poised over the keyboard, ready to type in the new title.

Lee came in.

He saw me at his desk, sitting in his chair, typing on his computer. Assumed I was trying to "destroy" his novel. Like I was about to write *Un-Make Me*. He had something in his hand. "A hollow-nose bullet," he said. "Have you any idea what it can do to your insides?"

I said nothing.

E-LOG

April 11 [2015]

Lee Child to andymartinink
re My final draft
Read-through with different font and spacing always illuminating. Cut 2,303 words—now 109,427.

  Strikes me Keever was a well-rounded and well-developed character for a guy who was dead the whole book.

Attachment.

April 12

andymartinink to Lee Child
Finished Make Me. *There are no grapes left in the fridge.*

AUTHOR'S NOTE

All the conversations in this book really took place. I made a lot of contemporaneous notes. In the interests of authenticity, any modifications are minimal. A few "um"s and "er"s got omitted just to speed it up. Expletives have by and large not been deleted. The timeline is as faithful as I can make it. The names are real (unless they are actually fictional). The quotations from *Make Me* are as I originally heard them or read them—they don't always correspond exactly to the text as it finally appeared. But they have an archaeological value.

ACKNOWLEDGMENTS

Thanks are due to all the people who appear in this book and a few who don't.

ABOUT THE AUTHOR

ANDY MARTIN is a native of Britain, where he lectures at the University of Cambridge for the Department of French. He is the author of *Waiting for Bardot, The Boxer and the Goalkeeper, Walking on Water, The Knowledge of Ignorance, Stealing the Wave,* and *Napoleon the Novelist.*

ABOUT THE TYPE

This book was set in Minion, a 1990 Adobe Originals typeface by Robert Slimbach (b. 1956). Minion is inspired by classical, old-style typefaces of the late Renaissance, a period of elegant, beautiful, and highly readable type designs. Created primarily for text setting, Minion combines the aesthetic and functional qualities that make text type highly readable with the versatility of digital technology.